KU-215-171

change

DEDICATION

For Harry and Felix

change

how to kick-start the future and refresh the spirit

ALISON HAYNES

God help us to change. To change ourselves and to change our world. To know the need for it. To deal with the pain of it. To feel the joy of it. To undertake the journey without understanding the destination. The art of gentle revolution. Amen.

MICHAEL LEUNIG,
COMMON PRAYER COLLECTION (1993)

CONTENTS

What you can do, or dream you can do, begin it; boldness has genius, power and magic in it.

ATTRIBUTED TO
JOHANN WOLFGANG VON GOETHE
(1749–1832), INSPIRED BY *FAUST*

1. TIME FOR A CHANGE

CHANGE: IT'S EXHILARATING, ANNOYING, CHALLENGING AND THREATENING. SOMETIMES YOU LOVE IT—A CHANGE IS AS GOOD AS A REST—SOMETIMES, YOU ARE UNCOMFORTABLE WITH IT. YOU RESIST IT, ENDURE IT, FEAR IT, CAUSE IT AND HOPE FOR IT. ABOVE ALL, AT TIMES YOU NEED IT.

THE CERTAINTY OF CHANGE

Life is change. Breathe in, breathe out. Smile, yawn, scowl. Move, lie still. A multiplicity of changes takes place at all times in your body: digestion, respiration, circulation. Growth pushes you up and out, ageing mellows you (sometimes). The possibility of changing yourself is always there. As Oscar Wilde put it: 'Every saint has a past, and every sinner has a future.'

Love it or hate it, you change, and the world changes around you. The Latin poet Ovid, born in 43 BC, said: 'All things change, nothing is extinguished.' He knew what he was talking about. His fascinating stories of change related in his *Metamorphoses* (or *Transformations*) remain compelling today. Take *Pygmalion*, Ovid's story of the statue that turned into a real woman. George Bernard Shaw turned this into a play, written in 1913, which formed the basis for the 1964 film *My Fair Lady*, starring Rex Harrison and Audrey Hepburn. In Shaw's play and the subsequent film, Professor Higgins falls in love with Eliza Doolittle once he has transformed her—like the sculptor creating the statue out of a block of stone—from flower seller to lady. Ovid also underwent his own transformations. Trained as a lawyer he turned to poetry and, for reasons which are unknown today, was banished to Tomi on the Black Sea when he was 51.

For most of us, change is much less dramatic. You may grow out of jobs and houses, leave partners and make new friends. Your life undergoes lots of small changes all the time. A new supermarket is built and the corner shop closes. Your sister has her first child and you realize you've become an uncle or aunt.

At other times you may be forced to take dramatic action: you realize you're not cut out to be a teacher at all and switch to a job in the financial markets; a spell of rheumatoid arthritis makes commuting impossible and causes you to reassess your lifestyle; one day you decide you're sick of the nine to five city life and head to the country to try your luck. There are sea changes, mid-life crises, adolescent crises, career changes and retirement.

Life may demand you make a new start. A husband of 30 years dies or leaves you when you never expected he would; the second child, who'll accommodate a progressive career, turns out to be twins; a fire destroys everything you own. The doctor says that unless you stop smoking your lung condition will turn fatal. Your inner city job gets moved out of town. Government policies can change dramatically in one generation, meaning the sons and daughters of those brought up on the pension ideal now find it's up to them to manage their retirement funds. The workplace changes, and you may find you're no longer permanently employed, with all the benefits that brings, but are part of the consultant/freelance world. The information you are able to access and the choices available threaten to overload you and you have to learn to find your own filtering systems.

Life demands constant adaptation. Sometimes you get swept along and wonder how you got where you are. Sometimes you feel life has got out of balance. You are unhappy, overloaded or plain fed up and something's got to change.

TYPES OF CHANGE

Change comes in many guises, both welcome and unwanted. Whether it demands you act or unfolds around you, change has many facets and characteristics.

TAOISM

The Chinese philosophy of Taoism centres on the *tao*, loosely translated as 'the way'. In simple terms, Taoism sees change as a constant, fundamental state. It requires you to 'go with the flow' of the universe, accepting that the world changes around you all the time and that to keep healthy, prosperous and happy, you need to be constantly changing yourself, sometimes subtly, sometimes more dramatically and quickly. One of the major Taoist texts, the *I Ching*, or *Book of Changes*, refers in a poetic, mysterious way, to the nature of change. There are times when it's best to sit back and do nothing, times to be bold, times to search your heart, times of prosperity and times of hardship. But these situations and positions are constantly evolving and changing as they move towards the next period.

DISCONTINUOUS CHANGE

The economist philosopher Charles Handy talks of discontinuous change in his book *The Age of Unreason.* War, technological leaps—like that witnessed in the Industrial Revolution—and even changing demographics can bring about sudden changes that can be hard to keep up with. For instance, during the Industrial Revolution in the late eighteenth and early nineteenth centuries, handloom weavers in Britain found work increasingly difficult to come by as factories introduced power looms that replaced their skills. The hardship and poverty the weavers experienced prompted historians to describe their plight as one of the starkest tragedies of the age. At the same time, mill owners enjoyed the substantial profits that the new technologies had made possible.

EVOLUTIONARY CHANGE OR CONTINUOUS CHANGE

Unlike discontinuous change, evolutionary or continuous changes are ones you feel comfortable with. Although these call for action too, you can become complacent about the need—like the frog in the gradually heating water that will not jump out even to save its life. Take waistlines, for example. A slim teenager becomes a well-covered twenty year old, then a plump thirty year old who should lose weight for health reasons—all because of putting on just a kilo or so each year from too much food and not quite enough physical activity.

LEARNING CURVES

There are times when you may feel you're struggling, but really you are absorbing and learning and your brain may be working overtime trying to figure out how to do a new task. Then there's the breakthrough and a rewarding improvement. Motivation and will help to overcome that discouraging initial phase; whether you're someone who's come to computers late in life, or have migrated to

Gandhi (1869–1948)

Mohandas Karamchand Gandhi was an undistinguished student. When he returned to India in 1891, after studying law in London, he was unable to find a suitable position as a barrister. That's when he went to Natal in South Africa and, experiencing racial prejudice for the first time, was persuaded to stay and oppose a Bill that would deprive Indians of the right to vote. He remained in South Africa for twenty years, using the same pacifist defiance that he became famous for later on when he returned to India—including leading the 320-kilometre march in 1930 to collect salt from the sea in protest against punitive salt taxes.

another country in your mid-life and find yourself grappling with a new language.

ADAPTATION

Adaptation is often an essential part of change: new situations call for new skills, attitudes and habits. Sometimes these come easily, sometimes you may fight them for a while until months later you realize you've glided into the new role and are managing well. It's something that occurs with the little:

When my first child started school I found the mornings horribly rushed and ridiculously stressful: getting the packed lunch together, making breakfast, coaxing two children to get dressed and out of the door. But after a while I was slotting the tasks together, had a better idea of how long everything took and we seemed to flow out of the front door rather than wrestle and squirm. AN

and the big:

Everyone assumed I'd become a doctor. I was accepted into a good medical school but once there felt like a fish out of water and failed every exam in sight. It was a shock to my system. When I failed a re-sit too, and that was it, I cried for three days. Then I got on with the business of working out what to do next. MH

A BALANCED LIFE

A shift of balance can make you miserable. Too much work makes Jack a dull boy and a depressed and unhealthy adult. It's a fine line: too much packed into the day and you're overloaded, tired and haven't got the presence of mind to enjoy anything to the full. Not enough stimulation and you stagnate, ruminate, bother the neighbours or eat too much chocolate. If the balance is out, you may need to introduce change in one or more areas of your life.

Balance comes down to having enough of the things that make us tick. And preferably, make us tick loud and clear. While the elements for a balanced life differ from person to person they usually include some of the following:

- money
- work
- exercise
- peaceful time on your own
- time with family and friends
- interest and stimulation.

At times, finding balance seems to involve managing a variety of conflicting needs: family and career; creativity and finances; adventure and security; enjoying the present while sacrificing for the future; a taste for gourmet delights and a regard for health.

VOX POP: What does a balanced life mean to you?

The challenge of balance is different for everyone. Here are a few people's viewpoints.

'I strive for a good balance between my family and my work, between leisure and the need to make money, and between practical matters (shall we buy a new microwave oven?) and soul-enriching experiences such as travel, family holidays, theatre and art galleries. I treasure time with my family and if the pressure of work is so great that I have to cancel out, I feel depressed, uptight and cheated and consider the amount of money earned to be inadequate compensation.' PN

'Balance means everything to me. I find it through swimming, talking, writing, music and creating.' FH

'I seek balance in all sorts of ways: work and study versus leisure; consumption versus saving for my old age (I should save more); being free and radical versus keeping up the appearances of normality.' HB

'Maintaining balance between socializing and solitude; rest and exercise; work and leisure; urban and rural; seriousness and humour.' ML

'Balance is so important—you only notice when you don't have it. But mostly I feel like I'm on a treadmill trying to keep up with the rest of the world. If I achieve balance it's a bonus, but if I don't then I figure I am doing the best I can anyway.' CT

'Seeking balance is the most important thing to me. I'm not interested in climbing the corporate ladder as I don't need the stress of it and am not willing to put in the hours. I seek balance in my life with paid work, publicity work on our business (in the arts, which I love), yoga and my family. At the moment my life is out of balance because I'm working full time which is not ideal. What's missing is more time with my husband and friends.' CS

The perils of being out of balance

Imbalance can have several negative consequences:

- Stress. Serious relentless stress can cause a spiral of problems at work, in communicating with people, and in health. Rest can help you renew and regain perspective. Sometimes tipping the balance in one area of your life—for instance exercise—can also help break a cycle of stress. It relaxes you, gives you time away from other problems and makes you fitter and more able to deal with difficulties.

- Burnout. When 'too much' becomes 'can't take it any more', you've hit burnout. Heeding the warning signs before you get to bursting point can save a lot of mental anguish.

- Relationship breakdown. When life is seriously out of kilter, relationships suffer—whether you are a workaholic who ignores her family's needs or a gambler who has lost his family's home.

- Health problems. Overindulgence, not eating properly and burning the candle at both ends can all increase your chances of developing numerous lifestyle diseases including heart disease and diabetes.

- Depression. Depression can strike when your life is out of balance and you're working overtime, have lost your vitality and are feeling stuck in a rut. Taking some risks, finding something to laugh about, and leaving the office on time for once can bring back a sense of control to help clear the blues.

- Sleep problems. Good sleep makes you better able to tackle what life throws at you—whether it's a toddler's tantrums or an unexpected tax bill.

'Much of my work involves using the computer or reading. I need to balance that cerebral activity with something physical that gets my hands dirty. Like gardening. Or pottery.' AN

'It means balancing what you have to do with what you want to do, and spending most of the time doing the latter. There's a balance between work and play (which I struggle with—I like work too much!), between spiritual and material; being physically active and slothful. It's important. Imbalance is harmful in any of these areas. I constantly monitor myself and adjust things as they go out of balance. It's a full-time job in a way.' DL

PRIORITIES

The ability to prioritize and work out what's really important to you can help you to change your life for the better.

It helps you shed surplus burdens, whether it's the school parents' committee that only winds you up so that you don't really contribute anyway; a compulsive friendliness that has you inviting people around for dinner when you are really pushed for time; or going out for drinks after work even though you don't enjoy the experience and feel awkward.

Prioritizing also helps you to focus and provides a rudder to direct you through the labyrinth of choices and decisions you must make. If you feel clear that your family comes first, you'll find it easier to accept that you'll put your career on the back burner for a few years while your children are young (or find other ways to maintain a toehold in the work force). If you hate clock-watching bosses, you might choose freelance work, knowing that the flexibility it offers is more important to you than fringe benefits or a company car (and anyway, cycling to appointments keeps you fit).

Sometimes it takes a crisis to highlight what really matters, focus your priorities and trigger change. A close shave with death may lead to a ruthless reassessment of where your life is going. One lost weekend too many may make an alcoholic decide once and for all that he can conquer his addiction. A confrontation at work may make you realize that it's time you moved to another job rather than continue to complain and undermine your position in an industry you dislike.

THE TIME OF YOUR LIFE

To master one's time is to gain mastery of oneself.
JEAN-LOUIS SERVAN-SCHREIBER, *THE ART OF TIME* (1988)

Part of the reason people feel it's difficult to find balance and focus on priorities is simply lack of time. Human beings have an uncomfortable relationship with time. Have you noticed it is elastic? Time passes unbearably slowly when you are in a traffic jam trying to get to the airport (no one likes waiting) but takes on a shocking pace on holiday (where did it go?). Sometimes, you take your time; at other times, it gallops past you.

The pace of life has quickened and with it a host of new vocabulary has emerged: fast food, grazing, speed dating, multitasking, sound bites, speed reading, instant replay, instant coffee, one hour photographic development and fast download. While there is an appreciation of the patina of the old we are not always prepared to wait for it: hence pre-faded jeans, distressed furniture and even mock-worn antique-look carpets in hotels. Candles, church bells and sundials have been replaced by the electric bulb, digital alarm clock and quartz watches.

George Green (1793–1841)
George Green was elected a fellow of Cambridge University, United Kingdom, in 1839. He'd taught himself mathematics while working as a baker and published several papers on wave motion and optics.

With this increase in pace, you lose time for reflection and digestion of information. Your life and often your work can suffer.

Rocks before sand

A common Buddhist parable recounts the following experiment. A monk took a glass beaker and a handful of rocks and placed them one by one in the beaker.

'Is the beaker full?' he asked his students.

'Yes,' came the eager reply.

The monk took out a small bag and started to tip gravel into the beaker until no more would fit.

'Is it full now?' he asked.

The students thought they were quick to have got the idea: 'No.'

'Quite right.' He continued to fill it with sand. 'Now?'

'There are still air holes', came the reply, so he poured in some water. 'What am I trying to illustrate?' the monk finally asked.

'That however much we pack in our day, we can always fit more in,' answered the students.

But that was not his point. If you want to put rocks in a beaker of gravel, sand and water, you need to put the rocks in first. Similarly, if you want your life to be full and rewarding, you must make sure your priorities are in place first, or you may find that your life is consumed by trivialities.

TAKING BACK CONTROL

If you want to improve your experience of life but the world won't change around you, then it's time to change the way you look at life.

FOLLOW THE SIMPLE LIFE

'I went to the woods because I wished to live deliberately, to front only the essential facts of life, and see if I could not learn what it had to teach…' explained American naturalist and writer Henry David Thoreau of his two years at Walden Pond near Concord, Massachusetts in the mid-1800s. There, he found the simple life: read books, wrote his diary, cultivated beans and walked in the woods. His thoughts on the value of wilderness and the need to live in harmony with nature are still relevant today, nearly 150 years after his death.

If going back to nature is a bit radical for you, there are other ways to simplify your life.

- Do one thing at a time. Concentrate on the exercise bike; don't try to read at the same time. Talk to your mother on the phone and leave the washing up until later, even if you can do it one handed.
- Don't let the phone interrupt meals or other special times. Use it when you want, and when you don't want the interruptions let an answering machine take over.
- Say 'no' more often. This will avoid bursting weekend schedules, overflowing cupboards, an overdraft and an overloaded life.
- Consider a blank day in the diary a necessity. You need some time for spontaneity and to allow for short-term plans.
- Learn when less is more. By cutting back on your living expenses, you'll find your budget looks a lot healthier and you'll be surprised at how much you never needed in the first place. Fewer belongings also leave you with less to dust, maintain and insure.
- Ignore media clutter. Entering competitions you won't win, filling in coupons for products you wouldn't usually buy, and becoming a slave to technology you don't need, all take up valuable time.

Keeping track of time

We have at our disposal 24 hours every day. That's 1440 minutes. Where do they go? Time-use analysis is not a perfect science. It runs into a variety of problems, such as how to record activities and how to deal with the human fact that we often do more than one thing at a time. Couples eat dinner and watch a film or a child might sit at the kitchen table while her mother cooks and supervises some painting. But it's an interesting exercise and the sort of figures that research on the use of the 24-hour day throw up show that you sleep for around eight of them and eat or prepare food for two hours.

Dressing and washing takes almost one hour. That's more than ten hours to meet your biological needs. You work for around eight hours a day and might travel for around an hour. That leaves three or four hours for family life, entertainment, learning, sports and so on. Housework eats an hour and a half or so into that time, and those who spend a couple of hours watching television may find that that's it.

But compared to our ancestors we enjoy more leisure time than ever. So, what has happened to the experience of time?

- Productivity. The demands of productivity put extra stress on those in work. You are asked to perform more tasks in a fixed amount of time.
- Commuting. Time lost in getting to work is time taken out of other activities. Many people choose to commute long hours so they can live out of a crowded city centre.
- Urbanization. In *The Art of Time* Jean-Louis Servan-Schreiber argues that because the supermarket has replaced the corner shop, you travel further to the shops. As neighbourhoods have become specialized, so shopping, entertainment and other errands have become more time consuming. Children go out of the area to

- Make some ground rules and stick to them. Even unwritten rules can help you carve out the life you want rather than the one that threatens to engulf you. Not working at the weekend; never arranging more than one social event in a day; and agreeing on a few basic family finance principles are all examples.

school; the dentist and doctor are several suburbs away; your parents live halfway across the continent.

- The cost of consumption. You are a consumer as much as a citizen, and have more worldly goods to show for it. But consuming takes time. Whether it's a boat, bracelet or bar fridge, you first have to want it, shop for it, then maintain it.

- Having it all. At times you may feel as if you devote little pieces of time to a multitude of pleasures rather than enjoying at leisure the ones that really suit. Rather like the pizza 'with the lot' which can be a mushy disappointment, whereas the simple but classic pleasure of the Margherita can be so much more rewarding.

- The envy economy. Instead of people being satisfied with the spare time they have (which many of their ancestors lacked), some commentators argue people have been corrupted by a new industry of envy. While your desires may have undergone a revolution, the time available to satisfy them has remained constant.

- Segmentation of time. You move house more often; jobs are no longer for life; divorces are more common. The slices of life are getting slimmer, it's harder to enjoy the whole cake.

- Everyone wants your time. More demands are made on your time than ever before. Knocks at the door offer free market analyses from local real estate companies. Phone surveys demand to know what soft drinks or margarine you use. Interruptions, both wanted and unwanted scramble your time. Long-haul air trips can be relaxing, even though you are cramped, because for the duration of the flight, life is simple. Eat, doze and wonder how much longer you've got to go.

- Take sleep seriously. What could be simpler than a good night's sleep? It keeps you healthy and lets you achieve more. Skimping on sleep is a false economy that can result in fatigue, anxiety, more colds and flu as well as a loss of productivity.

Time thieves

Time has a habit of running away from us. What's more, interruptions steal time until we're left with scraps. One study of managers found that the average period of uninterrupted time is seven minutes.

Writer and speaker, Alec MacKenzie conducted a time-management seminar for a group of chief executives from a range of industries and businesses and started off by asking them to list their biggest time wasters. Their answers form the basis of his book, *The Time Trap*, first published in 1972, now in its third edition ad credited with kick-starting a time-management boom. Some common time thieves identified by this industry are listed below.

EXTERNAL THIEVES

These thieves allow us to place blame on others:

- unexpected and prolonged phone calls
- co-workers stopping by to discuss problems or to chat
- open-door policies demanding availability
- visitors, clients and unexpected suppliers
- poorly trained or incompetent personnel
- the boss or several bosses
- business lunches, promotional cocktail parties and other entertainment for outside visitors
- personal or family business
- maintenance and machine repairs

LIVE IN THE PRESENT

The here and now is all you have. There really is no time like the present. However, the complexity of life constantly pushes the mind into the future. The new and unexpected is often exhilarating precisely because it brings your mind back to the present. How is it possible to exploit the invigorating nature of living in the present moment?

- Focus on the now. Take a moment every now and then to stop and listen to your body. For instance, follow your breathing or

- appointments (doctor, music lesson etc) for children
- housework, errands and cooking
- interruptions by the family.

INTERNAL THIEVES

These thieves are a result of our own shortcomings, whether poor planning or lack of discipline:

- confused and changeable objectives and priorities
- absence of a daily work plan
- no self-imposed deadlines
- tendency to do too much, perfectionism
- lack of order, messy desktops
- confusion and overlap of responsibilities
- insufficient delegation
- excessive attention to detail
- delay in dealing with conflict
- resistance to change
- scattered or too-numerous interests
- inability to say 'no'
- lack of information; insufficient (or excessive) communication
- indecisiveness or overhasty decisions (or decisions made in committee)
- fatigue, being out of shape.

take a tour of your body from toes to head, tuning in to how each part feels, whether relaxed, tense or uncomfortable. Stop and listen to the sounds in the same room or close environment, further away, in the distance. Give whatever activity you are involved in your full attention for even a few moments. It will bring your mind and body back to the now, whether it's savouring every morsel of a bar of chocolate, really listening to a piece of music or enjoying the buzz of a busy street market.

- Practise mindfulness. The Zen concept of mindfulness is all about living in the here and now. It requires you to maintain an intelligent alertness or heightened awareness. 'Live as you'll live forever, but live each day as though it were your last', as an old piece of wisdom advises. The Sanskrit word for mindfulness, *smriti*, means 'to remember'; one aspect of mindfulness is to remember that life is special and full of ordinary miracles every day, whether it's by appreciating dawn light on the trees as you go for an early morning run, the playful kiss on your cheek from a great-grandchild, the heat of strawberries in the sun or howls of excitement over watching rugby finals on the other side of the world. Another aspect of mindfulness aims to cultivate the liberating attitude that problems only become problems when they take over your mind. The Zen Buddhist will say that even if you are very sick and in pain, it is really the confusion and worry about what will happen to you and your family that is painful.

TAKE THE OCCASIONAL RISK

It doesn't have to be over anything important. Break your routine every so often. Try something you've always intended to, take up opportunities to try something new.

COUNT YOUR BLESSINGS

Carpe diem ('seize the day'). There are countless sayings and proverbs encapsulating the idea of enjoying what we have rather than mourning the past or worrying about what we don't have. The popular *Rubaiyat* of Omar Khayam, the astronomer-poet of Persia, who lived between 1050 and 1122, explains:

The moving finger writes; and, having writ,
Moves on: nor all thy piety nor wit
shall lure it back to cancel half a line,
Nor all thy tears wash out a word of it.

MANAGE YOUR TIME

Human psychology tends to push us to do first of all things that we enjoy doing, leaving those we don't enjoy until last—or never. We pick quick jobs over slow, easy tasks before difficult ones and familiar tasks before something new. In addition, we may delay self-imposed tasks until ones which others have imposed on us are completed. To combat this, try the following:

- Scheduling time for important tasks. Unscheduled tasks have a habit of being left by the wayside.
- Dealing with the most important or urgent problems first. This is not necessarily the order in which the problems appeared.
- Doing things at the time of day you best perform them. For instance, if you take a while to get going in the morning, leave the creative problem solving till after a coffee break. If you tend to slow down in the afternoon, make that your filing time or when you catch up on phone calls.

THE PROCESS OF CHANGE

Change is never an isolated incident. Even the challenge of giving up a single behaviour—such as smoking, for instance—is a process involving a number of phases of varying degrees of awareness, motivation and action. Like crossing a busy road, it's not as simple as merely deciding to do it. You need to find a pedestrian crossing, press the button, wait for the lights, and keep an eye out for cars even when you cross.

THE TRANSTHEORETICAL MODEL OF CHANGE

The stages of change are recognized in a tool called the Transtheoretical Model of Change, developed by clinical psychologists Dr James Prochaska and Dr Carlo DiClemente in the late 1970s.

The model is used by health authorities and many others interested in making people change. It's been used to help people quit smoking, reduce the fat in their diet, curb alcohol problems, regain financial health, and deal with organizational change. Its somewhat clumsy name comes from the fact that it draws on a number of different psychological theories including psychoanalysis, existential or humanist theories, gestalt or experiential theories, and cognitive and behaviour sciences.

After the death of his father, who suffered from alcoholism and depression and did not change, Dr Prochaska was interested in studying why some people successfully change their behaviour.

The TTM, as it is sometimes referred to, defines five different periods people experience before, during and after change.

- Stage one: Pre-contemplation. This comes before any awareness of a problem and people in this stage say they don't intend to make any changes in, say, the next six months. It is often accompanied by denial; denial that something needs to change, despite evidence to the contrary such as the bathroom scales, written warnings at work or truancy from a child. Health promoters may regard people in this stage as resistant or unmotivated. People may avoid reading or talking about problems. Sometimes people in this stage have tried changing before and have become demoralized as their earlier efforts failed.

- Stage two: Contemplation. You acknowledge changes are needed but you are not yet sure which changes and how. When asked, you may say you intend making a change within six months. While people in this stage are more aware of the need

Francis Howard Greenway (1777–1837)

The Australian $10 note once depicted Francis Greenway, an architect who started life near Bristol in the west of England. He was transported to Sydney in 1812 for forgery but soon gained 'ticket-of-leave' and established himself again as an architect. Greenway was appointed civil architect and designed many of the early colony's public buildings.

to change, they are also aware of the downside change may bring. In attempting to weigh costs and benefits, ambivalence may set in or—worse still—chronic contemplation or procrastination. 'Contemplation' can easily become 'stuck in the rut'.

- Stage three: Preparation. Preparing for change often involves researching options and their possible impact as well as searching for an understanding of the situation you face: the whys, wheres and whens. At this stage, people usually have plans—perhaps to join a health club or an adult education class or read a self-help book. They are prime candidates for health programs as the motivation is setting in.
- Stage four: Action. You've identified some solutions and you're giving them a go. A certain objectivity makes plans more effective. For instance, if smoking is a problem, total abstinence might be the real goal, not cutting back just a few. This is a stage where you might need vigilance against relapse or losing momentum.
- Stage five: Maintenance. Sticking to plans is half the battle. Keeping the weight down, not giving up on quitting smoking, continuing morning runs despite wintry weather. People in this stage are still working against relapsing into their old habits, but they don't have to apply themselves as much as in the previous stage because they are less easily tempted and now have more confidence in their ability to change.

Slipping up

As anyone who has tried to make changes in their behaviour knows, slip-ups (or 'regression', as psychologists call it) are common. You can regress to any stage in the process—entirely giving up and not intending to try again would be a regression back to stage one. But the good news is that usually you will only relapse a little down the scale and, before long, you're ready to start climbing it again.

OTHER MODELS OF CHANGE

Researchers describe another scale in relation to change: the Decisional Balance scale. Put simply, it means that at the beginning of the change process the cons of changing seem to outweigh the pros. However, as you move towards the next stage, the advantages gradually appear to be greater than the costs.

Another way of looking at this is explored in the Self-efficacy and Temptation scale. This demonstrates how at the beginning of a change, temptation is high and confidence is low, but as people move through the stages, they feel less temptation to relapse— whether through cravings or in particular social situations—and more confidence that they can cope with risky situations without relapsing.

This model describes another ten processes of change at play along the scale. These are divided into two categories: factors you experience and behavioural factors.

Factors you experience

- Increasing awareness. This process involves an increased awareness of causes, consequences and cures. For instance, you may recall information about professional training you could benefit from or realize it might be a good idea to start saving.
- Emotional arousal. This occurs when you experience an emotional reaction to a warning. The emotion betrays some concern, and is a beam of hope for positive change. Public health authorities often attempt to switch on emotions by

Caroline Norton (1808–77)

When Caroline Norton tried to take her husband to court—he had beaten her and gained custody of their three sons against her will— she was enraged to find that as a married women she had no separate legal existence. Her efforts to reform the law eventually bore fruit and she is now acknowledged as a significant, if not well known, early feminist.

making use of psychodramas and personal testimonies in their 'quit smoking' and road safety campaigns.

- Social reappraisal or environmental re-evaluation. This is when you take a look at how your personal habits affect others, whether directly or as a role model. For example, someone trying to curb angry reactions might finally acknowledge that they are causing problems with their relationships.
- Social liberation or environmental opportunities. Healthy food options at the school canteen give children a better chance for a good diet. The fact that water restrictions are introduced strengthens your resolve to conserve water at home.
- Self re-evaluation. This is where taking a look at your values and self-image can help. An acknowledgment that, for instance, being unfit is making you feel sluggish and bad about yourself.

Behavioural factors

- Stimulus control, also called re-engineering. This is all about removing cues for unwanted behaviour and prompting wanted changes: attractive stairwells can encourage you to take the stairs instead of the lift, for example. You don't buy ice cream because you know it's a weakness of yours and you're trying to lose weight.
- Supportive relationships. Buddy systems, counsellor calls and friendships can answer the need for trust, caring and acceptance. You need a friend to listen when you feel the need to talk.
- Substituting or counterconditioning. Sometimes people need to learn healthier or more positive alternatives. These might be relaxation exercises to help counter stress or assertiveness training to enable you to withstand peer pressure. It could also be as simple as making a cup of tea instead of opening a bottle of wine.
- Rewards, or reinforcement management. This is about enhancing the positive consequences of taking steps in the right direction. You reward yourself when you hand in a report on time.

- Commitment. You make the commitment to change. This is a genuine belief that you can change and you reinforce it again and again by resolutions, willpower and telling others about it.

PUTTING IT ALL INTO PRACTICE

So, you know you need to change and you understand the processes involved. How do you go about putting your plan into action and keeping it on track? Some tools of change—like taking responsibility for your decisions, owning a problem, setting goals, and maintaining a flexible approach—are essential parts of any transformation toolkit. These and others are outlined below.

RESOLVING TO KEEP RESOLUTIONS

Making resolutions is easy. Keeping them is the hard part. In a 1996 survey, the British consumer magazine *Health Which?* asked its readers how their New Year resolutions were going two weeks into January. Forty per cent had already given them up.

Motivation, rather than discipline, is the key to success. Resolutions likely to be kept are realistic, practical and from the heart.

Three's best for motivation

Motivation researchers show that, to a degree, the more choices you feel you have available in order to make a change happen, the greater the chance you'll see it through. People with two choices rather than one are more committed; those with three possibilities are more motivated still. But there doesn't appear to be any benefit to having four choices. Perhaps it produces indecision. A smoker trying to give up, for example, is more likely to succeed if they feel they have the choice of going cold turkey, nicotine fading or nicotine replacement.

- Realistic. PN usually gets up at 7 am but sometimes he dozes to 7.30 am. Every now and then he resolves to rise at 5 am to clear a glut of work. 'No, 4 am,' he says. So he lies awake for a few hours worrying about getting up early, the alarm goes off at 4 am and, exhausted, he rolls over and sleeps until 8 am.
- Practical. Pursuing pipe dreams undermines your ability to change what is within reach. You may not be able to afford a four-bedroom house in your suburb, but you might be able to upgrade from two bedrooms to three.
- From the heart. Beware of resolutions with overtones of 'I ought to…' or 'I should…' These are more likely to result from other's expectations than your own intentions.

THE ART OF PROBLEM SOLVING

Sometimes we are so absorbed in our own surroundings that we forget to look over the fence.

CHARLES HANDY, *THE AGE OF UNREASON: THINKING THE UNLIKELY AND DOING THE UNREASONABLE* (1995)

The ability to tackle problems successfully is a valuable one. Here are a couple of approaches to problem solving that could get you started.

Who, Where, When, Why, What Analysis

Whether you're trying to solve a particular problem or change your circumstances, it helps to look at the issue from all directions.

- Who? Who are the other influences? A parent who may not approve of a career move? Dependants who make you feel more conservative about financial issues? A boss who doesn't see you as 'management material'?
- Where? Where are the problems occurring? At home, work, the amateur dramatics society?
- When? Are there triggers to your behaviour that you want to

change? Can you pinpoint a time when you realized that you'd started to feel differently?

- Why? By uncovering the genuine reasons for your decision to change—end a relationship, leave a job—you can sharpen your motivation and your focus. You may also find out you're wanting to change for the wrong reasons, enabling you to change course before it's too late.
- Why not? What are the obstacles to change? What's stopping you? What would it take to, for instance, move to the country—winning the lottery, a job transfer? Write down everything you can think of, then cross out the ones that are out of your control and those factors that, on reflection, are impractical or unreasonable. You'll be left with those within your control.
- What? What can you change: the situation, your behaviour, your thinking, your attitude? What can't you change? Some things—like gravity, death and taxes—are inevitable, although you can try defying the odds.

Creative problem solving

Creativity is not just about painting, pottery or patchwork. You are more likely to find success by approaching a problem with an open, creative mind than with a furrowed brow. Here are some ways to switch on your creativity.

- Mind mapping. Diagrammatical ways of recording your thoughts, with branches of possibilities and consequences can provoke new ideas and insights better than linear writing.
- Lateral thinking. Thinking beyond the obvious and orthodox can bring inventive solutions.
- Time alone. Sometimes a bit of personal space is all that is needed to allow thoughts to flow.
- SWOT analysis. Taking a look at your strengths, weaknesses, opportunities and threats can help you choose between options.
- Ideas book. Capturing ideas as soon as they occur, whether it's in the middle of the night or on the train to work, saves you from the frustration of not being able to recall your breakthrough.

- Play and daydream. Brains need rest and play if they are to perform at their peak.
- Humour. You make faster connections and think in a more wide-ranging and creative way when you can see the funny side.
- Sleep on it. While bodies recuperate, the brain works overtime. A little time, coupled with removing your focus from a problem is sometimes all you need to determine the best course of action.
- Change your environment. Businesses are sometimes advised to change the layout of offices or factories to improve productivity. You may do it at home too: home renovation is big business. But there are other ways of changing your environment: a day trip, a bus ride to somewhere you don't normally go, a weekend away, a holiday.

STEPPING BACK

Sometimes you need to gain some objectivity and distance yourself from a situation before you can really assess and analyze it. This is where a therapist or a good friend can help. Talking about something and externalizing it can often help you to think more clearly.

BOUNCE

The world is not perfect and nor are we. M's diet goes well until his aunt's 40th birthday celebrations; J & K's house hunting looks promising but then a busy period at J's office means she's bringing work home on the weekends and cannot view properties; L has not lost her temper with her children for over a month but the news that her father is ill makes her snappy. Bounce and resilience mean you can use a setback to strengthen your resolve and prevent further deviations. Look at the trigger, the situation in which it occurred—many smokers, for instance, find it harder to refuse a cigarette after a few drinks—and recognize the cutoff point for your willpower. Maybe you need to change your expectations? And even if you've slipped a rung on the ladder of change, there's nothing to stop you climbing it again.

DIVIDE AND CONQUER

When you feel life's really out of kilter or you have several major problems on your hands, you may have to switch to survival mode until life calms down. Prioritizing takes on a new urgency. Act on any emergency situations; seek help when you're out of your depth, for instance, if you finally realize that you need help to stop gambling. Attack the problem one step at a time. The bigger and more overwhelming the task, the more you need to break it into its smaller components.

Discard the unimportant. Good friends will wait for you to get in touch later and it doesn't matter if the house is untidy, but the electricity will be cut off if you don't pay the bill.

DO NOTHING

Sometimes you need to ramble and potter and take things easy. While action gets results, there are times when it's best to wait, times for recuperation, relaxation and reflection. Sometimes you need to cogitate a little, compost and mature your ideas, lie low, keep still, regain calm and get ready to act.

LIFE AND OTHER PLANS

Life is what happens when you're busy making other plans, they say, but plans are what will get you going in the first place. Plans are the maps that guide you through life. Some people have an excellent sense of direction and don't seem to need them, but many others benefit from a sense of knowing where they are going. Plans map out the route to the destination or goal. Making plans and setting goals is just expanding on an activity you do to some degree every day, from writing a shopping list to choosing a flight for a vacation. In the broader sense, it can involve taking a particular course of study to reach a desired career, or picking your way through the administrative steps involved in migrating.

To some people, the idea of setting goals for your life has an artificial ring about it. But, like shopping for the ingredients for a chocolate mud cake recipe, rather than any old cake, the best plans come from clear goals. Goals help you focus on what you want to achieve, even if you detour along the way.

SMART goals

There are various versions of what the acronym SMART stands for, but all agree, SMART goals are more likely to be reached. Here is one version.

- S for specific. 'Buy some running shoes and jog three times a week' rather than 'get fit'. 'Put all books on shelves, put clothes away, clear the floor' instead of 'clean up the boys bedroom'.
- M for measurable. 'Lose three kilograms' is a measurable goal with an endpoint, rather than 'lose some weight'. 'Move to a three-bedroom house with a garden big enough to grow vegetables' rather than 'move to a bigger house'.
- A for attainable. Good goal setting is in tune with your strengths and weaknesses.
- R for realistic. 'Finish the thesis by Christmas' could be unrealistic if it's only a month away, whereas 'by Easter' might, with good planning, be possible.
- T for time frame. A time element focuses resolve: 'to visit relatives overseas before the beginning of summer term' rather than 'as soon as we can'. Many contracts include a time clause.

TAKING STOCK

Balancing the different aspects of your life, meeting challenges, solving problems…you may often feel the need to step back and review your daily life and how you feel the days add up together. Are you being swept along the river of life, sometimes going under and just managing to come up for breath or have you found a vessel to navigate it? Although people sometimes report turning points, perhaps crises, from which their lives emerge better and richer, most people need to address problems, conflicts and choices, and continually re-evaluate their lives along the way. Even those who've found a vessel need to keep it in good repair.

At times, you cannot even find a straightforward answer to the question 'What do I want?' Your desires can be muddied by concern for others in your life, fear of the consequences, generally being out of touch with your feelings, or being confused about your motivations. Here is a series of exercises to choose from— some short, some more involved—that might help you assess your life, focus ideas and oil the wheels of change.

EXERCISE ONE: DO YOU HAVE TIME FOR…?

- [ ] Your body
- [ ] Fun, pleasure, leisure and play
- [ ] The material world
- [ ] Travel
- [ ] Rest
- [ ] Love
- [ ] Friendship
- [ ] Family
- [ ] Reading
- [ ] Learning
- [ ] Creating
- [ ] Meditating
- [ ] Solitude

EXERCISE TWO: DO YOU WANT TO...?

- [ ] Reduce stress
- [ ] Write a novel
- [ ] Stop smoking
- [ ] Erode debt
- [ ] Get a promotion
- [ ] Move jobs
- [ ] Stop working overtime
- [ ] Relax your schedule
- [ ] Cut down your alcohol intake
- [ ] Get fitter
- [ ] Lose weight
- [ ] Gain weight
- [ ] Stop feeling tired
- [ ] Do some voluntary work overseas

EXERCISE THREE: IF I HAD A YEAR TO LIVE...

Take pen and paper and write down what you would do if you knew your time was running out.

EXERCISE FOUR: WHERE AM I AT NOW?

This flexible exercise is designed to help you step back from your problems and find ways to move forward. If you find it useful, it's worth doing regularly. Problems, priorities and balance change with time. While its focus is on the present, it might help identify future plans too.

The fact that you run through a series of aspects of your life adds another dimension. If you are feeling depressed and look at your answers, noticing that almost all have serious problems, then at least you can say 'no wonder'. On the other hand, if after taking a wider look you realize that you have good health, great relationships, and a home you are happy with, but are looking for work, then you might be more inclined to feel like thanking your lucky stars.

1 Take a sheet of paper and divide it into six columns:
   - Relationships
   - Health
   - Work
   - Finance
   - Home
   - Soul

2 Jot down a few thoughts under each heading. Consider the things that are going well in addition to the problems or things that are getting you down.

3 Next, take a step back from these scenarios. Maybe note if they are short term or long term, serious or trivial. Think about what's stopping you, whether the obstacle is mental or practical.

4 Finally, make a note of any actions you can take or think about.

An example of a completed form appears in Appendix A on page 386.

EXERCISE FIVE: THE 'DEEP AND MEANINGFUL'

For a more thought-provoking look at your life, consider some of these questions.

1 General

(a) How significantly do the following areas of your life impact on your happiness?
   - Big events, traumas and incidents (eg. adolescence, getting married, moving house or a major illness)
   - Relationships with family/friends/partner
   - Your living space and home
   - Work

- Finances
- The spiritual or non-material (eg. religious or political beliefs, creativity)
- Health

(b) Have you made major changes in any of these areas? If so, in what ways did you have to adjust? Was that difficult or stressful?

2   Seeking balance

(a) What does 'a balanced life' mean to you? Is it important? In what ways do you seek balance in your life?

(b) Do you feel your life is stressful? What is most stressful about it? What aspects of your life reduce stress?

3   Relationships

(a) Who are the important people in your life (eg. children, a partner, friends or extended family)?

(b) How would you describe the place they occupy in (or the impact they have had in) your life?

(c) Do you think relationships should be left to 'happen' or do you think they take work?

(d) What sort of 'work' do you think they need? Do others in your life share your attitudes?

(e) How do you deal with conflict within relationships?

(f) Have your relationships changed much over time?

(g) Have you ever been in a particularly bad patch, then had a breakthrough that really helped?

4   Home

(a) What aspects of where you live affect your lifestyle?

(b) Does the physicality of where you live affect other aspects of your life (eg. health, contentment, finances, relationships)?

(c) Do you think that where you live can make you depressed or stressed?

5 Work
(a) Where does work fit in your life? Would you stop if you could?

(b) What does working do for you? (Provide money only or are there other benefits?)

(c) Do you find that you need to balance your work with other interests?

6 Finances
Money is said to be one of the greatest causes of marital break-down, and the cause of much unhappiness. Keeping this in mind, ask yourself the following:

(a) How do you feel about money? Are you financially phobic (eg. do you hate opening bank statements, dealing with tax) or are you pragmatic?

(b) Do you worry about money or do you believe it will arrive when needed?

(c) Do you find it hard to save and/or invest for the future? If you don't, what is your motivation? If you do, what makes it hard?

7 Spirit
(a) Do you have strong beliefs that are an important part of your life (eg. religious, political, ethical or other spiritual beliefs)? How do these beliefs affect your life in practical ways?

(b) Do you think life has a meaning or is it up to us to give our lives meaning? What brings meaning to your life?

(c) Do you feel the need for a creative outlet? If so, what is it and what flow-on effect does it have to the rest of your life?

(d) Would you agree that we all need ways to transcend the daily struggle? In what ways do you make your life worth living?

8 Health
(a) How important is health to you?

(b) How do you keep as healthy as you can?

(c) Are there aspects of your health you could improve through, for instance, exercise, diet, sleep or other self-help possibilities?

9 Summary

Have you been able to identify areas of your life that are out of kilter? Try writing down a few steps you could take to bring your life back into balance. Use these categories as a guide:

(a) Home

(b) Health

(c) Relationships

(d) Work

(e) Finances

(f) Spirit

SOME OTHER EXERCISES TO CONSIDER

- Your obituary. Write your own obituary, imagining you are a friend who knew you well. What would you like to say?

- A wish list. Write it freely, then decide on some filters to help sort it. For instance, you could divide the list according to what's possible, likely, requires miracles, requires courage, short term, medium term, long term, and so on.

- If you won the lottery. What would you do if you won a lot of money? Could you take a few steps towards those ideas in any way?

- Your life in a day. Write a summary of what's going on in your life but stick to one page—as if you are writing to a good friend who's out of touch with what's going on in your life. Write about your job, your family, what's bugging you and what you're thrilled about.

- The value of values. What do you care most about? Do you have a life philosophy? How does it relate to people, money, status, the environment? What motivates you most?

Be not sad.
Be like the sun at midday.

I CHING (BOOK OF CHANGES)

2. LIVING THE DAY TO DAY

DAILY LIFE CAN BE DEMANDING,
NOT LEAST OF ALL WHEN
CUMULATIVE PRESSURES LEAD TO
STRESS OR DEPRESSION. THE
GOOD NEWS IS THAT THERE ARE
MANY WAYS TO LIFT THE CLOUD
OF DEPRESSION, QUELL ANXIETY
AND LEARN TO CONTROL STRESS.
CHANGE MAY NOT BE EASY BUT, IF
YOU ACHIEVE IT, YOU'LL REAP THE
REWARDS EVERY DAY.

IT'S ALL IN THE MIND

Marvin Staples, a cheerful Chippewa Indian from Minnesota, walks backwards. Everywhere. He says it makes him feel younger, and has cured him of backache as well as arthritis in his knees. It has also reversed the way he looks at the world: 'I used to want more and more, but now I think about how I can get by with less.' Al Joyner of Virginia Beach, Virginia, delights local children by riding around town on a half rocking horse, half bicycle that is his own creation. It bears the words 'disco kid' on one side, and pulls along a milk crate mounted on a golf cart. Ann Atkin, of Devon in south-west England, likes to wear a felt pixie hat. She also likes garden gnomes and has 7500 of them in her garden.

When Dr David Weekes, a clinical neuropsychologist at the Royal Edinburgh Hospital, realized that eccentricity was a facet of human behaviour largely ignored by psychiatry and psychology, he decided to research it himself. Ten years later, in 1995, he published his findings, including accounts of eccentrics like the endearing folk above, in a book entitled *Eccentrics*.

Weekes and his team studied more than 1000 eccentrics, mainly from Great Britain and the United States. They were interviewed at length and given standard personality evaluations, then underwent IQ tests and other tests used in psychiatry. Eccentrics are by definition non-conforming, but Weekes also found they were more creative, had more curiosity about the world and, in many cases, were contentedly obsessed by hobbies and interests. In addition, although it was not a quality he felt could be scientifically measured, he found eccentrics to be happier than the bulk of the general public.

Eccentrics have in common an indomitable spirit of hopefulness, a buoyant self-confidence and a persistently positive outlook. Not only do they suffer less mental ill health—such as stress and depression—they are also healthier all round, visiting the doctor at a rate that works out as sixteen times less than the average man or woman during their lifetime.

Much of the population could take a lesson or two from the eccentrics, it seems. Across the world, in both developing and developed countries, 1 in 4 adults will suffer a mental health problem of one sort or another during their lifetime, according to the World Health Organization. And research in countries such as Australia and the United States reveals that in any one year, 1 in 5 adults suffers a mental health problem. 'Times change, and we with them', states the proverb. But sometimes you may resist change or struggle to adapt. Enter stress.

THE MODERN CURSE

Stress has many faces and many causes. Battle fatigue in the 2003 Gulf War was reported to be the cause of friendly fire incidents, because after a week of reduced sleep and heightened stress, soldiers performed worse than if drunk. Medical researchers at Ohio State University College of Medicine in Columbus gave medical students a hepatitis B vaccine during exam time. Those with less social support were not only more stressed and anxious, they also showed evidence of a more sluggish immune system reaction.

Since our cave days, stress is the emotion as well as the biological state we experience when things get tough. If you slip while walking on a steep rocky path or encounter a big animal with big teeth, a fear of losing control (or your life)—the infamous fight or flight mechanism—is switched on. Your heart beats more strongly, your perceptions become acute, and your mental and physical prowess is at its peak until the danger passes.

But modern day stress is different, researchers tell us. Evolution has given human beings the gift of being able to deal with short-term stress arising from isolated incidents—what scientists call 'acute' stress—but we don't seem so well adjusted to chronic stress. This can build up gradually over time because of a psychological and emotional overload.

When you are stressed, your body adopts a range of emergency measures: your heart rate increases in order to feed muscles that might be called on for extra duties; you have the urge to empty

Florence Nightingale (1820–1910)

Florence Nightingale, the Englishwoman credited with making nursing a skilled profession—and who became known as the Lady of the Lamp for her work during the Crimean War—was no stranger to mental anguish. She suffered a nervous breakdown when aged 24 after her parents refused to allow her to train as a nurse. Another crisis came five years or so later, after she had refused a marriage proposal from a man she 'adored'. Despite assuring herself she'd made the right decision she was deeply depressed and thought often of suicide. Her middle years—in which she finally had the chance to work and prove herself—were fulfilling. But her old age was happy as she found personal relationships no longer clashed with other desires. In 1907 she became the first woman ever to receive the Order of Merit.

your bladder and digestive tract, to take a load off your body if not your mind; and you divert energy away from your immune system. In the short term this is fine, but in the long term, such a 'high alert' state causes heart disease, digestive problems (such as ulcers) and makes you more vulnerable to infection. Health authorities, such as the Australian National Heart Foundation (NHF), take stress very seriously. Although 'stress' is too vague a term, says the NHF, depression, social isolation and lack of social support are all on a par with smoking and physical inactivity for increasing the risk of heart disease.

If you feel stressed from time to time—or even, when you stop to think about it, most of the time—you are not alone:

- In Britain in 1999 there were 783 work-related stress claims, up by 70 per cent on the year before.
- In the United States, job stress is estimated to cost industry around $300 billion every year.

The Whitehall Studies, which began in the 1960s, revolutionized research into the causes of stress-related illness. Led by Michael Marmot, professor of epidemiology and public health at University

College, University of London, the project aimed to identify and analyze risk factors for cardiovascular disease. Ten thousand British civil servants were studied.

As the results flowed in, Marmot was surprised to find that those he considered to be employed in high-stress occupations—the bowler hat, black umbrella brigade pursuing high-pressure, senior executive jobs—showed lower rates of heart disease than expected. They ranked lower in other major causes of death as well. Those at the bottom of the bureaucratic heap—guards and messengers, for example—had the highest rates of disease.

The group in between presented a puzzle. Doctors and lawyers, one rung down from the top, had twice the disease rates of the topnotch job holders. The difference couldn't be explained by poverty or wealth, as this mainly middle class group excluded both the rich and the poor. The solution was found to centre on the matter of control. The degree of control people exercised at work explained the apparent anomalies, the researchers concluded: the greater the control, the lower the rate of disease. Issues such as whether workers were fairly treated and whether their work was interesting were also very important. Boredom at work can be damaging.

REDUCING STRESS

Not all stress is bad. A little stress helps you get up in the morning and face a day's work, whether it's a commuting distance away or involves caring for your children. A crisis can be a time of personal growth; stressful periods may also be rich ones. Some stress is fun—if you like sky diving or roller coaster rides. But the ability to reduce stress is a life skill from which everyone can benefit.

- Awareness. An awareness of stress symptoms can be the first step in reducing them. Tense muscles leading to backache, a tight jaw, over-tiredness, headaches and migraines can all be connected to a stress overload.
- Detective work. Working out what's causing your stress can help identify those situations you can change, and those you have to learn to live with. This does not necessarily mean you have to

Why are you stressed?

A 1998 General Social Survey in Canada asked people under moderate or greater stress to identify the source of their stress. Respondents, who accounted for just over half the Canadian population, nominated the following reasons:

- work   44%
- family   18%
- finances   11%
- school work   9%
- personal health   6%
- stress in general   4%

grin and bear it. But it might mean trying to find a way around the problem, or nurturing a new attitude towards it.

- Switching off. Becoming totally absorbed in an activity is highly relaxing, whether it's by going to bed with a good book, taking a weekly print-making class, or enjoying the camaraderie and physical activity of soccer practice.
- Relaxation exercises. Meditation, deep breathing, yoga and tai chi are all useful ways to reduce anxiety and therefore stress. See page 300 for ways to induce the relaxation response.

VOX POP: Are you stressed?

Doing too much, not feeling in control? The reasons people give for feeling stressed have a lot in common.

'I get very stressed when I see control slipping. What really stresses me out is not having the time to do everything I want— to do all my work to my satisfaction, see all my friends and keep the house clean. In the longer term I worry about how I can have a great career and fit in children and a husband as well, and how I'll ever afford to own my own home. If I have a problem, bed is the first place I head. Nothing can get to you while you are asleep.' CT

'I'm stressed because I'm doing too much. Still in sales…which I didn't think I would be at 40, but financial necessity rules at this stage. Home is also an "office" as I work on a business with my husband. Yoga, time on my own and time with my son reduce stress for me, also a good conversation with a girlfriend…rare these days, which saddens me.' CS

'Stress usually revolves around deadlines, which can be hateful, exerting horrid pressure. Working for myself also means tax is another stressful activity: the process of sorting out hundreds of small pieces of paper for some wretched purpose is boring, perplexing and frustrating.' PN

'My life is not very stressful, which is just as well as I do not cope well with stress. Rows with my wife (or contorting myself to avoid them) are the single biggest cause of stress. I also get stressed over professional exams, usually without good reason.' HB

'I don't feel my life is stressful but I've worked hard to achieve this. I used to experience panic attacks and anxiety disorder in the past but I learnt to control my thoughts, although it took a long time. Laughter, spending time with friends and family, walking in the country or travelling to different places all help reduce my stress levels.' ML

KEEPING IN EMOTIONAL TRIM

Emotions play an integral part in being human. They express our experience of life—the anger of being attacked, the grief of loss, the joy of play. But even more, they govern our ability to make decisions, motivate ourself and even think clearly. Horace Walpole, the eighteenth century writer, wrote in a letter to the Countess of

Upper Ossory on 16 August 1776, 'This world is a comedy to those that think, a tragedy to those that feel.' But humans are not 'either/or': emotion sits alongside reason as our guides through life, and we need both.

Emotions help streamline decision making by eliminating some options at the outset, and highlighting others. In his book *Emotional Intelligence*, Daniel Goleman, an expert in behaviour and brain sciences, shows how people who have experienced damage to their brain such that they can no longer experience emotion are surprisingly incapable of making even simple rational decisions. Goleman relates the story of a man he calls Elliot, who underwent an operation to remove a brain tumour. Elliot lost his job, his wife and his investments because he could no longer prioritize and use his time usefully. His neurologist ascribed his tragedy to the fact that, along with the tumour, a part of his prefrontal lobes had been removed, burning the bridge between his emotional brain and the thinking part. With no preference for one or other option even decisions as trivial as what time to make an appointment became impossibly confusing for him.

There is a tendency—especially among the 'stiff upper lip' brigade—to value logic over emotion, and to downgrade feelings as obstacles to be overcome. But increasingly we are learning that IQ and logic are only part of the story, and are by no means an indicator of success or happiness in life.

WHAT IS EMOTIONAL INTELLIGENCE?

Emotional intelligence takes you a long way along the road to 'knowing yourself'. It's about being aware of your own and other's emotions. It's also about keeping them under control or at least not letting them get out of control.

Be aware of your emotions

Recognizing your own emotions gives you a better chance of working with them rather than against them. It is also part of being in charge of your own life. Psychologists refer to three possible states of awareness:

- Self-aware. People's awareness assists them in shaking off bad moods quickly.
- Engulfed. People often feel swamped by their moods and lose perspective as well as the feeling of being in control.
- Accepting. People are aware of their moods and don't try to change them (those who are forever in good moods don't feel the need; others are resigned to feeling depressed).

Manage your emotions

The ability to soothe yourself, and shake off anxiety, irritability or gloom helps you to bounce back after a setback, whether it's big or small. Restraint allows you to express emotions in ways society deems appropriate—bottling up anger in public and screaming with frustration in private, or checking your temper at a toddler's antics and so refraining from giving a blow you know you'd later regret.

You may have little power over when you are swept by what emotion, but to some extent you can control how long the emotion lasts. For example, anger is one of the hardest emotions to control as it generates its own energy and can even call in a companion— exhilaration—for the ride. But there are some ways of diffusing it:

- Challenge the thoughts that trigger anger, the earlier the better. For instance, you might be ready to forgive a rude remark if you knew the person expressing it had recently suffered a personal tragedy. Timing is all. However, once you reach top scale rage, your ability to think straight has already gone out the window.
- A cooling off period is an excellent balm. A natural response to anger is to seek time alone. Long walks or relaxation techniques such as deep breathing and muscle relaxation also help by distracting you from what angered you in the first place. Effective distraction will shut off angry thoughts and help prevent you from stoking your anger.
- If out of control anger is a recurrent problem for you, write down your angry thoughts as they occur. This may help stop them escalating to rage, and can be a first step in challenging them.

Harnessing the power of emotion

Skills such as being able to accept delayed gratification and the ability to check impulsiveness are essential in order to meet goals, take control of your life and generally be productive and effective. If you've studied for a qualification then you know about having to work now in order to be rewarded later. Similarly, if you are able to refuse another drink—tempting as it may be—because you are driving, that's another sign that you can control your emotions.

A good mood does much more than put a smile on your face. Research shows it makes you think more flexibly and with greater complexity. These are handy skills to have when you are trying to solve a problem. Laughter is even better: it helps you think more broadly and freely, perhaps noticing connections you hadn't realized existed before.

By contrast, bad moods can lead to more cautious decisions, while out of control emotions can lead to bad ones.

Relating to others

Reading other people's emotions tends to feed altruistic feeling as well as enhance the people skills necessary for jobs that involve managing other people, teaching them, selling to them or caring for them. Leadership, popularity and how you interact with others all depend on understanding the complex world of emotion. Even considering others' feelings is a start—thinking about how colleagues may feel about certain comments or behaviour in meetings, for instance. Body language reveals a lot; for example, making eye contact drives a message home much more effectively than darting eyes (which invite mistrust) or simply looking the other way (which can easily be read as boredom).

THE BLUE DEVIL OF DEPRESSION

Blues music—credited with giving birth to rhythm and blues, and rock'n'roll—owes its origin to the plaintive singing of the Negro spiritual. 'The songs of the slave represent the sorrows of his heart;

Anger alert: why the last straw makes us snap, crackle and pop!

We've all experienced it—a trying day. One thing after another and snap! Something you might laugh off at another time releases your anger. Ever wondered why? Underneath the frazzled emotions lies a biological reason. Irritations and stress build on each other. They steadily arouse the adrenocortical branch of the nervous system, creating a background state of edginess, ready for action. For the overworked mother or the underpaid father, this aroused state lowers the threshold for anger. By recognizing and dealing with stresses as they occur, you can help to keep your level of anger under control and well below the snapping threshold.

and he is relieved by them only as an aching heart is relieved by its tears,' wrote the journalist Frederick Douglass, who escaped American slavery in 1838. But according to the *Shorter English Oxford Dictionary*, 'blue' has been used as early as 1550, in the phrase 'to look blue', meaning low spirited or suffering anxiety, fear or discomfort. A candle burning blue was once considered an omen of death or an indicator of the presence of ghosts. It's an interesting association, given that we often regard depression or a low mood as something that we'd like to 'shake off', almost as if it were an unwanted presence.

Where do the blues end and depression begin? Andrew Solomon, author of *The Noonday Demon: An Anatomy of Depression*, has battled with depression for many years. If you imagine yourself a soul made of iron, he says, while grief weathers and mild depression rusts, major depression is the collapse of the whole structure. It's an analogy that works on a number of levels: rust can be insidious and slow, but if chronic—and left unchecked for long enough—it can cause sudden collapse.

Depression encompasses everything from a sense of feeling down to debilitating despair, from intense sadness and isolation to lethargy and numbness.

The incidence of depression is rising. No one knows exactly why, but there are plenty of theories on offer: erosion of the nuclear family; soaring divorce rates; the reduced time parents spend with their children; and increased mobility, which means people don't know their extended families as well as they used to and can access neither their support nor the bolsters to identity they once provided. Some psychiatrists believe parenting styles that are not in touch with, or are even indifferent to, children's needs are a cause of increased vulnerability to depression. Another suggested cause of depression is the waning of religious beliefs and the rise of individualism, bringing with them a weaker sense of community. Too much focus on your own concerns can lead to a loss of perspective.

A range of theories attempts to explain why some people appear more susceptible to depression than others. For instance, psychodynamics theories look at events in early life and, among other factors, their effect on the development of self-esteem and the individual's ability to cope with stress. Behavioural theories cite circumstances that mould responses. A child may learn that being passive is the best response to unloving parents, for example. Physical theories explain depression by ascribing it to a genetic predisposition, or to changes in the brain.

Life events—such as the birth of a child or a period of overwork—can trigger depression, as can lack of stimulus leading to stagnation and boredom. Repression and suppression of a natural response to an event or situation commonly leads to lowered emotions across the board. For example, suppressing anger at being retrenched might create an emotional picture of lethargy, disinterest and helplessness. Many events provoke mixed feelings and it is natural and healthy to express and explore them. In other instances, some people may find they become depressed when they experience distressing situations over which they have little control.

Some medical conditions can lead to depression. These include stroke, dementia, hypothyroidism, Cushing's disease, Addison's disease and Parkinson's disease. Some medications' side effects include depression.

The lowdown on depression

- According to the World Health Organization (WHO), more than 21 million people worldwide suffer from depression.
- One in 5 people suffering depression attempts suicide, according to a seven-country survey by a research company called Datamonitor.
- Eighty per cent of suicides were suffering depression.
- An estimated 20 to 25 per cent of general practitioner patient visits involve those needing support or treatment for anxiety or depression, according to a 1997 community survey in Australia.
- An estimated 40 per cent of people suffering depressive disorders do not receive professional help.
- More women (1 in 6) than men (1 in 9) seek help for depression.
- More than one million prescriptions for antidepressants are written each year in Australia.
- Ten per cent of the US population suffers from depression, according to the the country's National Institute of Mental Health.

ARE YOU DEPRESSED?

Health authorities often make use of lists of specific symptoms in order to define depression. The list given below comes from the World Health Organization.

Someone suffering clinical depression would have at least two of the following symptoms for at least two weeks:

- an unusually sad mood that does not go away
- no longer enjoys activities that used to be enjoyable and interesting
- no energy, tiredness.

Other symptoms include:

- loss of self-confidence and self-esteem
- feeling guilty when there's no reason
- wishing they were dead
- increased difficulty in concentrating and in making decisions

- moving slowly, or sometimes becoming more agitated and unable to settle
- sleeping difficulties, including sometimes sleeping too much
- eating problems—either loss of interest in food or sometimes eating too much with either weight loss or weight gain.

The level of depression is then determined by the number of symptoms suffered by an individual.
- four of the ten symptoms in the past fortnight: mild depression
- six of the ten symptoms: moderate depression
- eight of the ten symptoms: severe depression.

DEFLECTING DEPRESSION

The good news is that there is much you can do to reverse the spiral of depression and lift a low mood. Dianne Tice, a psychologist at Cage Western Reserve University in the United States, interviewed over 400 people on how they shook off bad moods. One of the most successful tactics, she found, was seeing things differently—cognitive reframing, as it's referred to in psychology. Other related techniques include the following:

- Take responsibility. Even if it's only for a small aspect of life, taking responsibility can stop the slow slide of giving up that can accompany depression. Making your own decisions is energizing. Those who tend to look to an external authority for decisions and fulfilment have a greater propensity to depression.
- Find the feeling. Depression can be caused by repressing a natural response to a life event, such as the death of a loved one or a marriage break-up. Thinking through the emotions the depression may be masking, then working at expressing those feelings can be of help.
- Distract yourself. Just as wallowing in negative thoughts can perpetuate depression, a strong focus on something else can break the cycle. Sometimes indulging in a small pleasure is enough: a hot bath, a funny television program. Helping others

can also provide welcome relief from your own problems, whether it's volunteer work at the local old people's home or taking on coaching junior football.

- Do something. Being busy, staying active, doing exercise, all keep depression at bay and can help shift it too. It's surprising just how much of a lift doing something can give: getting out of bed in the morning even though you don't feel like it at all; going to the party even though you're feeling depressed and antisocial; going for a swim after work even though part of you just wants to get home.

THE POWER OF THOUGHT

One of the most praised therapies for lifting depression is cognitive behaviour therapy (CBT). Its premise is that many upsetting emotions are caused and perpetuated by negative or irrational beliefs. American psychiatrist Karen Horney coined the phrase 'the tyranny of the shoulds' in 1939 to describe this tendency. CBT aims to help people challenge the tyranny by identifying these beliefs— which can be as simple as 'life should be fair'; 'I must be approved of and loved by everyone in my life'; 'it's dreadful when things don't go as I'd like them to' or 'it is better to avoid problems rather than confront them'—then challenging them.

Challenging

The key to CBT is challenge. You can challenge the shoulds by saying, 'Why should…?' Why should you be athletic and slim? Why should your house be spotless? Why should people be kind to you?

Another challenge is to come up with a statement that directly opposes your thinking. For instance, you might be feeling lonely at a new job and feel disappointed that no one's asked you to join them at lunch. Your belief is that people should be friendly and like you. Your first challenge—'why should they be friendly?'—can be supplemented with the statement 'it would be nice if someone approached me in a friendly fashion but it doesn't always happen straight away and I can cope with it in the meantime.'

The next step might include some action: 'Maybe it's up to me to take the first step. S seems nice. I'll ask her tomorrow if she'd like to go to the cafe on the corner one lunchtime next week.'

Rational disputes help: 'this is inconvenient but it's not a disaster'; 'this is not my problem'; or 'everybody is wrong at times and that's OK'.

Reality testing involves testing your belief to see if it's true. For instance, if you believe your husband can't look after a baby and therefore you never get a second to yourself, you could leave him with the baby while you go to the shops. If he copes, then you have some evidence to challenge your beliefs and you may feel more confident leaving him with the baby for longer next time.

Goal-directed thinking forces you to ask yourself if behaving or thinking the way you do helps you get closer to your goal—whether it's getting on with the new CEO or relaxing at a social event. If you know you're close to a promotion it's hardly going to do you any good to be stand-offish with the new boss, even if you don't like his style. If you've arranged a gathering at home in an effort to make new friends in your new neighbourhood, you will only put people off if you fuss around and don't stand still long enough for them to talk to you and get to know you.

Some of the thinking that can feed depression and anxiety includes the following:

- Black and white thinking. The potatoes weren't done so the dinner party was ruined; you misread an exam question so you must have failed; your child's still up at 10 pm— 'he never sleeps'. This is polarized thinking where you refuse to see the middle ground: everyone seemed to have a great time and no one noticed the potatoes; the other questions were ones you knew off pat; your child's routine may be out of whack but he sleeps for eleven hours once he's succumbed.

- Overgeneralization. Drawing negative conclusions from limited evidence is often betrayed by using words like 'everyone', 'never' and 'always'. By saying, 'I'm always the last to leave the office'—when in actual fact it's only been for the past week while you worked on an urgent report—you make the situation seem worse than it is.

- Personalization. This involves taking things personally, such as a rude remark from an overworked shop assistant, when it's not intended that way; or interpreting someone's behaviour towards you as a rejection when it has more to do with their own worries or personality.
- Individual outlook. This occurs when you focus on information that confirms your own viewpoint, such as something you're already anxious about, rather than taking a more realistic perspective. You believe your neighbour dislikes you because he didn't say hello when you were bringing in your shopping yesterday. However, the truth of the matter is that he was helping his elderly mother out of the car and didn't notice you because he was worried about her hip fracture.
- Jumping to negative conclusions. Here you instantly assume your teenage daughter's had an accident when she's not home by the agreed time; that your work's going to dry up completely because the industry has suffered a small decline; that someone's snubbed you on the street, when in reality, they didn't see you.
- Blaming others. Blaming others rather than owning a problem is a serious obstacle to moving on as it hinders action and results in you harbouring bitterness and resentment—perhaps you blame family life for preventing you from attempting your first novel when, with a little creative problem solving, you could carve out writing time.
- Catastrophizing. Rather than focusing on all of the bad possibilities, or catastrophizing, you can attempt to accept uncertainty and concentrate on what you can do rather than that which is outside your control or unlikely.

DEPRESSION TREATMENTS: TRIED, TESTED AND TALKED ABOUT

The range of treatments people try for depression is testimony to its widespread existence. But does St John's wort really work? Is acupuncture appropriate? Will supportive counselling send depression flying? This section outlines some major treatments in different therapy fields and explains which ones have the stamp of approval from the scientists.

Medical treatments

Medical treatments include standard antidepressant drugs and other medications. Treatment might be made by referral from a doctor or in a hospital setting.

Antidepressants

These are drugs designed to treat depression and are available on prescription only. They work by changing the levels of neurotransmitters (chemical messengers) in the brain, several of which, such as noradrenaline and serotonin, are thought to be low in people who are depressed. Older generation drugs such as tricyclics do not seem to work with children and do not work well with adolescents. So far, little research has been done on the newer drugs with these age groups. Antidepressants may have side effects but they are not addictive. They can take up to four weeks to kick in.

Electroconvulsive therapy

Known as ECT for short, electroconvulsive therapy involves giving a brief electric current to the brain to produce an epileptic fit, while the patient is under general anaesthetic with a muscle relaxant.

It is only used for people with severe depression and is considered more effective than antidepressants. It has been little studied for mild or moderate depression. ECT carries a stigma, and it is mostly only used in extreme circumstances when all other treatments have failed—for instance, if the depressed person is considered suicidal or a danger to themselves.

Oestrogen

The naturally occurring female hormone can be given in a variety of ways: tablet, skin patch or gel. It is most commonly given in combination with progesterone.

Theories propose that oestrogen may act as an antidepressant in women, whether or not they have a low level of the hormone to start with. Studies have been patchy: some that looked at premenstrual syndrome sufferers showed the oestrogen patches helped; others that looked at depressed women around menopause were inconsistent. It may be worth considering oestrogen if other treatments don't work.

Transcranial magnetic stimulation

This treatment involves placing a magnetic coil next to the scalp. Strong magnetic pulses cause electrical changes in the brain next to the coil. Transcranial magnetic stimulation (TMS) is an experimental technique thought to stimulate a number of neurotransmitters in the brain which are at low levels in depression.

Tranquillizers

These drugs, mostly benzodiazepines, provide short-term relief of anxiety by making one of the neurotransmitters in the brain work better. However, they do not affect the neurotransmitters' serotonin and noradrenaline, which are believed to be in short supply in depression. Tranquillizers are addictive and not considered useful in the treatment of depression.

Psychological treatments

These attempt to change thought patterns and ways of seeing things—whether by overcoming emotional obstacles or talking over problems with a counsellor.

Bibliotherapy

This treatment involves reading books or using computer programs to obtain information on how to overcome emotional problems. The individual suffering from depression can work through exercises and homework. Studies have shown books on cognitive behaviour therapy to be more helpful than no treatment, and as helpful as therapy with a professional.

The research is limited and there has been none on the treatment's impact on severe depression.

Cognitive behaviour therapy

As cognitive behaviour therapy (CBT) is regarded as one of the most successful forms of treatment, this therapy has been discussed in detail on page 54.

Hypnotherapy

In hypnosis a patient can become so engrossed in focusing his attention that he is more responsive to suggestions. Hypnosis is used to induce relaxation, reduce anxiety, and overcome negative thoughts, but it is not considered a useful treatment for depression.

Interpersonal psychotherapy

This helps a depressed person solve problems that involve others—for instance, feeling lonely, disputes or long-term grief. Research shows that interpersonal psychotherapy helps mild to moderate depression. It seems to work as well as antidepressants but has not been studied as extensively.

Psychodynamic psychotherapy

Intended to help a patient understand the origin of her problem, this treatment requires the person suffering from depression to form a very close relationship with her counsellor. Studies show psychodynamic psychotherapy works better than no treatment at all, but that it is not considered to be as effective as, for instance, cognitive behaviour therapy.

Supportive counselling

Supportive counselling is where the patient talks over his problems with a health professional whose aim is to be a good listener and provide emotional support. Counselling limited to listening and providing support is not considered effective help for depression. It should be combined with other treatments such as cognitive behaviour therapy or interpersonal psychotherapy, which are designed to aid depression.

Lifestyle and alternative treatments

We'll try almost anything, it seems, to lift our mood. And there is much on offer. Some options, such as exercise, are a good idea anyway; others, including alternative medications, may require a little caution, especially if you are already taking doctor-prescribed drugs.

Acupuncture

A traditional Chinese treatment that requires needles to be inserted at precise points in the body to correct imbalances of energy, acupuncture is thought by Western medicine to possibly increase brain chemicals that are low in the brains of depressed people. Several studies show acupuncture to be as effective as antidepressant drugs but more research is needed to confirm this.

Alcohol avoidance

Cutting down on alcoholic drinks, or stopping drinking alcohol altogether, may have a beneficial effect. Heavy drinkers, especially alcoholics, are more prone to depression. If heavy drinking is linked directly to depression, then cutting down reverses this trend. In addition, cutting back may reduce the problems associated with heavy drinking such as difficulties with money, work and relationships. Cutting back alcohol does not seem to have any effect on the depression of people without drinking problems. Those with long-term drinking problems may need the support of a qualified drug and alcohol expert.

Alcohol for relaxation

One of the effects of alcohol is to reduce the emotional load of stressful situations that can cause depression. While studies show alcohol lifts people's moods and that moderate drinkers suffer less depression than teetotallers, heavy drinking is associated with increased depression.

Aromatherapy

This is a form of gentle massage that makes use of essential oils to increase the benefits. Essential oils may affect the brain through the pathway of smell, although the effects are not fully understood. While massage therapy can make you feel better in the short term, there's insufficient evidence to claim it as a depression treatment.

Caffeine avoidance

Cutting down on coffee, chocolate, cola drinks and energy drinks reduces a person's intake of the stimulant caffeine. Some people may be sensitive to caffeine, and find it makes them more anxious; in certain people, anxiety is linked to depression. In one study of people who thought their depression was due to diet, cutting out caffeine and sugar helped.

Chocolate

Chocolate is a comfort food that people turn to, to lift their mood. There is no evidence that it helps depression although there are reasons why chocolate could boost mood as it contains carbohydrates, which boost serotonin levels in the brain. This chemical is in low supply in the brains of depressed people. Chocolate also contains stimulants such as caffeine, while the sheer pleasure of eating it could release endorphins, brain chemicals that increase pleasure and reduce pain, like opiates.

Colour therapy

Mood may be affected by the colour of rooms, clothes and other objects. While there's insufficient evidence that colour therapy is effective as a treatment for depression, it might help you feel more at home.

Dance and movement therapy

In this form of treatment, a therapist helps people express themselves through movement in order to improve their mood.

The physical exercise can't be bad, nor the social contact, but there's no research yet on the long-term benefits as opposed to the short-term lift derived from attending a class.

Exercise

Theories as to why exercise works are varied: it could block negative thoughts; it might increase social contact; increased fitness could lift mood or increase the levels of neurotransmitters that are low in the depressed. It could also increase endorphins, natural mood lifters in the brain. Exercise is more helpful for depression than relaxation therapy, and in older people it is found to be as effective as antidepressant medication.

Fish oils

Omega-3 oils are found in oily fish such as tuna and mackerel as well as in dietary supplements.

There is limited evidence to show that countries with a low consumption of fish oils have higher rates of depression, and that

John Nash (1928–)

American Nobel Prize winner John Nash is almost as well known for suffering schizophrenia as he is for his mathematical genius. A lack of social skills had him labelled as backward at school, but by age fourteen he began to show an interest in mathematics. He received his doctorate from Princeton University, with a thesis entitled Non-cooperative Games. Described since a child as 'odd', Nash's behaviour became increasingly eccentric until he was admitted to hospital in 1959, the first of many forced visits. In 1994, after winning a Nobel Prize, he wrote that he appeared to be thinking rationally again, although this was 'not entirely a matter of joy'. But he still hoped to be able to add to his achievements, to create something of value through his current studies or new ideas he might entertain in the future.

depressed patients have lower blood levels of omega-3 oils. However, no studies have looked at whether increasing a person's intake of fish oils helps to combat depression.

Ginkgo biloba

Gingko biloba is a supplement made from the leaves of the maidenhair tree. It is claimed to improve blood supply to the brain, but the only study to look at gingko biloba and depression showed it to have no effect.

Ginseng

This Chinese medicine is made from the roots of the ginseng plant. Although it is claimed to improve energy levels and help the body deal with stress, there's no evidence to date that it helps depression.

Glutamine

An amino acid found in foods such as meat, fish, beans and dairy products, glutamine is used to make the transmitter glutamate, which is often promoted as being good for the brain. While there is some evidence it may help depression, this evidence is not yet conclusive.

Homeopathy

Homeopathy is an alternative medicine that treats patients with highly diluted substances that in their full concentration would cause symptoms of an illness. It aims to restore balance and health to the body by stimulating healing processes. There has been insufficient study so far to back any claims of helping depression.

Lemon balm

This is a type of mint with the Latin name *Melissa officinalis*. Used in herbal remedies, it is not known how, or indeed, if, lemon balm helps to relieve depression.

Light therapy

Involving exposure to bright light for about two hours a day—

usually in the morning—light therapy helps people with winter depression and works as well as antidepressant drugs. The brighter the light, the more effective the treatment. The therapy is often performed with a bank of bright fluorescent lights but you could get the same light exposure by taking a one to two hour walk outside in the morning, even if it is overcast.

Massage therapy

Gentle massage, particularly of the back, by a trained therapist, may produce changes in the activity of the brain and could lower the level of stress hormones. This, in turn, could help lower the level of depression. Studies show massage therapy helps those with anxiety—it also seems to help the person giving the massage!

Meditation

A form of quiet contemplation that focuses attention on, for instance, the breath, a phrase, an idea or an object, meditation has religious and spiritual connotations but is also used simply as a relaxation technique.

Its effects on depression have not been evaluated, but it is often practised to relieve stress and anxiety, which is why it is thought meditation could help depression too.

Music

Music conveys emotion and is known to have a positive effect on people. It is not yet understood how music affects the brain but initial research does not show any difference between listening to music, listening to any noise or sitting quietly. It may have more effect when used in conjunction with cognitive behaviour therapy.

Natural progesterone

A naturally occurring female hormone supplied as a cream or suppository from a naturopath, natural progesterone is not the same as the synthetic progestogens used in contraceptives.

The theory is that natural progesterone will help to counterbalance the falls in progesterone levels that a woman experiences after childbirth, a few days before a period and in menopause. Natural progesterone is thought to improve mood by increasing serotonin in the brain; however, there is no convincing evidence that it helps.

Negative air ionization

Fresh air contains more negative ions (atoms or molecules that have gained an electron and have a negative charge). Negative air ions are produced in nature by lightning, ocean surf and waterfalls, and by machine with an air ionizer.

One theory says that negative ions increase brain serotonin levels; serotonin levels decrease in autumn and winter and may be related to seasonal depression. While studies show a promising improvement in seasonal depression with high-density ionizers, there's no research on its effect on general depression.

Pain killers

Common pain killers are mostly taken in tablet form and many people take them when depressed. There is no evidence that they have any effect on mood. In addition, some, such as codeine, can become addictive. If severe pain is causing depression, it should be discussed with a doctor.

Pets

While owning or caring for a pet, especially ones that enjoy company and like to be stroked, is promoted as being good for your health, there is no scientific evidence that it helps depression.

Phenylalanine

This is an amino acid essential for life, found in protein-rich foods such as meat, fish, eggs and beans. It is used to make the neurotransmitter noradrenaline, which is believed to be in short supply in the brains of people who are depressed.

There is little scientific evidence as yet that phenylalanine helps depression, although one study concluded it worked well for women with premenstrual depression.

Pleasant activities

Identifying activities that you find pleasurable—whether kayaking, kite flying or eating Korean food—and doing them more often is an important part of cognitive behaviour therapy (CBT) for depression. While CBT is known to work, there's not much evidence that pleasant activities alone can help.

Relaxation therapy

This includes a number of techniques such as special breathing or progressive muscle relaxation and is aimed at teaching someone to be able to relax voluntarily.

Muscle tension is often associated with stress and anxiety, both of which are strongly associated with depression. In two short-term studies it was found to be as effective as cognitive behaviour therapy or antidepressant drugs, but longer term effects are uncertain.

SAMe

Short for S-adenoslylmethionine, SAMe (pronounced 'sammy') is a chemical that occurs naturally in all of the body's cells. It is present in numerous natural chemical reactions involving DNA, proteins and neurotransmitters (the chemical messengers between nerve cells).

Studies show SAMe works as well as antidepressant drugs for mild to moderate depression, although it is not entirely clear exactly how it works. More research is needed. However, it is not suitable for all as SAMe can cause mania in sufferers of bipolar disorder and should not be used in conjunction with anti-depressants unless under medical supervision.

Selenium

This trace mineral is found in soil and therefore food, and is essential for health. However, there is no evidence to suggest selenium is an appropriate treatment for depression, although one study found it improved the mood of people not suffering depression.

Levels of naturally occurring selenium are lower in some countries than others. It is toxic in high doses.

St John's wort

Hypericum perforatum, or St John's wort, is a small plant with a yellow flower and small oval leaves that is a traditional herbal remedy in Europe.

It is believed to work by increasing the level of chemical messengers in the brain (neurotransmitters) as these are thought to be at low levels in people who are depressed. While some studies show St John's wort is as effective as antidepressant drugs for mild to moderate depression, other studies are less conclusive. Care should be taken if a person is on other drugs as it can interact with some forms of medication.

Sugar avoidance

A theory that some people are sensitive to sugar, resulting in depression, has prompted one study. This showed an improvement in those who cut out caffeine and sugar, compared to cutting out red meat and artificial sweeteners. There's no real evidence that for most people cutting out sugar will relieve depression. The suggestion also flies in the face of biochemistry, which says that foods rich in carbohydrates give a temporary mood lift.

Tyrosine

Available as a dietary supplement, this is an amino acid that is used to make the neurotransmitter noradrenaline. Noradrenaline is believed to be lacking in the brains of some depressed people.

Vitamins

These nutrients are essential for normal metabolism in the body. Folate may prove useful for depression but the research is still in the early stages. Some studies have shown folate supplements help, but this may be because many people with depression have low folate levels. There is no conclusive evidence on the effect of other vitamins. As vitamins are only required by the body in microscopic doses, care should be taken not to take large doses which could prove toxic.

Vervain

Verbena officinalis, or vervain, is a small flowering plant the leaves and flowers of which form a traditional herbal remedy used for depression. There are no scientific studies on its effectiveness.

Vervain leaves can be used to make tea, and liquid drops are also available. Vervain should not be used during pregnancy.

Yoga

Yoga encompasses exercises for greater body and mind control and better wellbeing. Traditionally it covers philosophy and diet too, but in the West it tends to be limited mainly to the physical component. Its series of stretches, usually performed slowly, require concentration and can give a surprisingly vigorous workout. One study showed breathing exercises banished depression at a faster rate than no treatment.

FEAR AND ANXIETY

Fear has a strangely individual stranglehold. An article entitled 'Why We Fear Ourselves More than Asteroids' on the website Space.com describes planet Earth as vulnerable to unexpected attack which could wipe out a city, even destroy civilization as we know it. But people don't care, the writer gasps. On 8 March 2002 an asteroid the size of an eighteen-storey building swept by—at a distance of half a million kilometres, a little further away than the moon. The writer says that statistically human beings should fear death by an asteroid about as much as they fear death by a plane crash. But hang on, thousands of people have died in plane crashes in the last few decades. How many people do you know who've been smashed to death by an asteroid?

The point is, we fear things that are closer to the bone, and risk probability factors are only part of the perception. If you are unsure about newcomers to your suburb, you may fear being broken into. If you work in the food industry, you may have a heightened awareness of the dangers of food-borne illnesses.

According to the US National Institute of Mental Health, fear evolved to enable human beings to deal with dangerous situations. It causes an automatic, rapid protective response in many systems of the body, coordinated by a small structure deep inside the brain called the amygdala.

Anxiety is fear gone wrong. Instead of feeling fear for a real danger, you may worry over mundane minutiae or even suffer the pathology of panic attacks and phobias. Fear enables you to fix on a problem and start working out how to respond to it. But worrying, or anxiety, means you start rehearsing how to deal with problems before they've even arisen.

The saddest thing about worrying is that the quality of thinking you do when worrying is often not good enough to get you out of the trouble you imagine might happen. In other words, you'd be much better off if you reserved your energy, stopped worrying, and instead channelled creative, fresh thoughts to problems when they arrived. But 'never trouble trouble till trouble troubles you' can be easier said than done.

Anxiety at its normal level is a useful protective measure: it can help you avoid dangerous situations and solve everyday problems. But whereas we all suffer mild uneasiness at one end of the scale, terrifying panic attacks at the other end of the scale are experienced by an estimated 1 in 10 Australians.

HOW ANXIOUS ARE YOU?

The Goldberg Anxiety Scale is used by health professionals to assess anxiety levels. It looks at how you have felt over the past month and asks the following questions:

1   Have you felt keyed up or on edge?
2   Have you been worrying a lot?
3   Have you been irritable?
4   Have you had any difficulty relaxing?
5   Have you been sleeping poorly?

Edith Piaf (1915–63)

'The little sparrow', as Edith Piaf was affectionately called, was known for her poignant ballads sung in a heartbreaking voice. Many of the songs were her own, including 'La Vie en Rose', written during the German occupation of Paris in World War II. Her expressive music was said to have reflected a life of tragedy—her mother wanted little to do with her and left her in the care of an acrobat father and Algerian grandmother, and as a young adult she lost her own child to meningitis at age two. She battled with addiction and depression throughout much of her adult life. But when she died, tens of thousands of fans flocked to Paris to follow her in her last journey to Père Lachaise Cemetery—causing traffic to come to a complete stop for the first time since the end of the war.

6   Have you had headaches or neck aches?
7   Have you had any of the following: trembling, tingling, dizzy spells, sweating, urinary frequency, diarrhoea?
8   Have you been worried about your health?
9   Have you had difficulty falling asleep?

Score one point for each 'yes'. Most people experience a few of these symptoms—Australians, on average, experience four. The higher the score, the more likely it is that anxiety will intrude on daily life. About 12 per cent of adults score eight or more; these and other high scorers may have an anxiety disorder.

ANXIETY ALERT

The medical profession divides anxiety disorders into several categories. Some are more cause for concern than others.

Generalized anxiety disorders (GAD)

These are characterized by an overwhelming unfounded anxiety or worry and are accompanied by numerous physical and psychological symptoms. The disorder lasts for at least six months.

Panic disorders

People who suffer from panic attacks live in constant fear of them occurring. A panic attack is defined as a sudden onset of intense apprehension, fear or terror, often with a feeling of impending doom. Symptoms can include an increased awareness of the heartbeat; sweating; trembling; nausea; feeling dizzy, light-headed or faint; and a feeling of unreality or feeling detached from oneself or from one's surroundings.

Phobic disorders

These are phobias that result in the sufferer avoiding or restricting activities out of fear. An example would be agoraphobia—a fear of being in open or public spaces—which may result in the sufferer not leaving home, avoiding shops or never driving a car.

Social phobias

Social phobias can develop in shy children, and involve the fear of any situation where public scrutiny may be possible. It might be as simple as being too overcome by nerves to speak in an assembly or something more severe that means you could never be comfortable in a job that brought you into contact with the public, such as working in a shop.

Specific phobias

These tend to be less disabling as they involve very particular fears such as spiders or snakes.

Acute stress disorder and post-traumatic stress disorder

These occur after a distressing or catastrophic event, involving either actual or threatened death or serious injury. They can also occur if a person witnesses or learns about the catastrophic or distressing experience of a family member or close friend. See the section on post-traumatic stress disorder on pages 74–75.

Obsessive compulsive disorder

This is a disorder in which compulsions, such as washing one's hands or counting the number of paving stones on a pathway, are endlessly repeated. The sufferer is unable to control her behaviour—even though she knows that on leaving the house she checked the door was locked, the oven turned off and the answering machine left on, she cannot help but go back inside and check again…and maybe again.

OVERCOMING ANXIETY

Anxiety is best overcome by confronting fears rather than avoiding them, and by identifying and challenging exaggerated concerns and pessimism. In some cases avoiding feared situations allows your anxiety to grow. If you fall off your bike, or off a horse, people will tell you it's important to get back on again as quickly as you can to avoid anxiety brewing. Talking in self-help groups provides a supportive environment to explore problems. Daily relaxation methods such as meditation, muscle relaxation and deep breathing may reduce physical symptoms of tension. Adequate sleep, regular exercise, avoiding more than 300 milligrams of caffeine a day (an espresso or a cappuccino contains 80 milligrams) and a commitment to what health authorities call rather blandly 'pleasurable activities' also have a part to play.

In addition, there are a few other simple strategies that can help you control your levels of anxiety.

- Take it one day at a time. Doing something about the immediate problem at hand rather than grappling with a catalogue of possible disasters stretching out to the horizon has a calming effect on the worried mind. It also helps to change a worrisome situation. As the proverb says, 'Every day is a new life to a wise man.'
- Identify and analyze. Identifying exaggerated concerns and a pessimistic outlook gives you the chance to challenge them and even reverse them. Pinning down a worry can help you sort out in what circumstances it occurs and perhaps identify what the common triggers are.

- Probability. Break a worry cycle by using rational analysis (such as how probable an event really is) to challenge anxious thinking.
- Consider the worst case scenario. If you can narrow your anxiety down to one particular problem, try this exercise. Write down as clearly as you can what it is you are worried about. What is the worst that can possibly happen? Work to improve on the worst—it may not turn out so bad.

Although it's not always possible to change the way you think, you can try acting differently, which may change your thinking in the end.

- Relaxation. Relaxation exercises, if practised daily, can be called on to ease immediate anxiety.
- Make anxiety work for you rather than against you. Worrying about a job interview, public speaking or an examination is natural, but unchannelled anxiety does nothing but cloud your thoughts and prevent you doing your best. Channelling the energy and pressure you feel into preparing for the event has the double benefit of clearing your thoughts and increasing performance.

Born to worry

Those more prone to anxiety include:

- women
- people who had a very anxious parent
- emotionally more sensitive people who tend to see the world as threatening
- people who have had a difficult childhood; perhaps suffered abuse or had excessively strict parents
- people with medical conditions such as hyperthyroidism
- people with a vitamin B12 deficiency
- people on certain prescription drugs as well as those taking non-prescription drugs such as caffeine, cocaine, LSD and ecstasy.

POST-TRAUMATIC STRESS DISORDER

We used to call it shell shock or war neurosis, now we read about post-traumatic stress disorder, or PTSD. It is a phenomenon with which we are becoming increasingly familiar.

The US National Institute of Mental Health defines PTSD as an anxiety disorder that can develop after exposure to a terrifying event or ordeal in which grave physical harm occurred or was threatened. PTSD can be triggered by violent attacks such as rape and mugging; natural disasters like earthquakes, floods and hurricanes; and man-made accidents and calamities, such as military combat and terrorist bomb attacks.

As well as those immediately involved in a traumatic event, people witnessing the event and the family of those involved are also at risk of developing PTSD. Around 3.6 per cent of Americans aged between eighteen and 54 will suffer PTSD in any one year, according to the Institute. Just under a third of men and women who have spent time in a war zone will experience PTSD.

Recognizing the symptoms

Symptoms of PTSD usually occur within three months of the trauma, but sometimes do not surface until a year or more after the event. According to the institute, PTSD symptoms include any of the following when experienced for a month or more:

- repeated re-runs of the trauma in the form of flashbacks, nightmares and frightening thoughts (a re-experience may be triggered by seeing an event or an object that reminds you of the ordeal; the anniversary of the event is also a common trigger)
- emotional numbness
- sleep disturbances
- depression
- anxiety
- irritability
- angry outbursts
- intense guilt.

A wide range of other symptoms can also occur, including alcohol abuse, other kinds of anxiety disorders, headaches, gastrointestinal complaints, immune system problems, dizziness, chest pain, and bodily discomfort.

LF started to experience strange 'turns' a year after she had struggled to get herself and two children out of the house while a fire raged in the kitchen, blocking her normal exit. Smoke was building up and fireworks—the cause of the fire—exploded behind them. The combination of fire, smoke and the fire brigade's water destroyed almost all of her and her children's possessions, including photographs, books, clothes and toys. Fainting fits prevented LF driving on main roads for a year, and she underwent a battery of tests for diabetes and other gland disorders. No physical cause was ever found. At the time it was hard to believe the episodes had a psychological cause as she thought she felt fine and had recovered from both the trauma of the fire and other difficult personal matters in her life. Eventually, the episodes ceased and, looking back, LF now believes she was suffering panic attacks linked to the fire.

Treating PTSD

There are various ways of helping sufferers of PTSD. One option is therapy. Cognitive behaviour therapy, group therapy and exposure therapy are among the most used. They involve gradually and repeatedly reliving the ordeal under controlled conditions in order to work through the experience and reduce its power. A study of 12,000 school children who lived through a hurricane in Hawaii found that those who underwent counselling early on were doing much better two years down the track than those who did not.

Medication can help to treat the symptoms and is sometimes prescribed to ease the depression, anxiety and sleeplessness associated with PTSD.

THE POWER OF ACTION

In any fight against troubles of the mind—be it depression, anxiety or stress—you may find you need to use many of the same weapons: taking action, taking back control, and problem solving. In fact, researchers in this field believe that building up resilience to stress may be possible by improving problem-solving abilities. The power to challenge negative thoughts is also a valuable tool.

The Penn Depression Prevention Program sought to reverse pessimistic thinking and reduce depression in a group of US school children in Pennsylvania in the early 1990s. Over a twelve-week course, a treatment group learnt about:

- capturing negative thoughts and challenging them
- thinking about goals before acting
- coming up with alternative solutions
- weighing the pros and cons of each course of action
- relaxation techniques
- conflict management such as negotiation.

A body of evidence

Research in the field of PTSD is focusing on a number of biological factors and has found a few explanations for why PTSD might affect some people but not others:

- The hippocampus (the part of the brain critical to memory and emotion) is different in PTSD sufferers. This may explain the intrusive memories and flashbacks.
- PTSD sufferers tend to have abnormally low levels of cortisol and abnormally high levels of epinephrine and norepinephrine. These are all hormones associated with the stress response.
- Natural opiates that temporarily mask pain are produced when someone's in danger. PTSD sufferers continue to produce these when the danger has passed.

Such skills—which are similar to those taught in cognitive behaviour therapy—were aimed at helping the children to deal with reality in a productive way, rather than attempt to gloss over their difficulties. In a follow up six months later, a third of the children who had completed the program were no longer showing signs of strong depression.

In a broader sense, perhaps you can learn from the eccentrics: their strong sense of individuality means they care less about what other people think. This seems to break one of the weaker links in the stress cycle so that eccentrics experience very little of the stress build-up that many of the rest of us are prone to. In addition, they nurture a creative outlet and keep their intellect alive.

Taking charge—even if it's only by deciding to clear out and redecorate your bedroom so it feels like a haven once more, or taking the challenge to improve the communication between yourself and your spouse—gives back a sense of control. Actions speak louder than words and are far more powerful. They can ease stress, halt the spiral of depression and reduce fears. Taking control puts you in the driving seat of change.

TAKING STOCK

Take a few moments to jot down some thoughts in these areas.

1 Stress
(a) Do you feel your life is stressful?
(b) What is most stressful about it?
(c) What aspects of your life reduce stress?
(d) What else could you do to reduce stress levels?
(e) What could you change in your life?
(f) What can't you change?

2 Depression
(a) Would you say your emotions are on an even keel or do you experience ups and downs?
(b) Have you ever been depressed?
(c) What did you do about it?
(d) How did it end?
(e) Have you noticed any particular situations or circumstances that trigger depression or feeling down?
(f) What do you do to give yourself a lift?
(g) What else could you do?

3 Anxiety
(a) Do you waste time worrying?
(b) What do you worry about?
(c) Does the worrying help or hinder?
(d) What do you do to stem anxiety and worry?
(e) What else could you do?

4 **Vulnerability**

(a) Have there been times in your life when you have felt more vulnerable to stress or depression?

(b) Is there anything you can do to protect yourself in these times?

(c) Do you feel there are aspects of your personality or habits you've developed that help you move on, not get stuck in a rut, and hold on to perspective when you strike problems?

(d) Has your life ever reached a crisis point or a real low that you've managed to come out of?

(e) What did you learn from this experience that can help you now?

Life, and Death, and Giants

EMILY DICKINSON,
COMPLETE POEMS, BOOK 1, LIFE, XXXIX
(FIRST PUBLISHED 1924)

3. THE TRIALS OF LIFE

SOME CHANGES ARE MORE
DRAMATIC THAN OTHERS—A
BABY IS BORN OR A FRIEND
DIES, AND SUDDENLY THE
WORLD LOOKS DIFFERENT.
DEMANDS SEEM GREATER,
RELIEF AND RELAXATION A
LONG WAY OFF; BUT DOING
WHAT YOU CAN IN A PRACTICAL
WAY CAN SMOOTH THE
EMOTIONAL ROLLER COASTER.

DEALING WITH THE INEVITABLE

Christmas comes but once a year. Children love it, but many adults grin and bear it: 60 per cent of them find elements of Christmas stressful or depressing according to the UK's Mental Health Foundation. Somehow, if you are expected to feel happy, and you just don't, you feel worse than at other times of the year. E's first Christmas alone after separating from her husband was a time she dreaded and just wanted to get through. A couple of years later, however, she wrote that she was putting up Christmas decorations to celebrate being alive.

People who are separated from friends and family at Christmas time can feel that the day itself is a trial. It's often seen as a time to stop and reflect on where you are in your life and if the situation is less than ideal, then the 'celebrations' can take on a certain poignancy. Against the commercial illusion of perfect families enjoying harmonious time together, the imperfections of your own relationships are thrown into relief. There's extra pressure to be 'nice' to friends and family, to create wonderful food, buy presents, send cards. For some it is just too much.

MEASURING THE IMPACT OF LIFE EVENTS

Christmas is just one of 41 life events included on the Holmes Rahe Scale. Also called the Social Readjustment Ratings Scale, it was devised by American doctors Thomas H Holmes and Richard H Rahe and published in 1967 in *The Journal of Pyschosomatic Research*. The doctors assigned both positive and negative events a numerical value according to how much adjustment it required for people to adapt to them. Christmas has the value 12, a little more stressful than a minor violation of the law (11), but requiring less adjustment than the foreclosure of a loan (32), and much less than the top-rated stressor, the death of a spouse, which is given 100 points.

Holmes and Rahe followed a group of people over the course of two months and found that those who accumulated more than 300 points in the 12 months prior to taking the test had an increased risk of becoming ill. The pioneering ratings scale was the first to attempt to

Keeping the 'merry' in Christmas

'At Christmas play and make good cheer, for Christmas comes but once a year' is as true now as when Thomas Tusser wrote it 500 years ago in his *Five Hundred Points of Good Husbandry*. Christmas stress is a microcosm of things we worry about throughout the year. If Christmas stresses get out of hand in your household, try bringing back a sense of proportion.

● Debt. Avoid Christmas debt by making a budget and sticking to it. Allocate sums you can afford for presents and shop carefully for food. If you tend to run up credit card bills, leave the cards at home or make a concerted effort to pay it off quickly to avoid severe interest payments.

● The early shopper. Planning ahead and shopping well before seasonal deadlines can save time queuing and avoid the headaches of crowds as well as the pressure of running out of shopping days.

● Christmas spirit. Alcohol flows at Christmas—no doubt helping to fuel family tensions where they exist. Drinking a glass of water after each glass of alcohol can help keep alcohol consumption under control.

quantify and compare the effects of different life events. But it can only ever be a starting point to assessing levels of stress, as it does not take into account individuals' differing coping methods and abilities.

Using the Holmes Rahe Scale

The scale works by adding up the units assigned to events experienced in the past year.

● If you score 300 or more points in one year, you are at a significantly greater risk of developing an illness.

● If you score 150–299 points, you have a 30 per cent less risk of developing an illness than the top category.

● If you score 150 points or less, you have only a slight chance of developing an illness.

- When you don't want to be alone. One in 10 of the UK population suffers loneliness at Christmas. While some people don't mind being on their own on Christmas Day, others would rather have company. Thinking ahead and arranging a get together with friends can help. Volunteering is also a way of sharing the spirit of the day with others.

- Share the work. The expectation of a celebratory meal can mean hours in the kitchen. Spread the load by dividing up chores and responsibilities.

- The perfection trap. Don't fall into the trap of expecting everything to go smoothly. It rarely does and it doesn't matter.

- The convention trap. In Australia, picnics at a park or the beach are a relaxing alternative to cooking at home. In France, the main meal is after Midnight Mass on Christmas Eve. Christmas is celebrated in a variety of ways around the world—and for a variety of reasons, as a season of goodwill and peace as much as a religious festival. Find your own way of celebrating and observing the season. Doing it your way makes it more enjoyable.

LIFE EVENT	LIFE CHANGE UNITS
Death of spouse	100
Divorce	73
Marital separation	65
Imprisonment	63
Death of a close family member	63
Personal injury or illness	53
Marriage	50
Dismissal from work	47
Marital reconciliation	45
Retirement	45
Change in health of a family member	44

Pregnancy	40
Sexual difficulties	39
Gain of a new family member	39
Business readjustment	39
Change in financial state	38
Change in number of arguments with spouse	35
Major mortgage	32
Foreclosure of mortgage or loan	30
Change in responsibilities at work	29
Son or daughter leaving home	29
Trouble with in-laws	29
Outstanding personal achievement	28
Spouse begins or stops work	26
Begin or end school	26
Change in living conditions	25
Revision of personal habits	24
Trouble with boss	23
Change in work hours or conditions	20
Change in residence	20
Change in schools	20
Change in recreation	19
Change in church activities	19
Change in social activities	18
Minor mortgage or loan	17
Change in sleeping habits	16
Change in number of family reunions	15
Change in eating habits	15
Vacation	13
Christmas	12
Minor violation of the law	11

A number of attempts have been made to expand on the Holmes Rahe Scale. The following are just a few examples:

- According to Canadian General Social Survey (GSS) 1998 data, two- thirds of Canadians aged fifteen and over had experienced at least one traumatic life event in the previous twelve months.

Events looked at included the serious illness or injury of a close friend or family member; the death of a family member or close friend; or someone leaving or moving into the home, including the birth of a child or a new relationship. Almost one-quarter experienced two or more traumatic events and one-sixth experienced three or more. People who reported three or more events were significantly more likely to be unhappy, feeling stressed, and more dissatisfied with their current state of health.

- A stress vulnerability model developed by scientists Joseph Zubin and Bonnie Spring shows how the effects of stress depend on how well equipped a person is to deal with it. They proposed that every person draws on three main resources: biological, psychological and social. A person without strong supports or characteristics in these fields—for instance, poor family support and a genetic susceptibility—may become 'ill' in response to a stressor, whereas someone with strong buffers will not.

- Sociologist Suzanne Kobassa is credited with developing the idea of 'hardiness factors' that build resilience to stressful events. These factors are commitment, control and challenge: commitment to yourself and your work, a sense of control over the choices in your life, and seeing change as a challenge rather than a threat.

Syd Cunningham (1926–99)

Australian Aboriginal community stalwart Syd Cunningham made a name for himself as 'Black Santa'. For 30 years he delivered toys at Christmas to Aboriginal children in remote parts of New South Wales. Teaming red overalls with a red pyjama top and gumboots for the first time in 1960, he persuaded Sydneysiders to donate toys—6000 or so in his last years—and took them by helicopter to Wellington, Dubbo, Peak Hill, Gilgandra and Bourke. He also helped pensioners with gifts of food, clothing, party fare, fridges and televisions, and in 1989 was awarded the Order of Australia medal.

Life throws a variety of events at us to test our resilience and ability to adapt. Most of us will have to deal with the death of someone close at some point, and many of us experience big changes when we start a family.

THE SHOCK OF THE NEW: BECOMING A PARENT

A child's a plaything for an hour

MARY LAMB (1764–1847), PARENTAL RECOLLECTIONS

When asked, 'What do children bring to your life?', PC, weary father of three, answered, 'Children bring disease into the house.'

Yes, children certainly do bring germs from day care, viruses from school and no doubt a host of stress-related heartaches and pains. But they also bring laughter, spontaneity, playfulness and chaos; elbows and knees in the bed; peanut butter on the sofa; jigsaw puzzle pieces on the floor.

Where do you start when trying to express what it's like having a child? It's like attempting to describe what it's like to be alive. You sleep less, maybe cry more. There's less time for relaxed sex with your partner but you're on 24-hour cuddle call for the under fives. Evenings in smart wine bars are harder to arrange, but first-release kids' movies are easy.

But where does all the time go? How come with the arrival of a tiny baby, it's suddenly a major challenge to get the washing-up done from the night before, let alone the extra washing, the thank you notes, and cleaning the bath. Any women's magazine article that says 'spend a day indulging yourself, maybe stay in bed with a book and a box of chocolates' is enough to bring tears of self-pity to your eyes.

FITTING IT ALL IN

Lyn Craig, senior researcher at the Social Policy Research Unit of Sydney's University of New South Wales, has spent much of the past five years analyzing time-use data from two Australian Bureau of Statistics Time Use Surveys. She became interested in how parents use their time, especially compared to people without children, because of her own experience as a new mother:

I was surprised at how relentless it all was. Especially when the children passed the baby stage, there just didn't seem to be any down time. I found particularly difficult the lack of time to think, mainly because of fatigue and incessant talking. My brain space was invaded. But it was a complicated interdependency as I was so attached to my babies as well. It was all so absorbing and involving that I couldn't see how the new cultural ideal of working mothers managed it all. How to fit everything into a few hours a day?

What interested me was how such a huge job had become culturally invisible. Another aspect was how having children cemented the gender roles. We had shared domestic stuff much more equitably before the children were born. It felt like something structural was going on—but it had to be solved on a personal level. So I became interested in finding out how common these experiences were. Was every new mother trying to personally carve her own path up the same hill?

While depressing figures totting up the financial cost of having a child seem at the ready, time costs have until recently been largely ignored because they are so much more difficult to quantify. Craig believes much time-use analysis has underestimated the time taken in caring for a child because it's often something done in tandem with another activity. But, as all parents will confirm, it's not quite the same doing shopping with children, especially young ones, and a picnic calls for continual vigilance.

A time-use diary could, for example, record 'cooking dinner' as a main activity. But it's not the gleaming, all-smiles and glass-of-wine-at-the-ready kitchen of advertisements. It's more likely to be combined with the secondary activities of helping a child with homework, comforting another who's just fallen over and taken a knock, putting on a load of washing and trying to listen to a news segment on the radio.

Craig analyzed how nearly 3000 parents aged between nineteen and 68 used their time and compared them with non-parents of a similar age. Her findings—in two discussion papers entitled 'The Time Cost of Parenthood' and 'Caring Differently'—showed that:

- All parents work longer hours than non-parents when you look at paid and unpaid work as the main activity. Mothers worked a total of 9 hours a day and fathers 9 hours 12 minutes, compared to childless women's 7 hours 8 minutes and childless men's 7 hours 16 minutes. That's two extra hours' work every day just for being a parent.
- When you take secondary activities into account as well, the divide between childless people and parents gapes larger still. Men without children average 7 hours 25 minutes in unpaid and paid work, while those with children average a total of 10 hours 42 minutes. Mothers average 12 hours 34 minutes work, compared to childless women's 7 hours 27 minutes. In other words, the mere fact of having a child is likely to add an average of more than five hours to your daily workload.

Two key points emerge from the statistics:
- Parents do more than one thing at a time more often than non-parents. Everyone 'multitasks' but fathers do it for around an hour longer than men without children, and mothers do nearly two hours more multitasking than fathers.
- Part-time women workers carry a greater total workload than any other category because they tend to do a disproportionate amount of the total child care. The statistics also point to a greater degree of juggling by women who work part time.

These women tend to have the highest amount of secondary activity; in other words, they multitask the most.

There are many ways of assimilating these figures. On the one hand, they are dry and analytical and can only ever reflect a shallow image of life. On the other hand, it may help you accept that when you are a parent spare time really is a luxury. Maybe the figures can also help bridge the understanding between parents and non-parents: no wonder your house looks a mess compared to your childless friends—children make more of a mess, faster, and you have dramatically less time available to sort, tidy and clean. The result is not always what you'd like it to be. And no wonder parents are trickier to pin down to girls' nights out or after-work drinks. The need to divide attention between tasks also explains the build-up of stress throughout the day, and the relief that the children's bedtime can bring.

SLEEP DEPRIVATION

The strange world of babies' sleeping patterns is a common obsession for parents in a child's first year. This too is represented in the time-use analysis. If it's hard to imagine where mothers get their time from, consider this statement from one of Lyn Craig's papers: women add extra time to their workload by 'redirecting paid work time into unpaid work time and redirecting sleep and leisure time into unpaid work time,' adding extra domestic duties as well as direct childcare time. Lack of sleep in new parents can lead to feelings of stress, irritability and depression, as well as plain fatigue. When you are exhausted, it's much harder to feel in control of your life, to take pleasure in the here and now and keep on an even keel.

Theories as to why babies don't sleep through the night and what you can do about it change regularly and opinions vary widely. Some schools of thought advise that you comfort your baby whenever they need it; others say go and talk to them, reassure them, but never pick them up.

What's right for your baby also depends a lot on his age and health. If you're fairly confident as a parent you'll probably feel best following your instincts. However, if nights seem to have become unmanageably disturbed and sleeplessness is taking its toll on your health and maybe your relationships, you should talk to your doctor or an early childhood nurse, screen out illness and discuss some possible strategies (perhaps community programs or training, or sleep theories).

There may come a time when sleep deprivation takes on enormous proportions and emergency action is required. This is a time for calling on help:

- You might go to bed ridiculously early, when the baby is asleep, and ask your partner to get up the first time the baby wakes. This will allow you to get a few hours' sleep on the trot.
- You could take up a friend's offer to take the baby for a walk, to allow you to catch up on your missed sleep.
- If you are lucky enough to have a willing and able grandparent at hand, they could come around for a weekend visit and take over wherever possible, making parents' sleep the number one priority for the household.
- Ignore the housework and other tasks that can wait. And, if all else fails, take comfort in the fact that the one sure thing about babies and children is that they will change!

So, parents can expect more work, less pay and less sleep. Add to that the everyday miracle of pregnancy, which puts a considerable strain on the body, the marathon of birth and a change in household dynamics. No wonder this puts a strain on relationships.

COPING STRATEGIES

'Be prepared', as the boy scouts say. A little forward planning on the practical side can, at the very least, leave more room for emotional play once a baby's born. To ease the first few weeks with your newcomer consider the following:

- Pre-birth pampering. Once a baby arrives it can be uncannily difficult to find even ten minutes to yourself, let alone time for a yoga class or a massage. Many women continue working for as long as possible before the birth, but try to leave at least a small window open to enjoy yourself in the time before the birth. Catch up with some friends; see an exhibition you've been meaning to or just relax with a book.

- A baby network. Find out about parent and baby groups, babes-in-arms sessions at local cinemas, and so on. You might cringe at the thought of drinking coffee with half a dozen new parents with nothing but babies in common; but then again, you might forge valuable new friendships.

- Being kind to yourself. Unless you want to prove yourself a superwoman, give yourself a chance to ease into your new life and, for a few weeks at least, don't invite people around for lavish lunches. Let people make their own tea and coffee when they visit, and put sleep before a gleaming house.

- Cooking ahead. Cook up and freeze some casseroles or other food you can heat in the oven for quick and nutritious meals.

- Two's company. Setting aside some special time for you as a couple makes sense, whether it's meals out or afternoon outings.

- Learning about babies. Babies are not like us. They flap their arms and cry when tired. They need food very frequently and feel desperate when it doesn't arrive on cue. Buying or borrowing a couple of baby advice books and reading them before the birth might help to start you off on the right foot. As MN says:

My first baby was a poor feeder, but if I knew what I knew about breastfeeding by the time my second arrived, I might have fed the first myself for longer.

LOOKING AFTER THE NUMBER ONE RELATIONSHIP

Much of a child's experience of happiness depends on the relative happiness of the parents and especially on the quality of that partnership. So, difficult though it might be, it is important for you to try to find ways of nurturing your primary relationship.

Emily Lennox (1731–1814)

One of four sisters depicted in Stella Tillyard's biography of an English upper class family, *Aristocrats*, Emily Lennox had nineteen children to her first husband, Lord Kildare. After he died, she had another three to a second husband, William Ogilvie, whom she'd engaged some years previously as tutor to her brood. She had her first child, George, less than a year after her wedding, when she was still sixteen and the last when she was almost 47 and a grandmother too. Emily believed in leading a normal life while pregnant—with plenty of good food, rest and exercise. Preparing for a birth involved gathering together the attendants she'd need: a trained male midwife, or accoucheur, a nurse-keeper to wash and clothe the baby, a wet nurse, servants and sisters. Once labour was over and a baby despatched to the nursery, Emily was officially 'in confinement' for a month. This meant rest and the relinquishment of all social and managerial duties and, at the end of the month, the ceremony of churching, which signalled the return of a woman back to daily life.

As was common at that time, only half of Emily's children survived into adulthood. She and her husband loved their huge family and mourned each child's passing.

Time together

The arrival of a baby puts extra pressure on your abilities to prioritize. When the baby drops off for twenty minutes do you clear the dining table or sit down with your partner and talk uninterrupted? If you don't carve out the time, the days slip by and you'll gradually find your couple communication has ceased. A little child-free time is ideal—right from the early days if you can arrange it—even if it's just for an hour's walk or a coffee. Small rituals you build into your life can also make the difference between managing, just coping or enjoying and treasuring this time in your life. It could be something as simple as always sharing a cup of tea with your partner in the morning, or a quiet conversation before turning over to sleep. Babies are intensely demanding but children take time too—they don't need nappies changed, but they might insist you play chess with them—so the earlier you get into the habit of putting aside time for the two of you, the better for all the family.

Sex—with and without it

Pregnancy, childbirth, breastfeeding and the presence of a new member in the household have the potential to play havoc with a woman's libido. A new father's confused feelings about the intimate relationship between mother and baby, and a shift in relationship dynamics, can add another twist to the situation. To borrow a phrase from Dr Rosie King, sex therapist, a couple must transform from Romeo and Juliet to Mum and Dad in a matter of months. Quite apart from hormonal changes that can affect the sex drive, there are some practical considerations to deal with: lack of opportunity, interruptions, fatigue and physical discomfort, to name just a few.

The knowledge that it is common for women to be uninterested in sex for a few months after childbirth can be a comfort to a new father who fears that the new low priority given to sex is permanent and personal. If the hormonal changes that accompany breast-feeding make intercourse uncomfortable, aids such as vaginal lubricants can help. It's a time for trust and patience. And, as Steve and Shaaron Biddulph, authors of *The Making of Love* point out, you won't die if your sex life wanes for a few months! But be sure to consider whether there are communication problems inhibiting intimacy and, if there are, address them sooner rather than later.

Creating harmony

Sharing the responsibilities of bringing up children adds strength and an extra dimension to a couple's relationship. A woman left to deal with everything—extra shopping, feeding, caring and getting up in the night—will begin to resent her partner. A few basic habits—such as eating meals together or, as the children get older, making sure the television doesn't dominate—helps keep the communication lines open within a family.

Essential baby equipment

Thinking about what you will need for your baby means you are well prepared before his or her arrival.

- Transport of some sort. Pouches and slings are ideal for the first few weeks and months, depending on how heavy your baby is and whether you are comfortable using them. They're especially good for walking on beaches and anywhere else that a pram or stroller can't go. They are also handy for comforting a crying baby in the house, or for pacing your baby to sleep while getting on with a few chores. Strollers and prams are good for long walks in the city and provide the chance for a little personal space between baby and parent, which can be welcome at times. A newborn needs to be able to lie down in any carrier. If you intend to travel by car, you'll need an approved baby capsule.

- Nappies. Whether you decide to buy cloth nappies or use disposable ones, it's handy to have a few of either on hand just in case you run out. Cloth nappies make good wipes and children's hand towels even if you don't ever use them for their intended purpose.

- Wraps for calming and warming. If you plan to use these, consider selecting a variety of weights to cater for changes in the weather. Many little babies find being wrapped calming, but your little one won't want to be swaddled in brushed cotton on a sweltering summer's day. Muslin is much more appropriate for hot weather. Wraps, or bunny rugs as they are called in some countries, are also perfect for adding light layers on a sleeping baby, especially when you are out and about together.

- First aid. The last thing you want to do with a sick baby or infant is traipse around the shops looking for standard medicines and first aid equipment. Consult a good baby book and start your home infant medicine cabinet: a digital thermometer is accurate, reliable and easy to use; a suitable infant pain killer is good to have on hand. You may also be glad of a good nappy rash cream, cotton wool to wipe eyes, a mild baby bath and baby lotion. A dozen or so face washers, or flannels, won't go amiss either.

Solo strategies

Being a single parent is tough. Some don't have a choice—when a parent dies, perhaps unexpectedly, soon after the birth of a child. Some choose to go it alone. Here are some of the ways single parents can lessen the load:

- Organize contact with other adults, particularly of the opposite sex, whether friends, relatives or neighbours. Adult conversation is important for a parent and socializing as a child is an important part of growing up. Keeping in touch is good for both of you.
- Consider joining parenting groups so you have someone else to talk to about the ordinary problems and situations that arise in parenthood. It's useful, for instance, to recognize that some unwelcome and even infuriating behaviour is a perfectly normal part of child development.
- Enlist help if you need it to make sure you are getting what's yours by right in the way of maintenance payments from another parent if there is one, or government benefits if you qualify.

LOSING A LOVED ONE

At the other end of life is the grief of loss. Death, the great leveller, is something everyone faces at some time or other—the death of a parent, a spouse, or perhaps most painfully, the death of a child. It doesn't help that much of Western society is uneasy talking about death. Social etiquette seems to have failed to provide us with a way of dealing with death beyond rituals such as funerals, wakes and memorial services. And while these may help you, they occur early on in the journey of grief, with little opportunity for you to continue to talk through your experiences beyond the first few months.

Bereavement is highly individual, and one of the most private experiences you can go through. Your reactions may range from simple deep sorrow to overwhelming relief when you know that your loved one's suffering is now over. Bereavement is often described as being like a deep raw wound. It heals with time, but in the meantime it needs protecting.

EARLY DAYS

While each person's experience of grief is unique, bereavement and grief often follow common patterns that help you gradually to adapt to new circumstances. A generalized feeling of numbness and shock is usual on the first day. Denial is also common. Even when you accept a death at the logical level, it can take quite a while for a real sense of belief to seep in.

Some people need to cry when they hear of a death, some will scream or kick, while others may feel the need to withdraw. Grief counsellors such as Mal and Dianne McKissock, authors of *Coping with Grief*, stress again and again that it's best to give way to emotion. 'A bereaved person who has not successfully grieved is more prone to illness, both physical and psychological,' they write.

In the first few days, feelings of sorrow are often overwhelming. Thoughts and images of the person who has died may fill your mind. A common experience is for the moments of sorrow to become gradually but increasingly interspersed by less troublesome thoughts, or even moments of 'normality'. But grief comes in waves and often hits at the oddest times, when you're least expecting it. And when it does, the intensity of the feeling is very often as great as ever. It's as if your mind has a compartment where it keeps the feelings of sorrow and loss; as time moves on you may find you don't visit that place in your mind as often, but when you do, the feelings are still there in all their intensity.

The physical response

Soon after learning of the death of someone close, changes take place in your entire body. No part is untouched by grief, opening up the possibility of a wide range of physical symptoms such as heartburn, migraine and chest pain. Sometimes people develop a 'sympathy reaction' where they feel pain in an organ or part of the body which was involved in the loved one's death.

Loss of appetite is common for a couple of days. And reactions such as nausea, restlessness and agitation, sleeplessness, headaches, backache, vomiting, diarrhoea and period pain also fall well within the realm of 'normality'. MN's reaction to her mother's death is a typical example of the physical impact an event such as this can have on you:

When I heard my mother had died, my appetite took a dive for a couple of days. I had a headache just above the bridge of my nose and for many days woke around 4 in the morning without being able to go back to sleep. I had to travel halfway around the world for her funeral, and for the few

Frank Manthey (1938–)

One-time kangaroo shooter turned conservationist Frank Manthey had lost his wife and, in his own words, was 'doing it pretty hard'. He went to work, ate and slept but found life had become fairly meaningless. One night, over a few glasses of 'snake juice' in far northern Queensland, zoologist Peter Macrae persuaded Frank to go spotlighting with him to look for bilbies, small furry—endangered—animals with a pointy nose and large pointy ears. Frank was struck by their grace and beauty, and he and Peter decided to join forces to, somehow, save the bilby.

Overnight Frank regained his sparkle and would think and talk of nothing else. Macrae said what was needed was a large fenced-off area in which to release bilbies bred in captivity. Manthey came up with the idea of selling off fence panels at $20 each in a nationwide 'Save the Bilby' appeal. Building the $300,000 fence began in 1999 with helpers from Conservation Volunteers Australia. The bilby conservation area officially opened in 2001. When they first hatched the plan it seemed too big but now as Manthey said on the television documentary series, *Australian Story*, 'It's made all the difference in the world to me.'

nights before her funeral I never slept more than a couple of hours. strangely though, I did not feel exhausted, and I felt very relaxed, almost as if I was drugged. I believe this was a mixture of tiredness and body chemicals helping me through. The fact that although I felt distressed, I was also 'mellow' helped me glide through some of the strange situations that occur after a death, and in particular helped me stay out of a nasty fight between my sister and father that came out of all the tension surrounding my mother's death.

Your body also produces a number of chemicals during the intense experience of grief. These chemicals include the following:

- Pain killers. The body produces a number of narcotic-like chemicals similar to heroin and morphine. These create the numbing effect common in the first few days and are released through tears. The production of these chemicals gradually decreases over the weeks following a death, until reaching much lower levels around six weeks later.
- Relaxants. The chemicals released also have a relaxing effect on muscles, including ones used in digestion. One outcome of this is a reduced appetite, as the gut is not emptying at its usual rate.
- Adrenaline. When under stress, you produce adrenaline to help you fight or flee danger. Adrenaline primes your muscles and heart, making the muscles tight and the heart beat more strongly. It also makes it harder to sleep, a normal, sometimes infuriating, symptom of grief.
- Cortisol. The pituitary gland secretes adrenocorticotropic hormone (ACTH), which helps produce adrenaline in times of bereavement and also produces the immunosuppressant cortisol. This has the effect of decreasing the number of white blood cells, called T-lymphocytes, which help fight off viruses and bacteria. This accounts for the vulnerability of the bereaved to flu, colds, cold sores, urinary tract infections, and the like.

The emotional response

Even the most stoic person feels the currents of grief. Those who repress their feelings may be prone to depression, as well as physical illnesses. Some of the common elements included in the cocktail of grief are as follows:

- Anger. This is a common, if unwelcome, emotion around the time of death. You may feel angry with the deceased for leaving you or perhaps you may feel he didn't entirely 'look after' himself. You may also direct your anger towards other people whom you feel could have done more. M was on holiday with her girlfriend J when she received a phone call to say her husband was in hospital following a heart attack. M quickly returned home and spent a day or so with him before he died. She has never quite 'forgiven' J, 40 years on, even though her husband's death had nothing to do with her friend. Anger often emerges as the initial defensive numbing mechanisms wear off.

- Guilt. This is a common emotion to feel after someone close has died. You may wish you'd done more to prevent your loved one's death, that you'd called her one last time, that you'd said goodbye or 'I love you', or even that you hadn't said something unkind.

- Sadness. Grief is usually accompanied by what some counsellors describe as 'passionate sadness', a lowering of energy and motivation, and sometimes a questioning of the value of life. Although it shares some characteristics with depression, this type of sadness differs in that it is an understandable response to a terrible blow. If expressed—by, for example, weeping, or talking about the deceased—the 'depressed' state should gradually lift.

- Despair. 'No one can prepare you for the finality of death,' says S, twenty years after the death of her father. The longing to see the deceased again, to hug and to hold them, can be over-whelmingly powerful. You may feel as if you will never be able to 'come to terms' with a loved one's death, but usually, eventually, time heals.

THE LONG AND WINDING ROAD OF GRIEF

It is not uncommon to find that just as you think you are 'coping' and heading back to normal, your mood takes a dive and you feel more upset, spend more time crying and generally feel worse about the whole thing. This can be explained as reality setting in, and numbness and shock wearing off. Many grief counsellors emphasize that a resurgence of powerful feelings and episodes of weeping several weeks after a death should not be seen as 'going downhill' but should be recognized as part of the process needed to let feelings surface and heal.

While we may hope to be 'back to normal' a year or so after someone's death, grief is not necessarily a dead-end road: the feelings of loss may never fade, but we learn to weave them into our life and move forward. Dreaming about a deceased person is a common way to remember them beyond the first year of death. Some people feel they have moved out of a disorganized, despairing phase three months after the death, others would put it at more like five years. There are no time limits.

OTHER ASPECTS OF GRIEF

While every person's experience of grief is unique, those who find themselves living through circumstances such as terminal illness or the death of a child may report similar feelings.

Preparatory grief

In some ways the healing process of grief is a separation process. When someone is terminally ill, that separation can start before death. It can be helpful for both you and the person who is sick to talk frankly about the future. Some people find that prior knowledge of a death helps very little, as the gulf between being alive and dead seems so infinite. Others find that at the very least it helps them 'rehearse' the practical arrangements they will be called on to make.

The anniversary reaction

The anniversary of a death is hard for some people, while others see it as no more or less of a hurdle than any other day. Sometimes the physical reactions that developed at the time of your loved one's death—such as headaches or nausea—may resurface.

Children and grief

Children need to express emotion just like adults, but they may not do it in the same way. They may seem unaffected and even unable to cry. At the same time they can switch to play mode and laugh with friends. However, in time, they may want to talk about the death. An understanding ear will encourage them to voice concerns, while familiar routines will reassure them that life goes on despite family bereavement.

When a child dies

Charles Darwin described the death of his eldest daughter Annie, aged nine, as 'our bitter and cruel loss'. He said it caused the final destruction of his Christian faith. Darwin's marriage—unlike his faith—remained strong, but the death of a child is a severe test to any relationship because neither parent has sufficient resources to nurture the other. Additionally, explain the McKissocks, while both parents initially grieve the loss of a child, in time, while the mother's focus remains on the child, the father's may centre on his wife's emotional unavailability. Women may experience feelings of guilt and responsibility, while men are more likely to feel anger and want to blame someone.

PRACTICAL CONSIDERATIONS

Dealing with someone's memoirs can wait until you feel better equipped, but other tasks following a death cannot be put off.

Death duties

After the death of someone close, there is much that you will need to organize and decide upon, depending on the local laws. You may choose to enlist the help of a professional and, between you, you may need to give consideration to the death certificate, whether to bury or cremate, what form a service should take (if you decide to have one), and the wording of newspaper notices, to name just a few potential issues. Although these may seem surreal tasks at times, their practical nature can be a relief. At least you are 'doing' something. And as they usually follow close after death, there may still be a sense of connection to the deceased, and a feeling that you are doing something to assist them on their final rite of passage.

Viewing the body

Seeing the body can help dispel feelings of denial. It also offers you a last chance to see your loved one. While it can be a disturbing experience, many counsellors believe it to be beneficial in the long term. If you are viewing a body, ask whoever will show you into the room to describe the scene to you before you walk in. A dead person's body often looks waxlike, or in some other way quite unlike the person you knew when alive. Some degree of 'make-up' is usually applied, which may or may not look natural to you; sometimes padding is placed inside the face, which can distort the appearance.

Speaking at the funeral

A good fall back plan if you intend speaking at a service is to write out a rough plan of what you wish to say and give a copy to

Supporting a grieving person

When someone close to you has lost a loved one, they don't need platitudes and are not asking for any magic words. All they want is for someone to listen.

- Do encourage them to express their feelings and emotions and 'permit' them to be open.
- Do let them talk. It's an important part of organizing their feelings.
- Do listen.
- Don't try to fix their feelings of guilt or grief.
- Don't say, 'Is there anything I can do?' Do it.

Good counsel

Here are a few things that counsellors advise you to do following the death of someone close:

- Use up adrenaline by doing housework, gardening and other useful jobs, or taking long walks.
- Have a massage, especially if you have a regular therapist with whom you feel comfortable. Massage eases tense muscles and can facilitate crying and the release of emotion.
- Avoid making major decisions—such as remarriage, having another baby, moving house, leaving a job—for at least a year after a death.
- Don't be bullied by well-meaning people who wish, for instance, to help pack up the deceased person's house, when you'd prefer to do it yourself at your own pace. It can be an important healing activity, and something you can look back on and be glad that you did in your way and in your own time.

another person. That way, if you find it too difficult to continue to speak, the other person can continue your words. A trial run before the funeral may also help.

VOX POP: Life after death

Death is a taboo subject in many ways. But it's one we all have to deal with at some point.

'I feel worse about my mother's death now, twelve years after her death. I am sorry she never got to cluck around my children.' LF

'When my mother died, I found I could operate on a day to day basis almost without hitch, but her death was a blow, even though it was somewhat expected, and took the wind out of my sails for some time.' MN

'"I'll always be sad that Granddad died," I told my children. "But I won't be sad all the time."' AN

'I didn't sleep a wink the night before my dad's funeral. I'd been travelling for three days and nights and was exhausted too. But I got there in time to speak at the funeral along with my brother. At the cemetery, Dad's brother told me, "I'm proud of you" and shook my hand, which meant a lot to me. Dad lived long enough to meet my sons, one of whom is named after him. He was 84 when he died, wise and optimistic. I miss him deeply.' PN

'I spent too long grieving over the loss of my sister, and my partner started to give me a hard time over it. Through her I saw the loss had become part of my identity and I decided to do something about it. So I went to a fire festival on New Year's Eve with a list of all the things I was wrestling with mentally. I threw the list into the fire. Let go of the whole lot. My partner noticed an immediate change for the better, and so did I.' DL

LIFE AND DEATH

Religious faith helps a lot of people at the time of death. A belief that you'll see a person again, albeit in another dimension, is of great comfort. The Tibetan monk Sogyal Rinpoche explains in his book, *The Tibetan Book of Living and Dying*, how shocked he was when he started to understand the Western world's relationship with death: half denial, half terror, he surmised.

Death reflects life. When contemplating the death of someone close, you may find that its finality acts like a sounding board, reverberating back through the details of their lives—like an obituary. How many times have you heard that someone has come close to death, only to find afterwards that they are able to start living more fully, by really appreciating the gift of being alive? People who have worked extensively with the dying end up emphasizing the quality of how we live—however long we have— especially in relationship to our friends and family. Forgive now, not later. Tell them you love them now, not when it's too late.

In tarot, the death card, with its spindly skeleton and the scythe of the grim reaper, is not as ominous as it might first appear. It does not symbolize death, but rather a new beginning. At death, the focus is on doors closing, but as weeks become months, and months become years, some people are able to look back and see that out of a sad situation, life has continued to blossom. Take JS's story:

I lost the sense of who I was during the first year I married. My husband was 33 years my senior, an overwhelming character who made all our decisions. We spent 30 years travelling from country to country making a living from professional gambling. I was totally immersed in him and always at his beck and call.

When he died, I felt relieved and freed, as if a load had been lifted from me.

My sister, who has Down's syndrome, taught me to see the silver lining. The morning after my husband died I was sobbing in bed. She marched in and said, 'I need to talk to you.' 'Right,' I said, mopping up.

'Now,' my sister continued. 'Bob's gone...so I'm going to have his chocolates!' With that, she leant over, picked up a box of chocolates that had belonged to my husband and marched out of the room. At first I just sat there, then I laughed.

It took me four years to find my feet after he died. I was surprised at the anger and resentment locked up inside me— at having had to live his life, that we didn't have our own home...There were times after talking to him that I would feel like a wet rag and exhausted. He could press my buttons because he knew my weaknesses, and because I felt I couldn't live without him, I let him take advantage of me.

After he died I completed a course to become a financial planner, passed all my subjects with distinction. I'd never have been able to study with my husband around. I'm now a spiritual kinesiologist and run workshops to encourage people to come from the heart, not the head. I found I had the knack to help people move on in their life.

Six years on I still miss my husband...his advice and his humour, that wonderful energy. He could see ahead much more than I can. I still loved him so much. But I've reclaimed myself.

TAKING STOCK

The big events, or dramatic changes, can take quite a toll in terms of mental and physical health.

1 Major changes

In the past year have you experienced major changes or losses in the following areas?

- at home
- at work
- in your personal relationships
- in family life
- in your health
- in your financial situation
- in other areas of your life

2 Your reaction

(a) How did you react at first?

(b) Has your initial reaction changed at all as time has moved on?

3 Adjusting

(a) In what ways have you adjusted?

(b) How difficult was that?

4 Flow-on effect

How did the change affect other aspects of your life?

- other relationships
- finances
- health
- home
- work

5 Emotions

(a) Have the changes lead to extra stress, feelings of depression or anxiety?

(b) What, if anything, have you found eases these feelings?

6 Helping yourself

Is there more you can do to ease the transition into a new era, whether through finding emotional outlets or practical assistance?

For life, with all its yields of joy and woe,

And hope and fear—believe the aged friend—

Is just a chance o' the prize of learning love

ROBERT BROWNING,
A DEATH IN THE DESERT (1864)

4. RELATIONSHIPS

GOOD RELATIONSHIPS ARE AT THE CORE OF HAPPINESS. RESEARCH SHOWS THERE'S A CLEAR LINK BETWEEN SATISFACTION WITH RELATIONSHIPS AND SATISFACTION WITH LIFE IN GENERAL. RELATIONSHIPS ARE ALSO A MATTER OF HEALTH. THOSE THAT FOSTER A SENSE OF BELONGING AND CREATE A FEELING OF INTIMACY NOT ONLY KEEP YOU HEALTHY BUT MAY EVEN PLAY A PART IN YOUR SURVIVING SERIOUS ILLNESSES.

MIND AND BODY

'A faithful friend is the medicine of life', it says in the Bible (Ecclesiastes 6:16). Two thousand or so years later our medical fraternity is trying to measure the effect of that medicine, and the results are fascinating.

Close personal relationships and feeling part of your community help guard against the stresses of life: whether assaults are biological, environmental or interpersonal. For instance, Dr Lisa Berkman, a social epidemiologist, led a series of studies from the mid-1970s that measured the quality of social attachments and looked at how they related to a range of illnesses, including heart, respiratory and gastrointestinal disease. In almost all cases the most socially isolated individuals were at increased risk of developing illness that led to death. In one study, people who'd suffered a myocardial infarction—a heart attack in layperson's terms—and who felt they had two or more people they could talk to were half as likely to die over the next six months as those who said they had no one to turn to for support.

There are a number of ways relationships get under the skin. Mechanisms that influence our immune system are one possibility. The neuroendocrine system (that is the system of nervous and hormonal bodily control) is another. In one study looking at the reactivity of the heart and the circulatory system, volunteers who were accompanied by a supportive partner showed reduced heart pressure and blood pressure compared to those who came to the test alone. It seemed the mere presence of a friend had a soothing influence, acting as a safety signal that altered the neural messages to the brain and heart during the test.

A Swedish study showed that when a man has a network of support such as a wife and close friends, he reacts to major stressful events in a much less harmful way. For men without social support there was a close link between high stress levels and death rate, but those with good relationships seemed protected.

Just as good relationships are good for you, relationships with problems can be bad news for your health as well as happiness. John Cacioppo, a psychologist at Ohio State University, looked at the relationships between roommates and health. Among his findings, he discovered the following:

- The more they disliked each other, the more prone they were to colds, flus and visits to the doctor.
- The people you see day in day out are the ones who end up influencing your health.
- The more significant a relationship is to you, the more it matters for your health.

GOLDEN NUGGETS OF RELATIONSHIPS

Relationships are intriguing. Mix one complex piece of biology called a human with another—or, even better, a few families or

Laugh and the world laughs with you

Moods are contagious. If you see others laughing, it makes you want to laugh. The sadness of others can bring tears to your own eyes, even though you don't share their cause of sorrow. A coffee with a friend who's depressed and complaining leaves you feeling down yourself; while seeing a colourful, joyous circus act sends you home feeling ebullient.

In the Vietnam War, the quiet courage of a group of monks, calmly walking beside some paddy fields during a battle, stopped soldiers shooting and took the fighting spirit out of them.

You send subtle signals the whole time, and you pick them up too. In one laboratory setting, researchers found that when people look at a smiling face their own facial muscles show signs of picking up that good mood; on the other hand, they reveal a slight move towards anger when looking at an angry face. These are not changes that would be visible to the naked eye, but they can be measured through electronic sensors.

groups—and you have the dynamics of epic novels, Shakespearean tragedies and soap operas that run for decades. Your dealings with the people in your life—whether they're churlish children, demanding dads, meddling mothers, generous grandparents, worrisome work colleagues or awkward acquaintances—demand a range of social skills and abilities. You need empathy to tune in to and understand other people; and you need a certain measure of self-management. It's easy to notice children learning the latter—the difficulties they experience in learning to wait for something they want, the concept of taking it in turns, negotiating skills, the ability to control their impulses, whether physical or verbal.

Many other virtues and skills come into play when relating to others: respect (of others' views, rights and individuality), and intimacy (shared feelings and experience, letting someone 'in'). At times relationships test our willingness to commit. Compatability is an issue for couples and friends, but good communication skills help you get your message across even to those you do not necessarily feel are 'on the same wavelength'.

VOX POP: Should relationships be left to happen or do they take work?

'I've always favoured leaving them to happen but my ex-wife said we had to work at it and I didn't work hard enough. For me, if a relationship takes a lot of work, you have to ask if it's really right. I think my best relationships just flow. That's not to say I take them for granted, but there's a naturalness around a good relationship where neither party has any doubt at any time where they stand within it.' DL

'I think they take work like staying in contact through letter, phone and email, arranging meetings, sharing food and drink together, discussing things.' PN

'More and more I believe that any relationship worth having is worth working at, because those I just leave to develop tend to founder. I certainly believe that many relationships just happen to begin with—that's their beauty—but when we know they are worth maintaining and furthering, we have to step in and take a role in that.' FH

'They take work: patience and tolerance, sloughing off one's own sharp edges, understanding how the other feels and what they need.' HB

'Relationships take work. If there is no work, there is no relationship. Work is being at my daughter's trumpet concert or my son's soccer game. It is going to the school to argue their case when they are faced with injustice; it is sleeping on the floor beside them in hospital because they are scared. It is taking my mother to endless doctor's appointments, washing, cooking and cleaning for her because I remember when she did it for me.' SG

'Time is everything. Spending time with people is what matters, whether it's an aunt who enjoys your cooking, a child who wants you to go to the playground with him, or a husband who wants some free time with you. Taking the time to keep in touch, with postcards, emails, phone calls and visits, is a concrete way of showing people you are thinking about them.' AH

CALLING FOR COMMUNICATION

If relationships are at the heart of happiness, communication is at the centre of relationships: it's how you connect, share your experiences and feelings, build the bonds of love and goodwill.

Communication is not a science; it is an art. And everyone has their own style. You encounter a joyous variety of people in daily life and in your lifelong communications. It's one of the spices of life: the endless chatter of friends; the banter of the market stall owner; the careful tones of a teacher; and the dry humour of the gossiping neighbour. The way people get their messages across makes you laugh, irritates, soothes and entertains. But some ways of communicating can get you into trouble, whether it's marital breakdown, missing out on promotions or inciting aggression every step of the way. Communication is often a critical aspect of problem solving so it pays to consider how you communicate with others.

BODY LANGUAGE, WORDS AND OTHER MEANINGS

Words are only a part of the communication repertoire at your disposal. Some say they're only 1 per cent of the message, the rest—the 99 per cent—is body language. The tone, volume and quality of voice tell a tale: assertion classes often help people develop a firmer, louder voice with which to deliver their messages. Politicians are sometimes coached to soften their voices and soften a hard image at the same time. Posture betrays true feeling—the cowering of fear, the towering presence of oppression—but when you can control your posture, it can lend authority. Gestures too, are giveaways that can be controlled. Fiddling with keys at an interview looks like distraction or anxiety, banging a fist on the table is a sign of aggression.

Words too are open to interpretation. And, confusingly, you don't always say what you mean. Sometimes you need to get underneath the layers to know what's really going on. You're probably aware of times when your lips were mouthing one set of words, but your mind was thinking along different lines. In the longer term, you may find you say one thing, but do the opposite. Words provide a powerful communication tool but it's important not to always take them at face value. Silence can also be a powerful form of communication: who hasn't felt the strength of feeling emanating from someone who is brooding, sulking or who has cut you off? The things that hurt us most, or that we feel most strongly about, can be the ones that are hardest to talk about.

GOOD COMMUNICATION: GOOD VIBRATIONS

While tips on communication might not help you solve problems overnight, they might lead you in the right direction. Many self-help books include dialogues that illustrate helpful ways of confronting a spouse, boss or difficult teenager. Unfortunately real life doesn't seem to go to script—people don't even always talk in full sentences—but the ideas can be helpful. Sometimes the dialogue may take place over a few days instead of during one conversation. Keeping the communication lines open can be a challenge at times; if you need a few extra ideas, these may help.

Be assertive, not aggressive

Sarah Edelman, teacher of cognitive behaviour therapy and author of *Change Your Thinking*, defines being assertive as a willingness to honestly express thoughts, feelings and wants in a way that also takes into account the rights of other people. It is an idea based on equality—other people's interests and rights may be important, but yours are just as important.

Look for the win–win

The ideal situation is when, at the end of an exchange, all parties involved feel OK and no one feels they've come off badly. By being conciliatory, you can avoid the stress of a conflict and you are also more likely to achieve your aims.

Talk it over

Giving vent to your feelings, rather than harbouring them—especially when they concern another's behaviour—expresses your concerns, communicates that problems exist and also what they are, and gives you a chance to fix them. Not only can airing your concerns help you to understand them, it also gives the listener a better chance of understanding your viewpoint. Sometimes merely voicing a concern or thought makes you realize how unjustified those concerns are.

Learn your ABCs

One way of reducing the potential threat of a statement is to use the word 'I': 'What aspect of someone's behaviour am I upset about? What emotion does it trigger in me and how do I feel about it? What are the consequences of the behaviour for me?' By structuring the message in this way, it brings the problem back home, to you, rather than forcing it on another person.

Sometimes you need to use the ABC trick: 'I feel A when you B and I wish you would C instead'. For example, 'I feel like a slave when you throw your dirty clothes on the floor and I wish you would put them in the washing basket instead.'

The whole message and nothing but

When you've got something sticky to say, or something you feel will be greeted with conflict or disproval, it can help to have a structure to your statements. Consider including these elements:

- Objective statement. Just state the facts without any emotional embellishment. 'You have practised the piano only twice this week although your teacher says four times is the minimum needed.'
- Thoughts. Use interpretations, opinions and perceptions. 'I wonder if your heart is in your piano learning.'
- Feelings. Describe how you feel. 'It makes me cross that you're not making an effort when the lessons are so expensive.'
- What you would like. Conclude with an expression of preferences or a request. 'I would like you to practise four times a week. If you do not, I think we should talk about stopping the lessons.'

Don't stew

Confronting issues now rather than delaying and brooding on them avoids escalating tension. Bitterness and resentment grow while you do nothing and the problem itself seems to increase. The exception is when you need to cool down before tackling a problem that makes you feel very angry.

Share good feelings

Give positive feedback. Tell people—whether your colleagues, your partner or your children—when you really appreciate something they've done. It reinforces positive behaviour, strengthens the bonds between you and makes them feel good.

Take the first step

When you're unsure why a friend has not been in touch, or why your husband has been scratchy, approach the person instead of assuming they are fed up with you. The direct approach can help to diffuse bad feelings and tension.

Be honest

Lies cloud relationships, prevent you dealing with the real issues and, most importantly, they make trust difficult.

VOX POP: How do you deal with conflict in a relationship?

'Arguments happen but I try not to let them be too bitter or protracted. I dislike quarrelling and try to resolve matters by compromise and sometimes by giving way. I try to remember that I just might be wrong!' PN

'I deal with conflict badly. I try to avoid it. I try to talk things through. Communication is my best weapon, I guess. I hate sulkers.' DL

'Either I deal with it with dogged patience, or I bottle it up and it finds destructive outlets.' HB

'Parents fighting is a big no. Always explain when you are in a bad mood with the kids. They'll accept it if you explain. Always be prepared to say sorry, to hug and be silly and happy.' SG

'I'm a "last straw" person, so most of the time I remain calm and make a mental note to bring up an issue at a good time. If I can, I approach with "What about...?" or "How about trying...?" It's not always like that though and there are times when pressure mounts and voices are raised. But if I've shouted at my children, I always explain why I am upset and tell them that even when I'm cross with them I love them very much.' MN

CRITICISM: GIVING IT AND TAKING IT

One particularly difficult area of communication is that of criticism, both giving it and being on the receiving end. It is, however, an important skill to master. Off the cuff criticism can be unintentionally hurtful, yet it is often necessary to give negative

Pablo Picasso (1881–1973) and Henri Matisse (1869–1954)

Described as the twin giants of twentieth century art, Picasso and Matisse were not only rivals but also friends who criticized, admired and were inspired by each other's art. They met in 1906 in Paris at the studio of Gertrude Stein, where they were both regular visitors and, a year later, exchanged paintings. Matisse moved to Nice in the south of France, but Picasso remained in Paris during World War I, moving south afterwards. Matisse had abandoned a career in law by the age of twenty, but suffered severe poverty and self-doubt until he was nearing 40. Picasso, on the other hand, was recognized as a precocious child artist and gained fame, later fortune, quickly. While Picasso is known for cubism and political statement, Matisse is often referred to as the master of colour. Both strayed from realism but never too far into abstract art. In 2002–03 the sellout exhibition Matisse Picasso, featuring 132 of their artworks, toured London, Paris and New York, allowing a glimpse into this half-century long friendship.

feedback at home, at work and in many other social situations. A little forethought can lessen the blow.

Attack the deed, not the person

A piece of advice that comes up again and again, whether in the context of positive parenting or communicating among couples, is that criticism should always be levelled at the action—'I felt so angry when you turned up late for the dinner party'—rather than at the person—'The only thing you can be relied on is to be late. I can't stand it.' The former states the case without being vindictive, while the latter method is a sure-fire way to drive rifts in relationships.

Be specific

Always mention a particular incident rather than make a sweeping generalization. For example, 'You were late for work four days out of five last week' instead of 'You're always late.'

Offer a solution

If you don't open the door to solving the problem, you leave someone feeling frustrated and down. For example, 'I know you find it hard to write letters, but how about a postcard once a month?' instead of 'You don't keep in touch—you never write.'

Keep it personal

Face-to-face criticism may be harder to give, but impersonal methods like emails and notes are much harder to take. A face-to-face exchange also provides the opportunity to communicate and makes the problem easier to fix.

Have a little care

Some sensitivity and empathy in how you deliver your criticism helps the person on the receiving end and helps the final outcome too. Put-downs and negative feedback delivered in a hurtful fashion, on the other hand, create resentment, bitterness and defensiveness, and push parties apart.

When you are on the receiving end

While it's not easy to bear the brunt of criticism, some strategies are more constructive than others:

- listen
- respond constructively
- try to reach an understanding
- work co-operatively at finding solutions
- keep it in perspective
- ask for clarification if needed
- realize this may be valuable feedback that could help you in future
- don't take it personally
- don't become adversarial
- take responsibility; avoid defensiveness
- take time out if you feel the need to recapture your cool before proceeding with a conversation; ask to resume a meeting later or excuse yourself to get a drink of water, or explain that you need a little time to think.

FIGHT THE GOOD FIGHT

Fighting need not be all negative. In the heat of the moment you may often express emotions and feelings that you find difficult to mention in calmer times. You might speak more clearly and deeply, in a way that demonstrates what you are thinking. Fighting is the opposite of apathy and disengagement. As long as it is not cruel or out of hand, fights can bring you closer rather than push you apart. What works for one person, one couple or one situation, won't necessarily work for another, but here are some ways of fighting fairer.

- Express feelings directly and squarely. 'I'm angry you left me to do the washing up after the family came over' is far more effective than 'You don't do anything around the house!'
- Be clear about what you want. 'Can you do the dishes before I get back from work?' works better than storming off in tears with the words 'I suppose I'll have to do them again when I get back.'

- Stay on the goal. Stick to the topic in hand and don't get diverted to last week's or last year's debacle.
- Don't be abusive. It doesn't help to nurture a long-term relationship.
- Consider an interval. A break, especially if you can go off and do something that takes your mind off the fight, can help regain perspective and help you sort out the aspects of your conflict that really matter as opposed to the ones you are prepared to let go of.
- Be flexible. Give and take, from all parties, smooths conflicts and helps everyone get on with the job of living. Compromising yourself—rather than reaching compromises—is different. Compromising yourself can lead to resentment, which leads to bitterness and doesn't help anyone. Recognizing which issues could lead to resentment is an important part of finding solutions to them. Even if the answer doesn't appear overnight, at least you're on the right road.
- Admit mistakes. Saying sorry and admitting to mistakes when you make them is a great communication tool. It shows you can see the other person's perspective and demonstrates you are not letting pride or stubbornness get in the way of a solution.
- Accept the present and let go of the past. You may well need to talk about the past and express your feelings about it, but you certainly can't change it. It's the present that you can work with.
- Remember what it's all about. Fighting in a close relationship clears the air and spring-cleans the communication process. It's about taking responsibility and not blaming others.
- Listen, and show you are listening. In particular, listen for peace offerings and be open to them.
- Learn to recover quickly. Bouncing back from an emotional attack brings back clarity of thought and expression and lets you carry on trying to fix the problem.
- Challenge your thinking. For example, a husband who feels that his needs are always ignored might remind himself of a number of thoughtful things his wife has done for him in the last few weeks.

- Mirror, mirror. A technique used in marital therapy, called mirroring, involves one partner stating her cause, and the other repeating it in his own words, trying to catch the meaning and feelings involved. As well as enhancing the feeling of being listened to, mirroring can also help couples attune emotionally.

FRIENDSHIP

And in the sweetness of friendship let there be laughter, and sharing of pleasures.
For in the dew of little things the heart finds its morning and is refreshed.

KAHLIL GIBRAN, *THE PROPHET* (1926)

Friends hold a special place in your life. While you can't choose your relatives, you can choose your friends. It can be hard to keep in touch, but not so hard if your heart is in it. Virginia Woolf (1882–1941) wrote in *The Waves*, 'I have lost friends, some by death…others through sheer inability to cross the street.'

Friends will—if you're lucky—help you in times of need. Whom you turn to when in trouble can be revealing; sometimes you may discover you have fair weather friends. A betrayal by a friend is seen by many as the ultimate betrayal.

Friendships come and go throughout your life, become stronger then fade as circumstances change—you leave school, change university, move country; they start a family, jobs change, interests alter. Samuel Johnson advised in 1755, 'If a man does not make new acquaintance as he advances through life, he will soon find himself alone. A man, Sir, should keep his friendship in constant repair.'

Friends stretch you by introducing you to new experiences; they support you by listening and offering practical help; they give you companionship and help you deepen your understanding of the world by letting you into theirs.

MAKING FRIENDS

If keeping friends is hard at times, making them is even harder for some. Learning to make friends is an important part of growing up. It's how children learn many basic social skills such as joining in, participating in group problem solving, coping with competition and conflict, and learning to interact with peers. Being rejected by peers at school has been linked to depression and to problems such as dropping out of school.

VOX POP: What does friendship mean?

'It means communion on some level with another person. This can be intellectual, spiritual, physical, personality or humour based, circumstantial or a mixture of all these. I value most the ones where we're closer and easier with each other, but I really appreciate the less significant kinds as well.' FH

'I have a few close friends who accept me as I am, without me having to keep up appearances of normality. They accept the real me and I accept the real them: a transparent relationship sometimes of great depth.' HB

'My writing colleagues are my deepest friends and we share the richness of a profession filled with angst and the creativity of a brilliant life. Life without friends is empty. Lots of friends would be great but impossible. Family and partner are your main friends because they share your daily life. Outside friends are important too but you can't spend too much time with them.' SG

'Friendship is about connecting. Sometimes I wonder why I'm friends with someone, as on reflection we seem to have little in common, but then I think if somebody offers you friendship, you should treat it as special. No one can be everything you seek in a friend, they all bring out different aspects of your personality, and all have different things to share—whether it's wine, laughter, or child care.' MN

'You're rarely ever alone. You've got people to care for you. It's fun!' HN (age seven)

The good news is that it is possible to teach some social skills which help ease the way into friendship. Psychologists such as Steven Asher, director of the Bureau of Educational Research at the University of Illinois, says that being aware of the skills a child has, and those that are lacking, as well as understanding how children choose friends is the first step in helping them overcome social problems. When deciding whether to befriend another, children ask themselves—consciously and unconsciously—questions along the lines of the following:

- Is s/he fun to be with?
- Is s/he trustworthy?
- Does s/he make me feel good about myself?
- Is s/he similar to me?

Asher has developed a social skills coaching program which helps children who have difficulty making friends, particularly in situations where a child does not know what to do. The program centres on four interaction concepts, which are explained in the context of game playing:

- Participation. This means getting involved, getting started and paying attention to the activity.
- Communication. Here Asher means back to basics stuff like talking with another person, saying something about yourself or the game, asking questions about a game or about a person. Children learn to listen when someone talks, look at the other person to see how they are doing, discover alternatives to insulting others or arguing, and find new ways to respond to teasing.
- Co-operation. This includes ideas of sharing (taking turns, sharing games or toys), and solving conflict—making a suggestion if there is a problem with a game, or coming up with an alternative when there's a disagreement about the rules.

Playground skills

Children employ a range of skills to manage relationships in the playground. Many of these come into play in adult friendships too:

- joining in
- coping with success or failure
- managing conflict
- defending yourself
- staying involved
- sharing
- cooperating
- sticking up for others
- coping with rejection
- responding to requests
- making requests
- helping other people
- making and maintaining conversation
- coping with teasing
- being supportive of others.

- Validation. Children are taught that support is friendly, fun and nice. Support means giving attention to the other person, saying something nice when the other person does well, smiling from time to time, offering help or suggestions.

A few other concepts have been found to help such as 'being a good sport', 'being a good team member' and 'keeping your cool'. Kids can be helped to keep on top of emotions by being reminded to grin, make jokes and keep their voice calm and quiet.

Programs such as Asher's have a 50 to 60 per cent chance of raising the popularity of children who have been rejected by peers.

LOOKING FOR ROMANCE

Marriage rates are down and divorce rates are up, but a special relationship with a partner is still highly valued whether you are in one or not. School leaver, single parent, gay or straight, young or old, the search for a soul mate can be fraught with heartache and disappointment as well as hope and delight. It's a tough learning ground. In the more formal days of chaperones, contact between courting couples was a controlled affair—now many teenagers and young adults experiment with different partners, and on their own terms. Along the way they may learn much about their own insecurities, the power play within a relationship and the unfolding complexities and challenges of intimacy—as well as the rules of safe sex.

We often meet partners at work or through friends, when our guards are down or we're just getting on with life. But sometimes there's a feeling that time's running out, and waiting to meet someone special is just not enough. When new acquaintances are thin on the ground there are dating agencies, lonely hearts advertisements, dinner for sixes, and the like to turn to. Two recent developments are speed dating (an organized event where you meet a group of singles, talk to each of them for a set time and tick whether you'd like to see them again; if they tick you as well, you receive each other's contact details) and Internet romance.

ROMANCE IN THE FAST LANE

FL, a single mother in her late thirties with two teenage daughters, has been separated for five years and feels stuck in a rut, without the likelihood of meeting other singles. She signed up for a speed dating event as she saw it as an efficient way of meeting around twenty single men in one evening, with the added bonus of only having to talk to someone for four minutes if she didn't like them. 'I don't want to spend the rest of my life on my own, so I thought I'd better take some positive steps or else the years could slip by.' The first two events were cancelled for lack of males, but the third went ahead. FL describes the evening, which was held in a smart bar:

The main thing was that no one was ugly or strange—just normal people. I latched on to two women and started chatting to them—I was a bit scared of going and it did seem a bizarre situation.

We had four minutes with eighteen men. Sometimes the four minutes went really fast and at other times it seemed like forever. Actually, it was a laugh all the way through and it is amazing how you can talk easily to some people but others really struggle at communication. Among the males were three farmers, three lawyers, one doctor, a cable layer, an e-commerce bod and someone in finance. Unfortunately there was no one there that I felt physically attracted to but there was one man for whatever reason, whenever we spoke, we were laughing hysterically, so I ticked his box for 'friends' and 'date' and ticked one other person who I now can't remember face, personality or anything. The men seemed to be ticking loads—like ten or so—whilst the conversation in the ladies loo was that most women had ticked between none and three.

The girls I spoke to said they had been single for four to six years and had not met many single men in that time. A few of the ladies are going to meet up again—we all agreed that if your friends are coupled off, it makes going out hard. I haven't had any responses back, so I don't know if I got any ticks...then of course you have the almost blind date experience on top of the speed dating experience!

RELATIONSHIPS ON LINE

Chat rooms, email, dating sites, cyber sex...the Internet is the latest technological communication device used to join people together. It pulls people apart too. Relate, the UK marriage guidance organization, says that the use of Internet chat rooms is the fastest rising cause of relationship breakdown in the United Kingdom. The

Internet follows in the wake of mail, the phone and fax. But as well as a way of 'talking', it is also a means of 'meeting' someone for the first time, albeit on screen rather than in the flesh.

Relationship guidance organizations warn of the risks of Internet dating: disguise and deception is very easy in cyberspace as you have only the words someone chooses to write to go on. The same applies to your own revelations: at the keyboard, you need not worry about what you look like or how you respond to somebody's body language as you would in a face-to-face situation. It is an egocentric activity, and some people find it easier to express their emotions and feelings on line than with the 'whole' person. Moving the relationship into the real world requires caution:

- If you agree to meet someone for the first time, choose a public place and consider bringing along a trusted friend.
- Once you meet, think of the relationship as starting afresh. It is quite a different matter to meet someone in person. People act differently off line—sometimes not as honestly or expressively— and it's worth protecting yourself a little to begin with.
- Find ways to feel in control of the situation. Importantly, work out a safe way for you to take your leave.

WHEN LIMERENCE FADES

The American psychologist Dorothy Tennov coined the term 'limerence' in 1979 to describe that high emotion felt at the beginning of a relationship. Call it the glow of falling in love, euphoria or infatuation, it tends to be experienced in the first twelve months or so of a relationship, when all's exciting and overwhelmingly positive. It's not just an emotion but also a biological reaction. A number of chemicals flood the brain: arousal neurotransmitters such as acetylcholine, which produces a feeling of excitement; dopamine which induces a feeling of wellbeing; noradrenaline, which helps create pleasure and a feeling that you can do anything in the world; phenylethylamine, which creates heightened excitement; and serotonin, which soothes, creating a feeling of security. But as limerence is based on seeing a partner through rose-coloured spectacles, once those spectacles are removed—as they inevitably are at some point—a person doesn't always look so good in the cold light of reality. This is where, hopefully, real love kicks in to help a couple resolve the problems, practicalities and emotions of living with someone day in, day out.

The fading of limerence can coincide with sexual problems in the relationship. Clinical psychologist Judith Wallerstein interviewed couples who had been married for at least nine years and on average 21 years. She found many couples had experienced problems in their sexual relationships at one time or another but had helped each other overcome these difficulties. Sex lives tended to suffer when a couple's life became more stressful. Studies show, however, that with time couples can learn to adapt to the changes in levels of desire and activity in one or both spouses. The issue is no longer a source of conflict as psychological intimacy becomes more important than physical intimacy. The couple's intimacy grows—based on mutual trust, love and understanding—and, while the frequency of sex may diminish, enjoyment does not.

Sexual problems can emerge at any stage of a relationship. While there are various approaches, the idea of desire discrepancy is a helpful concept that removes blame and offers a way of altering dynamics within a relationship, whether you're young, old, gay or straight. Desire discrepancy, or desire mismatching, means simply a difference in sex drive. Without a good dose of mutual under-standing, desire discrepancy can start a chain reaction of negative feelings: a higher-drive partner may blame the other for a low libido; the more the higher-drive partner presses for sex, the more the other wants to withdraw and avoid sex. Demands may turn to impatience and anger, and the relationship may become bitter and resentful. Breaking the cycle, by challenging a few assumptions and attitudes, and rethinking the way you relate to and behave with each other can help you and your partner find a happy medium.

Helping yourself

The roots of desire spread wide. Sex drive depends on a complex network of biological and psychological factors: your physical health, how you are feeling 'in yourself', fatigue, and how you are feeling about your relationship. But, if you feel this is an area of ongoing concern in your relationship, there are many solutions at hand that don't necessarily involve seeking outside help and visiting a sex therapist:

- Turn on/turn off. Identify the factors in the relationship that are inhibiting (from arguments to unemployment or lack of spontaneity) and enhancing (from candlelit dinners to someone else putting the garbage out). Partners may have quite different enhancers and inhibitors. They don't have to be mutually exclusive, however. Maybe you can find some middle ground.

- Communication. Find the time to talk openly and without pressure about these and other factors of your sex life. It helps to keep a relationship alive.

- Understanding the gender divide. *Vive la différence!* While equality certainly has its place, let's face it…men and women have different needs and drives when it comes to sex. Of course, individuals vary, and we don't all fit the stereotypes, but there are some generalizations that might help you. Women need sex drive enhancers on a daily basis—it's no good turning up with a bunch of flowers after months of neglect and expecting an automatic jump in the sex stakes. Women tend to rate emotional closeness and affection higher, too. Men on the other hand, are typically more visually orientated when it comes to sex, hence the commercial success of erotic magazines and lingerie retail. Nudity and variety of lovemaking also tend to be rated highly by males.

- Relationship repair. The happier and healthier a relationship is, the more likely it is that sex problems can be worked out. Working at the relationship—whether that means ensuring more time together, improving communication or reorganizing the shared workload—will also help a couple's sex life.

Sometimes romance vanishes, leaving little feeling between a couple, sometimes it fades and is replaced by different, stronger shades of love—perhaps in a committed long-term relationship, perhaps in marriage.

Sex myths

- Rampant, frequent, passionate sex—such as that experienced in the early days of a relationship—is normal throughout a relationship. Wrong. Lust is often strong with limerence but can fade once reality sets in.
- Loving partners have matching sex drives. Wrong. As a relationship moves on, couples may find they want sex at different times and the intensity of their desire may vary too.
- Sex drive is a constant. Wrong. Sex drive fluctuates in the short term—over the day, the week, when you've got a headache—and in the long term—as you juggle the demands of children, stress or illness. Given these variations, desire discrepancy is inevitable at some point of a relationship.

MARRIAGE

It is common knowledge that men do well in the mental health stakes from marriage and women do poorly. Or is this a common misconception? David de Vaus, senior research advisor at the Australian Institute of Family Studies, trawled the data collected by the Australian Bureau of Statistics in 1999 when the institute conducted one of the most comprehensive mental health studies in the world: the National Survey of Mental Health and Wellbeing of Adults. The study interviewed a random sample of nearly 11,000 adult Australians, asking, among other things, about people's marital status and family structure. The data revealed that married people are the least likely to suffer from any particular class of mental health disorder. (In the study, 'married' included those in both de facto and legal partnerships.) Divorced and separated adults are the most prone to mood and anxiety disorders, while adults who have never married are at most risk of drug and alcohol disorders.

The proposition that married women are worse off than their single counterparts was first suggested in the late 1970s by sociologists Jessie Bernard and Walter Gove. But even then they blamed the role of full-time housewife rather than marital status itself. While their findings are still being supported by other studies, marriage has undergone a revolution, says de Vaus. The rate of marriage is down; there is less pressure to marry; it's easier to end a damaging relationship; family planning means fewer babies; and more women are in the paid work force. These are changes that have occurred in many Western countries, including the United States, and corresponding changes in mental health patterns have been found; however, the findings often remain within the academic world.

Even though finding time and energy for work, children, husbands and houses would seem taxing for anyone, married women with children are less at risk of mental health problems than single working women. Perhaps it's the fact that with more juggling to manage, they have less time for introspection or perhaps the relationships, while demanding, are also rewarding in deep ways.

THE EVOLUTION OF A MARRIAGE

Marriages and other long-term relationships typically move through a number of stages: from the excitement of 'the honeymoon phase' with its idealism to a more realistic phase when differences become apparent. After a time of feeling safe within the relationship—hence feeling able to put energy into work and family—couples often report 'finding each other again', enjoying increased intimacy having made the transition from being 'in love' to 'loving' each other.

Milestones in a relationship may require practical changes too: becoming a couple often involves moving away from a family. The days of moving straight from a parental home to wedded, domestic bliss are all but gone, but there may still be the sense of a change in identity from, for example, a son, brother or flatmate to a husband or partner. The transition from partners to parents requires another change in focus and a shift of energy from being a couple to taking on the responsibilities and labour of children. The adolescence of children is often a time when parents re-examine their own relationship in the light of their children's emerging sexuality. It's also a signal that the children will soon be leaving the nest. Retirement can throw people back together for hours on end when they've been used to days spent apart at work or in separate pursuits; in addition, finances may be tight and domestic chores may be reallocated.

Wherever an individual has to make an adjustment so too does the relationship in which they are involved. Many life changes are a challenge to a relationship too: migration, inheritance, business failure, serious illness, the death or illness of a child. The more open a couple are with each other and the more direct their communication, the more able they are to ride the changes of life.

BARRIERS TO INTIMACY

Sometimes intimacy comes naturally; sometimes it seems to slip away. According to Relationships Australia, which provides relationship support services including counselling, there are some common reasons why distance develops in a relationship:

- Lack of communication. One or both partners may find it difficult to put into words how they feel and what they are going through. They may fear rejection or may simply be unused to talking about their feelings.
- Emotional differences. When emotions like anger, hurt or resentment are not resolved, it's hard to feel safe enough to be intimate. Lack of trust and feeling unappreciated by your partner are also barriers.
- Practical difficulties. Financial worries, pressure at work, difficulties with children, or just being too busy can also get in the way of a couple's closeness.
- Childhood experiences. Adults who were badly hurt as children—whether by abuse, or a loss or death that was never fully mourned—may find it hard to trust other people. Self-doubt and a feeling of unworthiness that may have arisen in childhood can also impinge on a person's adult relationships.
- Contempt. According to marriage researcher John Gottman, contempt is very bad news in a relationship. Contemptuous

words, tone of voice and facial expression combine insult and injury in a visceral as well as emotional way. Gottman found that a spouse who is subject to regular expressions of contempt from their partner is more prone to frequent colds and flus, bladder problems and other health problems.

TILL DEATH—OR SOMETHING ELSE—DO US PART

Thomas Moore—an American psychotherapist who spent twelve years as a Catholic monk and is the author of *Care of the Soul* and *Soul Mates*—regards marriage, like religion, as unfathomable and mysterious. He suggests that you put back the soul in your exploration of relationships, and put behind you all notions of perfect partnerships and unruffled relationships. Work at a relationship, yes, he says. But observe and attempt to understand it rather than expect quick fix solutions. Open discussion, yes; dry analysis, no.

Although undertaking research into marriage could be considered the antithesis of Moore's spiritual approach, studies into what qualities contribute to a lasting marriage seem to support his description of a mysterious mix of magic and realism.

In one study by writer and lecturer Francine Klagsbrun, published in 1985, 87 couples who'd been married for more than fifteen years were interviewed at length about the qualities of their partnership. Klagsbrun came up with eight consistent characteristics in these marriages:

1   Ability to change and adapt to change. Marriages are always works in progress and even ones built on solid foundations need constant maintenance. Marriage, or any long-term partnership, involves ups, downs and plenty of compromise and sharing—whether of goals, love or children. Over the decades, external forces such as social change can also challenge a relationship. For instance, in many of the marriages studied, increased access to education and increased participation in the work force by women were seen as something that needed to be dealt with by the couple in a positive light.

2 Ability to live with the unchangeable. Do you believe that spouses can be trained to put dirty socks in the washing basket or not to tell the same joke endlessly at dinner parties? Some aspects of people are best accepted in the first place and that's an attitude that comes through in research of long-lasting relationships. Accommodating differences, enjoying the relationship rather than expecting to be able to change someone, not expecting perfection, and not even expecting resolution of every single disagreement are keys to survival.

3 Assumption of permanence. Alongside an ability to compromise and take a realistic view, successful couples believe in marriage as a solid institution. They accept that 'give and take' may waver over the years but will balance out in time. At times this may require a fair dose of faith. It is common for a mother to feel she's giving more than her partner in the early years after the birth of the first child. However, this can even out when children are of school age, or even later, as some mothers decide to take up studies again or invest time in a personal interest.

4 Trust. This is the essential glue that keeps a marriage together. For the couples in this study, it remained strong through ups and downs, sustaining the marriage with a sense of safety, security and fidelity, and providing a basis for intimacy.

5 Balance of power. This requires the couple to develop a mysterious mix of space and intimacy. In the marriages that were studied, a mutual dependency on each other was seen as a strength, but also as something that shifted depending on which partner needed more nurturing at the time. Couples reported a deep attachment at the same time as being able to survive outside the relationship.

6 Enjoyment of each other. This would seem to be where a successful marriage starts. Partners in happier long-term marriages enjoyed each other's company, talked, argued and listened. They had found a balance between time together and time apart. While they often shared the same values, they did not agree on everything. They accommodated their differences

and, in some cases, the pursuit of different interests helped them stay interesting to each other.

7   Cherished, shared history. When you can look back together at times you enjoyed as a couple, or problems you solved and survived, you bolster your marriage. Joint experiences that you both value give perspective to the marriage. In this study, couples reported it also helped to prevent rash decisions when they were faced with new difficulties.

8   Luck. No more or less important than any of the other characteristics, couples believed luck had had some part to play in holding their marriages together. (Klagsbrun believed it was as much to do with their positive outlook and an ability to make the best of things!)

SURVIVING THE UPS AND DOWNS

A central aspect of staying together is not so much how well you 'get on' but how well you and your partner deal with your differences and what life throws you. Marriages can certainly survive rough patches and many do. In Long Island, New York, a study of nearly 600 couples who'd been married for 50 years or more revealed that 1 in 5 of all spouses had at some time contemplated the failure of the marriage, but by far the majority now considered themselves happily married. While a hard life can be hard on a marriage, if partners are able to adapt, communicate with, and support each other, it need not break it.

Coping with crises

Small problems can eat away at a relationship. Larger ones sometimes seem to bring you closer to each other, but at other times can threaten to drive you apart. In times of crisis, take a deep breath and for the sake of the partnership remember the following:

- Keep the crisis in perspective.
- Contain fears to the actual event; don't allow them to overwhelm and intrude on the relationship.
- Be realistic; gather information to work out how best to respond.

- Avoid self-blame.
- Take action to prevent small problems becoming enormous ones.
- Don't apportion blame to either party.

Even strong relationships have their ups and downs. But, as a couple becomes more experienced at dealing with stressful circumstances, they see their relationship in a better light—which in itself has a positive spiral effect. Long-married couples are more satisfied with their marriages and seem more able to manage their emotions. This could be because of three factors:

- They have learnt to knock off the edges of conflict with affection.
- Conflicts may resolve themselves or disappear with time.
- They feel less need to resolve every issue.
  Finding the funny side also helps keep a relationship together. Intimacy grows alongside lighthearted banter; in addition, happy couples use humour to defuse conflict and hostility, and to soothe wounded egos as well as add a spark of playfulness.

Paul Newman (1925–) and Joanne Woodward (1930–)

Actors Newman and Woodward met when they were understudies on Broadway and married in 1958. Newman's second marriage is celebrated as one of the longest in Hollywood. The couple's acting careers span their marriage, and include several shared performances—from The Long Hot Summer in 1958, to Mr and Mrs Bridges in 1990.

Both Woodward and Newman are known for charity works, and while Newman is reluctant to reveal the marriage's secret of success, he is more open about Newman's Own food company, which has, since its foundation in 1982, donated $150 million to charities.

The language of love

More than 600 couples from eight countries (the United States, Canada, Israel, Chile, Germany, Netherlands, Sweden and South Africa) took part in a study by researchers Sharlin, Kaslow and Hammerschmidt. This looked at couples who had been together—whether in marriage or simply living together—for twenty years or more. The qualities the couples nominated as the foundation of a happy relationship were:

- love
- sharing
- mutual trust
- respect
- support
- give and take
- fun and humour.

Endings

Relationship problems are the stuff of women's magazines, television dramas and counselling rooms alike. The ending of a relationship can be sad, a relief, expensive—when joint finances have to be untangled—and messy. Are there warning signs along the way?

Negative behaviour can ultimately crush a relationship—but good relationships can bear a degree of negativity without folding. Dr John Gottman, founder of the Family Research Laboratory—otherwise known as 'the Love Lab'—at the University of Washington, attempted to pinpoint just how much. He observed hundreds of couples over many years, asking them to address areas of conflict while he recorded a series of reactions including heart rate, facial expression and gestures. Gottman's research showed that a couple can withstand one bit of negative behaviour to five positive bits, but tip the balance and serious problems develop. In other research he also identified four types of negative behaviour

Are same-sex relationships different?

Many of the issues that crop up in same-sex relationships are the same as those in heterosexual ones. Communication is communication whatever your sexual orientation. However, homosexual individuals are much more likely to bring extra burdens to a relationship. Feeling you are part of a minority can be isolating and frightening, especially when first 'coming out' or acknowledging a homo- rather than heterosexual orientation. One partner may feel comfortable about being demonstrative in public whereas the other may feel uncomfortable; and many homosexual people feel they cannot acknowledge their homosexuality in the workplace, so end up leading a somewhat double life. Then there is communal grief over the death of so many people with AIDS and the fact that same-sex couples feel there is a lack of role models for how their relationship should work.

Neil Rodgers, a psychologist with a practice in Sydney with a 20 per cent homosexual clientele, says:

I come across a lot of people who are disowned by their families or beaten up on Oxford Street, and that's in Sydney which is supposed to be relatively tolerant. If you've grown up

that he found to be particularly destructive, calling them 'the Four Horsemen of the Apocalypse'. They are: criticism, which leads to contempt, which leads to defensiveness, which causes stonewalling, or withdrawal.

Other early warning signs that a relationship is in trouble include:

- living parallel lives, having abandoned joint activities
- recurring, unresolved arguments
- dissatisfaction and unhappiness
- preoccupation with interests and activities outside the relationship so that one partner feels neglected
- losing feeling for each other
- an affair.

in a small country town and felt you've had to hide your sexuality, it's very difficult to have an easy relationship with yourself, let alone other people.

In addition he points out that 'containment of sexuality' is more of an issue in homo- than in heterosexual relationships. The expectation of sexual fidelity is not so strong, whether from society or from the individuals in the partnership, but that brings with it another problem of how to hold a relationship together and maintain intimacy.

John Gottman, a well-known US marriage researcher, agrees that gay and lesbian relationships are comparable to straight ones in many ways, but research from his gay and lesbian couple study highlights some differences:

- Same-sex couples are better able to include affection and humour in a conflict situation.
- Equality and fairness seem to rate higher—they seem to use less controlling and hostile emotional tactics than heterosexual couples.
- Homosexual men seem less able to bounce back from negative behaviour in a fight than heterosexual and lesbian couples.

THE FINALITY OF SEPARATION

MA was facing his tenth wedding anniversary and his 40th birthday in the same year. While he and his wife were 'good friends', that's all they were; he did not believe there was anything deeper to salvage in the marriage and announced he was leaving. After a few weeks of anger and tears, the couple were talking amicably and started to plan separate lives, which involved putting a house on the market and dividing up their belongings. LJ and WR had been together for sixteen years and enjoyed the first few years after having a son but, when LJ began to voice desires to have another child, WR got cold feet and began to think about all the things he wished he'd done and felt a two-child family could not accommodate. A rift had opened

and, just a few months later, the relationship had run
its course.

Relationships end for all sorts of reasons. Dynamics change,
love fades, everyday conflict can breed contempt. Separation may
involve finding a new home as well as detaching from someone
with whom you've shared much. Anger, even rage, is not
uncommon, nor is guilt, remorse, fear, insecurity and rejection…
emotions run high and can be difficult to manage. They can result
in sleeplessness, a reluctance to show up at work, turning to alcohol,
and the feeling that you've lost everything—from financial security
to lifestyle or a full-time parenting role.

Counsellors recommend a few strategies to help you cope and
get over the worst:

- Be prepared for an emotional ride for all involved.
- Be open to friendship and help from family, friends and, if
  necessary, community-based counsellors.
- Put the past behind you and try not to dwell on revenge and guilt.

WHEN THERE ARE CHILDREN

How children react to a separation depends on their age and the
degree of animosity between their parents. Separation can come
as a surprise and they are likely to grieve. Fantasies that their
parents will get together again are common, so too are fears that
the remaining parent will leave them. Children often have to deal
with other changes: new schools, new house rules, new boyfriends
and girlfriends of parents. Being sensitive to their needs can make
a big difference.

- Consider trying to set up a 'lifeline' for your child or children—
  let them spend time with other trusted adults, let the school
  know what's going on, and so on.
- Find out what support facilities are available if appropriate, such
  as legal aid, cash grants, temporary accommodation, and so on.
- Don't leave children in the dark about what is happening in the
  family—but don't give them more information than they can
  handle. Fear of the unknown can be far more damaging than
  knowledge of a harsh reality.

- Avoid character assassinations of your former partner where at all possible and don't demand loyalty to the point of excluding the other parent. Building a new, though different, relationship with a former partner—one with your children's best interests at heart—will help children to deal with the split. Love may have gone from the picture, but respect will help you and your former partner make mutual decisions about your children's future and will help smooth access and care negotiations.

FAMILY LIFE

What is a family? The word comes from the Latin term *familia*, which referred to everyone living in the same household. It was a simple enough definition and, for the Romans, included servants too. Paul Keating, former Prime Minister of Australia, made headlines when he was widely reported as commenting that, in his opinion, two poofters and their cocker spaniel did not constitute a family. Pets aside, families are a diverse bunch, as this snapshot of Europe taken by the Economic and Social Research Council in 2002 demonstrates:

- In Italy, almost half of all men still live with their parents at the age of 30, while in Finland half of young men have left the parental home by 22. The UK halfway mark for men leaving home is 23.5.
- The average Irish household is four people, the largest in Europe. In the United Kingdom it is 2.8 and Sweden has the smallest households with an average of 2.2.
- Between the ages of 23 and 27, British men are five times more likely than Italian men to be in a partnership—42 per cent compared to 9 per cent.
- In southern European countries such as Italy and Spain, a third of women over the age of 65 live with one or more of their children. In northern and central European countries (Germany and the Netherlands, for example), 1 in 10 lives with a child, while in Nordic countries this figure dives to 1 in 30.

CHANGES IN THE FAMILY

Change is the very nature of family life—a baby's needs are different from a school child's and different again from those of a teenager preparing for university. The arrival of siblings shifts focus and brings new dynamics, new routines and relationships. Grandparents age, cousins are born.

More families are undergoing a radical change in structure, too. In Australia, for example, a third of marriages involve at least one person who has been married before—and who often already has children. But, assures Relationships Australia, 'contrary to their bad image, step families can provide a rich and rewarding environment for the adults and children involved.'

While those in second marriages are often more aware of the difficulties ahead, and are more committed to the family unit, there are also hurdles. What sort of approach should a parent take to discipline? Is there a danger of overcompensating when showing affection and attention? What's more important: the existing family's pattern or your own expectations? How will you deal with and feel about the parent that's outside the family home? Are you ready for the emotional barrage you may face from children who are struggling to adapt to a new home life? Counsellors often recommend the following:

- Waiting longer rather than jumping into a second marriage. Explore any doubts, make sure you've come to terms with your first marriage ending, ask yourself what issues contributed to its breakdown. Some studies suggest it takes at least two years to adjust to the end of a marriage and regain the emotional freedom to begin a new marriage.
- Trying to identify why exactly you want to remarry. Is it so children have a two-parent home?
- Identifying what aspects of your previous partner were incompatible with you. Should this affect what you look for in a second choice of partner?

Another form of family unit on the rise is one headed by a single parent. This parent is likely to be under more stress than someone in a two-parent family and is also less likely to be satisfied with life. In a survey by Relationships Australia, 29 per cent of single parents were satisfied with life compared to between 53 and 71 per cent of people in other relationships.

WHAT DO HAPPY FAMILIES HAVE IN COMMON?

Family life impacts on how well children learn at school and how their social skills develop, on the family's health—both physical and mental—on economic wellbeing, and on each member's happiness and contentment. One of the first pieces of research to try to identify what made a happy family—one with good outcomes, not negative ones—was entitled No Single Thread. The name was intended to highlight the diversity within 'healthy' families. 'Happy' families are not perfect. They, like other families that are more or less troubled, have their weaknesses and strengths. They also encounter crises and rough periods. But, while research has found many models of happy families, they all appear to have some golden characteristics in common.

Communication runs deep

In happy families, members are not afraid to express themselves and let others know what they are thinking. But they often wait until the right moment to express something negative. The dynamics seem to work to avoid a build-up of emotion, so that fiery, damaging outbursts are avoided. It was found in No Single Thread that in the 'healthiest' families, family members interrupt each other a lot more than in other families. In not so healthy families, the pattern was for only one or two members to be interrupted; however, in the happy families, members are interrupted equally.

In your family you might consider when the best moments arise for letting down your guard and ensure you build more of these moments into your lives. They could be first thing in the morning when everyone piles onto the family bed; at meal times; on relaxed outings like picnics and bike rides; or at bath and bed time if you have young children.

Queen Victoria (1819–1901)
and the Empress Frederik (1840–1901)

'Oh, Madam, it is a princess,' announced the doctor attending the birth of Queen Victoria's first child. 'Never mind,' the Queen replied, 'the next will be a prince.' Named Victoria Adelaide Mary Louisa, 'Vicky' to the family, her mother regarded her—like all babies—as 'frightful' when undressed and a mere little plant for the first six months. But seventeen years later the Queen farewelled the newly wed Vicky and her husband, Fritz, the Crown Prince of Prussia, and later described how her breaking heart gave way.

Being a wife gave her daughter new status in her mother's eyes but, with Vicky now in Germany, confidences were shared by prolific letters. Child rearing was another subject of letters after the birth of Vicky's first child (who later became known as Kaiser Wilhelm)—a breech birth so traumatic that obituary notices were on their way to the newspapers before it was over, as the worst had wrongly been assumed. Letters continued to cross the English Channel between mother and daughter until the last weeks of Queen Victoria's life. After her mother's death, in a letter to her sister, Vicky asked what life would be like without the comfort and support of their mother. But Vicky was very ill with cancer and the Queen's eldest daughter died only a matter of months later, with the wish that she be buried as an English princess.

In praise of praise

Members of happy families demonstrate their appreciation of each other and all members know they belong and are loved. Although praise without genuine reason is not considered beneficial to child development, Moira Eastman, family welfare authority and author of *We're OK! Secrets of Happy Families*, believes that children thrive on well founded praise. She refers to a study in which researchers asked a group of teenagers whether in the last 24 hours their parents had hugged or kissed them, praised them for something they had done, told them they loved them, talked with them about what they had done that day, or helped them with their homework. The better the student, the more likely they were to answer 'yes' to all five questions. The question that revealed the most direct link to school performance was 'Did your parents praise you for something you did?' The more praise a child received, the better they did at school.

Putting this into practice could mean trying to catch children while they're being good and making sure they know you've noticed; or, if you correct or tell your children off, making a point of praising them for something else soon after.

Affection's OK

Happy families are open and clear about expressing affection, whether it's through hugs, kisses, wrestling or gentle teasing. Some parents make a point of kissing or hugging their children as they send them off to school or when they see them again in the afternoon. Others make time for close contact when reading together or watching a film.

Parents in charge

In 'healthy' families, parents share the power between them and regard it as their job to guide and limit their children's behaviour. They have high expectations of their children and are willing to make a stand, but will use humour, persuasion and following up rather than threats and punishments.

You can set high standards and let everyone know what the house rules are. For young children these could be as simple as: no balls in the house; no eating on the sofa; no mauling the kitten. For older children, house rules might be: always letting at least one of their parents know where they're going and what time they'll be back; finishing homework before watching television; clearing the table after each meal or snack.

A loving couple

The source of a family's strength is a loving relationship between the parents. Children's development suffers when parents bicker or when one undermines or bullies the other. An intimate and supportive relationship avoids the situation where a parent feels more comfortable turning to a child—rather than their partner—when they are faced with a problem or crisis. This is a dreadful experience for a child and puts them in an uneasy position between their parents.

As SG found, 'Children stretch the husband–wife relationship to the maximum.' For most couples, looking after the relationship means making sure you spend time alone together. This could be after the children have gone to bed in the case of younger children; dinners out or weekends away together when the children are older; or lunches and other short daytime outings when the kids are at school.

Commitment to values

The happy family has its own values, beliefs and rituals, whether stemming from spiritual, religious or other bases. A US study called Back to the Family found a strong link between family wellbeing and a belief system of one sort or another. This included religions ranging from Christianity, Judaism and Islam to New Age spiritual beliefs. A commitment to politics or social movements had the same effect.

What values do you and your family hold dear: religious, environmental, social or charitable? Do all members of the family know what the others feel strongly about? Are you open about religious and spiritual matters?

The lighter side of family life

Happy families have fun. There's a lot of humour in their lives and the family members show signs of happiness and contentment. Some families think up games for special family events or make up poems for people's birthdays; others have a family tradition of rising to the occasion of a bad event by always having something witty to say.

What does your family consider to be fun? Bearing in mind that what's fun for one person might be hell for another, it could be going to the beach or park with a ball and a picnic; digging out old records and dancing to them (it doesn't matter if you look silly); arranging a photoshoot with your kids and their cuddly toys; cooking together; organizing a board game night with other families.

Be there

Forget about 'quality' time, ordinary everyday time is what counts. Happy families value family time and make sure they have it. Hobbies, community activity, television and work are just some of the family time eaters. Some people keep work out of family life by refusing breakfast meetings, for example. Others make the evening meal a priority for every member of the family.

The tyranny of television

Research shows that happy families limit the time 'the box' is on. They know that television is not wallpaper and should not remain constantly on.

If you haven't already done so, you could develop a few rules for when the television is allowed on. For example, no television on school mornings; important things must be done first, whether that's writing thank you notes or practising the violin; and no television during meal times. Many parents are concerned about content, and make sure an adult is present if they're uncertain about what might be on. Teach your children to turn the television on for a specific program—and to switch it off again once the program is over.

Above all, in relationships it helps to be clear about what we can change and what we can't. While it's best not to count on changing people themselves, maybe we can change our own attitudes first. The good news is that dynamics between people are quite volatile and small changes can bring about rewarding transformations within friendships, with work connections and with family members.

TAKING STOCK

There is no scoring in this questionnaire, nor are there any right or wrong answers. These are simply a few questions to stimulate your thoughts about relationships in your life. Some questions you will want to gloss over, others may act as stumbling blocks that set you on a new course.

1 General

(a) Who are the important people in your life? These can include your partner, children, immediate family and close friends. Next to each name jot down a few words to capture how you are feeling about your relationship: perhaps one of your children is going through a clingy phase; maybe you have deep concerns about your marriage; or you might not be on good terms with your father.

(b) How would you describe the place they occupy in your life currently and the impact they have had on your life overall?

(c) Do you think relationships should be left to 'happen' or do you think they take work? What sort of 'work'? Do you feel you are doing the right work with the people in your life?

2 Children (if applicable)

(a) What's best about bringing up children?

(b) What are its hardest challenges?

(c) What attitudes helped you create a positive family life during its different stages?

(d) If you were asked by someone thinking of having children, 'What's it like?', how would you attempt to answer?

(e) Have you ever been through a particularly bad patch in family relationships and then had a breakthrough that really helped?

3 Partner (if applicable)

(a) Describe your relationship in a few words (eg. married/de facto couple/living apart, etc).

(b) How long have you been with your partner?

(c) How did you meet?

(d) What are the good points about your relationship?

(e) What aspects call for compromise or adaptation on either part?

(f) Why does your relationship work?

(g) How do you deal with conflict?

(h) Has your relationship changed much over time?

(i) Have you ever been through a particularly bad patch then had a breakthrough that really helped (eg. solved constant arguing over housework or survived an affair)?

4 The family you grew up in

(a) Describe your childhood in a few words (eg. only child/youngest of four/brought up by aunt and uncle, etc).

(b) What aspects of your childhood family life have helped you in your adult life?

(c) Would you/do you attempt to repeat these in your own family?

(d) What aspects of your family life would you seek to avoid again if possible?

5 Friends

(a) What does 'friendship' mean to you?

(b) What do friends contribute to your life?

(c) Are there different kinds of friendships?

(d) Is it hard sometimes to keep in touch with people?

(e) Do you think it's important to have lots of friends, or just a few you can count on?

seek home for rest
For home is best

THOMAS TUSSER, *FIVE HUNDRED POINTS OF GOOD* HUSBANDRY (1580)

5. HOME

HOMES ARE PLACES TO ENJOY BOTH
BECAUSE THEY DON'T CHANGE—YOU
KNOW WHERE TO FIND THE BOOKS YOU
WANT TO READ OR YOUR FAVOURITE
TEA—AND BECAUSE, TO A CERTAIN
EXTENT, THEY CAN CHANGE. THEY ARE
A SMALL CORNER TO CALL YOUR OWN
WHERE YOU CAN—WHETHER BY
RENOVATING, DECORATING OR LIVING
ECOLOGICALLY—MAKE A DIFFERENCE
TO YOUR WORLD.

A HOME OF YOUR OWN

The Californian poet Robinson Jeffers spent four years building a massive stone tower for his wife, Una, a lifelong student of medieval Irish towers. Named Hawk Tower, it stands over 12 metres (40 feet) high, boasts walls over 1 metre (4 feet) thick, and two stairways—one outside and a secret, narrow one inside. The middle room features a three-windowed 'oriel'—just big enough to place a chair in—from which to admire the spectacular coastal view. Included in the walls are relics from around the world: from towers in Ireland, cathedrals in England, the Great Wall of China, a piece of lava from Mount Vesuvius, and so on. Jeffers started building the tower in 1920, a few months after completing the adjacent family home, Tor House, also constructed from enormous stone boulders. Both the tower and the home stand on the wild rocky knoll known as Carmel Point in California.

The passion with which Jeffers created his home and tower is unusual in its intensity and determination. But many of us feel a similar pride, and seek self-expression in a related, if quieter, way in the dwellings we call home—we renovate, extend, fiddle, decorate, clutter, clear, mess up, and spring-clean our homes. 'For a man's house is his castle,' said Sir Edward Coke, the English jurist remembered as prosecutor of Guy Fawkes and the other Gunpowder plotters of 1605. His statement is still true today. We are territorial about our homes and careful who we allow in, whether through the front or back door or across a drawbridge.

When in 1923 architect Le Corbusier wrote, 'a house is a machine for living in', he wanted to emphasize the function of a house as a specialized shelter. Yet hotels and hostels provide shelter and are not necessarily homes. A home serves spiritual as well as material needs—at its best it also provides a sense of belonging and security. The ancient Romans recognized this when they used the word domus. It meant 'house' in the expanded sense: the people and their dwelling. Interestingly, the legal term 'domus' implies an intention to return to a place—to return home.

Your home is the stage and backdrop to your life. It changes with you and despite you. Even when you have running water at the turn of a tap and electricity at the flick of a switch, houses take a lot of work to keep in repair, clean, stocked up with creature comforts, and organized, maybe even tidy. For health and safety, houses demand attention and labour. But they are a source of joy as well as work and an important means of self-expression; whether you are the civil engineer who takes pride in the straight lines of your flowerbed edges, or the librarian with a home studio spilling over with paints, canvases and sketches.

Sometimes you can feel defined by the spaces you live in and, true or not, you may nurse the idea that if you make a major move—to a bigger house, to the country, overseas—your life will change dramatically too. You expect that by changing the four walls you'll also feel a change in thinking.

Much of the balance we seek in our lives is played out at home; and for most of us, our homes represent a balance of different interests and needs:

I live in Sydney because it's neutral ground for my husband and I. He's from New Zealand, I'm from England. Only my children feel Australian. My ideal home would provide an outlet for balancing my work and family commitments— I'd like a decent office and somewhere I can stretch out for yoga. My husband would like a garden. AM

AT HOME WITH THE ENVIRONMENT

How you keep house can impact on your health. For instance, ventilation keeps a place dry, helping to reduce the growth of moulds and dust mites, which is particularly important for those with allergies to them. It also ensures that new air replaces stale air that can be high in a number of gases produced in the home, whether as by-products of cooking and heating or from furniture finishes or new carpets.

Ten ways of reducing greenhouse pollution

It's never too late to change your home and your lifestyle to a cleaner, greener one.

1 Use green energy. Many electricity retailers have an option to use green-generated power. While it does usually cost slightly more, not only is your pollution contribution reduced, you are also supporting the development of more environmentally friendly sources of power.

2 Install a solar or energy-efficient hot water heater. Water heating accounts for up to 50 per cent of a home's energy use; installing one of these heaters reduces your energy bills and cuts down on pollution.

3 Install a water-efficient showerhead. The shower is the largest user of household hot water and accounts for around 20 per cent of the greenhouse pollution in the average home. These heads use less water—reducing pollution and heating costs—and usually pay for themselves in the first year of use.

4 Buy energy-efficient white goods. Top-rated fridges, freezers, washing machines, dryers, dishwashers and air conditioners produce much less pollution and are cheaper to run.

5 Insulate your home. You'll save on heating and cooling bills as well as cut down on the pollution these processes produce.

6 Install energy-efficient lighting. For each compact fluorescent light bulb you install, you will prevent the emission of half a tonne or ton of greenhouse pollution and save on energy bills.

7 Drive less. You can choose to shop locally where possible, use public transport or walk or cycle.

8 Use an efficient car. Fuel-efficient cars can produce up to 30 per cent less greenhouse gas than inefficient ones. Keeping a car engine well tuned keeps emissions down too.

9 Compost your waste. In landfills and poorly managed compost heaps where there is no fresh air, food scraps break down anaerobically (without oxygen), producing the greenhouse gas methane.

10 Recycle. Recycling means less energy is required for manufacturing and also cuts down on landfill methane. Aluminium, steel, glass and paper are just some of the materials that can be recycled.

Children around the world

Barnabas and Anabel Kindersley travelled the globe during 1994 and 1995 with 242 kilograms (533 pounds) of photographic and studio equipment, visiting 31 countries to interview and photograph dozens of children and their families with coordinating help from UNICEF, the international children's charity. The resulting book, *Children Just Like Me*, documents an amazing variety of ways to live.

- Celina lives in a mud brick house with a wooden roof in the Amazon rainforest in Brazil. When light falls, her family turns on a gas lamp. She fetches water from the village well, sleeps in a hammock and washes in a nearby stream.
- Nicole, of Los Angeles, enjoys swimming all year round in the family pool, while Taylor, who lives in an apartment with two bathrooms in New York, goes to the park when he wants to play outside.
- Ari from Finland lives in a brick house lined with wood and enjoys a sauna at home twice a week.
- Daisuke lives near the town of Ogawa, Japan, on an organic farm run by her family. They produce their own electricity, using biogas from animal manure to power a generator.

How you choose to run your home also says a lot about your philosophy in life. Environmental concerns are becoming more of a concern for everyone as we face increased pollution and reduced resources. Caring for the environment begins, like charity, at home. You can choose to use less energy, less water and contribute less to global and local pollution. Paints, household cleaners and pesticides all have the potential to pollute air and waterways, but environmentally friendly choices are available. If you're building a house, there is an increasing range of low-impact technology to choose from, such as grey water systems for recycling at home water (why use drinking-quality water to flush the toilet?). Following the three 'green' Rs—reusing, recycling and reducing—at home as well as at work is essential if we are to minimize our impact on the environment.

- Rachel lives in a French chateau that's been in her family since 1715 and is surrounded by vineyards.
- Yannis, from the Greek island of Crete, has lemon and mandarin trees in his courtyard garden, and a large grapevine which provides shade in the summer as well as grapes.
- Bakang lives with her family and close relatives in a group of houses with walls of soil and dried cow dung and a thatched roof of dried grass, in a village in Botswana in southern Africa. Her mother collects wood for the fire, water for drinking and cow dung to repair the house. They light the house at night with paraffin lamps.
- Esta belongs to the Masai people in Tanzania and walks 6 kilometres (4 miles) every day to collect water for her family. The family lives in a group of huts called an *enyang*, which means 'homestead', built in a circle with space for animals in the centre.
- Thi Lien is a member of the hill tribe people called Dao who live in the mountains of northern Vietnam. He lives in a wooden house with a tiled roof and a thatch-covered porch. The community is self-sufficient in food and much of their clothing and has a hydro-electric power supply.

SOCIETY AT HOME

Houses intrigue and fascinate—perhaps because they offer a window into people's lives. Old houses, foreign ones, eco-houses with clean lines, those with vast kitchens or old servants' quarters wound around tight spiral staircases, rambling houses, and cosy cottages with low beams and big fireplaces all have appeal.

However, what's right for one part of the world, or one location, is not necessarily right for another. Working within the constraints of money and time, the ideal house is one adapted to its location and built with local materials. People the world over have created all sorts of homes to live in: the English Victorian house with its careful zoning of children and servants; the Mediterranean whitewashed house with its cool courtyard providing security and privacy as well as comfort; or the American log cabin with its pioneer symbolism of courage, frugality and independence—a house design that, while still copied today, goes back to old Norse, German, Scottish and Irish building traditions.

With time, the functions of a house have become more varied and sophisticated. Initially just a shelter and somewhere to prepare food, houses are now places of recreation, hospitality, storage and communication. As the form of the house changes, so too does what goes on in it.

Apartment living is popular in many cities, but it's not new. Most residents of Rome in 300 AD lived in four-storey apartments on blocks of land known as *insulae*—or islands. The apartments ranged from single rooms on the upper floors to luxurious multi-roomed apartments on the lower levels.

Compared to the relative sophistication of Roman times, living in a medieval house may have been more akin to camping. The rich moved from house to house, taking their household with them as they went. Medieval homes were sparsely furnished and consisted predominantly of one large chamber or hall open to the ceiling. The middle classes transacted business as well as domestic affairs at home, and needed a flexible space. They did not agonize about permanent arrangements of furniture: it was a haphazard, practical affair where tables, chairs and beds were moved, put up, and dismantled as needed. The poor had miserable homes. All classes lived in a crowded fashion, with households of 25 being common: the immediate family, employees, servants, apprentices, friends and protégés. A room might contain many beds. Richard Toky, a London grocer who died in 1391, had four beds in his hall as well as a cradle. When private rooms where people could retire from public 'view' evolved, these were called 'privacies'.

The way we use dwellings is personal—hence the curiosity in visiting, or reading about, others' homes where they do things differently. It's also highly cultural. When an earthquake struck the Kütahaya province of Turkey in 1970, destroying 15,000 houses and rendering 70,000 people homeless, new houses were swiftly provided. Villages were rebuilt using a single-storey compact house design with four rooms. Years later entire villages remained empty; in others the original houses were heavily adapted. The homes were greatly disliked by their new owners, but the reasons were complex. In some cases, the houses that stood vacant had been built too far from farmland or in places where there was no water supply. However, the main reason was that the houses were culturally inappropriate. The compact houses were fine for nuclear families, but didn't suit the extended families of the peasants; they were forced to choose between being overcrowded or breaking up the family unit. The houses lacked a salon, or reception space, so there was no transitional space in which to welcome visitors. In the homes that remained occupied, and where space allowed, many families had built an extra room on for this purpose. They had also added screens to block the view to the toilet, outbuildings for their animals and an enclosed entrance, although many of these additions made the houses more vulnerable to earthquake.

VOX POP: How does where you live impact on your happiness?

'Our living space is a four-bedroom house in a village—two shops, two pubs. I have lived in student accommodation, council flats, bed sits...I feel the sense of privacy and peace is important. I'm not sure about feng shui, but I think how space is used is important.' TS

'It's vital. My home is a haven, a place of peace and I can get quite fussy about who I let into that space. I'm going down the minimalist route, getting rid of clutter and unnecessary furniture. Clear space in the place equals clear space in the head! I like to have easy access to the countryside—preferably wilderness. Climate's important, though harder to control.' DL

'We live in a small two-storey house in a convenient and pleasant inner city suburb. Furniture, books and bicycles take up much of the limited space, which makes the house somewhat cluttered and constricted—it also makes it cosy.' PN

'My peace and quiet at home is essential…it's where I am able to connect with myself.' JS

'If a place is cosy and comfortable, then I'm really happy to spend a lot of time at home rather than go out.' FH

'My home is small but perfectly formed. Wish it was tidier!' HB

'I am such a homebody. My home is my haven and I love to spend time in the comfort of my own space. Some people say your body is your temple. I'd say my home is my temple.' CM

'Living in a house built for me, my tastes and needs is wonderful.' JS

VOX POP: Can where you live make you depressed or stressed?

'Absolutely! Cities do that for me.' DL

'Most definitely. I feel better in a place that's light and airy so we keep our curtains open during the day and have lots of lamps around. It's also important to me to be familiar with the area I live in, and to have local support such as a GP, chemist and friends.' FH

'I need more space now—that's contributing to stress, partly because home is a home office as well.' CS

'I didn't feel depressed when I lived in the city though when I go back I'm amazed at how much time I spend at traffic lights.

Where I live now is so beautiful I often sit back just to absorb it—it's the distraction factor.' JS

'I find dark, closed-in places depressing. I also need to be able to walk out my front door somewhere or other. I hate feeling trapped.' AH

HOME AND COMFORT

Home is where, within limits, you are free to create your own version of 'comfortable': whether it's beige walls or bright red ones, state-of-the-art bathrooms or the original 1950s version which you feel does the job just as well. The rest of the road might be converting terraces like yours into open-plan living spaces, but if your family appreciates rooms with doors you can keep it that way and spend your money on extras like insect screens and bike shelters. Renting may cramp your style, but furnishings and the space within a space you create can often feel like home too, especially if you have a good relationship with your landlord.

The way we use the word 'comfort' is relatively recent. While its Latin root is *confortare*, which means 'to strengthen or console', its meaning has expanded to include ideas of 'sufficient' or 'ample'. The first use of 'comfort' to denote a level of domestic amenity was not until the eighteenth century. Today 'comfort' wraps up a host of meanings: domesticity, with its ideas of devotion to home, intimacy and family; privacy; homeliness (by no means neatness), cosiness; and, when it gets hard to pin it down, 'lack of discomfort'.

Scientific inquiry into comfort at home is minimal. Some research has been undertaken in the workplace because of the belief that a comfortable worker is a happier, more efficient—and therefore more productive—worker. In a study by the pharmaceutical company Merck & Company in 1982, 2000 staff were questioned about their working environment—its appearance, safety, work efficiency, convenience, comfort, and so on. The findings revealed that employees felt most strongly (negatively, that is) about lack of conversational privacy, air quality, lack of visual privacy and the level of lighting. If given individual control, they said they'd like to choose room temperature, degree of privacy, chair and desk, and lighting intensity. Control over decor was not seen as important.

Many traditional ways of life and building styles are about meeting the challenge of finding comfort, often in the face of extremes of climate, as the two following examples demonstrate.

Coping with cold

The igloos of the Central Inuit people, who live north of the treeline in northern Canada, were built as winter dwellings and as shelters for hunters. They were feats of climate and heat control. The entrance was lower than the floor level so that cold air remained trapped outside. A combination of blubber lamps and body heat meant the inside could be raised to 15.5°C (60°F)—when temperatures outside were –40°C (–40°F). A small hole in the wall ensured ventilation; the shape of the dome prevented stale pockets of air forming and also conserved heat. A layer of cold air trapped between insulating hides on the internal surface prevented the snow from melting.

Tenzin Palmo (1943–)

Diane Perry lived her first 21 years above a fish shop in Bethnal Green in cockney London. She was ordained as a Buddhist nun in 1964 and changed her name to Tenzin Palmo. Between the ages of 33 and 45 she gained fame for living in a remote cave in the Himalayas. Comforts were few: a wood-burning stove, table, bookcase and meditation box. She planted potatoes and turnips—the only vegetables that rodents left alone—on a small terrace at the front of the cave. A storeroom held goods, which porters and donkeys carried up to her on a two-hour climb: kerosene, rice, lentils, flour, tea, sugar, and so on. When she finally left the cave she thanked it for being so supportive during her retreat.

Handling heat

Many pastoral nomads, who wander the thinly vegetated areas of
Africa and Asia, live in black tents made from strips of material
woven from goat hair. The darkness casts a dense shade and
insulates from radiant heat. As the yarn still contains the goats'
natural oils its weave remains open when dry and lets air pass
through, but when damp, the yarn expands and keeps water out
of the interior.

The basic considerations of climate are an important part
of current Western building practice where houses are designed
so that they are comfortable to live in yet impinge as little as
possible on the environment. These are so-called eco-, or
sustainable, houses.

Once the basics have been achieved, comfort is about little
things—a place to put your tea where you can reach it but not
knock it over; somewhere comfortable to sit while you talk with
friends or read a book; a towel within easy reach of the shower.
Creature comforts—the sort you don't usually have when
camping—are hot water, heating, a comfortable bed, better than
basic cooking facilities, and a fridge to keep food and drink cool
and fresh.

THE COMFORT ZONE

Somewhere between sweltering heat and icy coldness, debilitating
humidity and harsh dryness, stuffiness and wind, lies what's known
as 'the comfort zone':

- As a rule of thumb, rooms should be as cool as is comfortable.
  Most people feel comfortable between temperatures of 18°C
  (65°F) and 24°C (75°F). But making tea in a cooler kitchen or
  soaking up the sun on a warm, but shaded balcony can also feel
  fine for short periods. Older people, on the other hand, can
  suffer hypothermia at even slightly lower temperatures of
  between 15.5°C (60°F) and 18°C (65°F). (Inactivity, illness,
  medication, susceptibility to flu and other viruses play a part in
  making them more vulnerable.)
- Rooms need some gentle air movement to prevent stuffiness.

- Relative humidity—a measure of the amount of water vapour in the air with 100 per cent indicating that the air is saturated—starts to make people feel uncomfortable when it reaches above 70 per cent. As humidity rises, the temperature at which you feel comfortable drops; in other words, when it's humid you feel the heat more.
- The average temperature of internal surfaces should be the same as, or above, the air temperature.

Heading for the comfort zone

How can you adapt your home so that it stays within the comfort

The meaning of comfort

During the six years Witold Rybczynski, author and professor of urbanism at the University of Philadelphia, studied architecture, he remembers the concept of comfort being mentioned once only: by an engineer referring to the scale of temperatures and humidity values known as the comfort zone in the context of air conditioning and heating. When Rybczynski began his career designing and building houses for clients, he was surprised to find that many of the architectural ideals he'd learnt disregarded conventional comforts. While building his own home, he says he discovered the fundamental poverty of modern architectural ideas and so, with these thoughts in mind, he set about discovering what 'comfort' means.

In 1986, he published the result of his research: *Home, A Short History of an Idea*. Comfort, he concludes, is like an onion, a layered thing. It is experienced personally, but within broad norms that change with the times; it is therefore somewhat objective but culturally based. At the same time, aspects of it—such as intimacy—are impossible to measure. It is the whole experience and effect which comes together to create comfort rather than a list of technical criteria. In short, it's what works for you, incorporating convenience, efficiency, domesticity, physical ease, privacy and intimacy.

zone? Air conditioning is one way to keep temperatures and humidity under control, but there are also ways you can work with nature to achieve the same result, but at a reduced cost to the environment and your pocket.

- Let the air in. Have windows that open, French doors that let air in, and walls that breathe. These will all help to create air movement in the house.
- Hang curtains, especially lined ones. These can be pulled across an overly sunny window to help keep excessive heat out in the summer; they can also be closed to keep warmth in during the winter evenings.
- Create shade. Balcony blinds, slatted roofs, and roof timbers hung with fruiting and flowering vines are all great ways to shade your outside decks and verandahs.
- Let the sun in during winter. Pull back curtains, raise blinds and, when it's warm enough, open up balconies.
- Create a courtyard. This helps to keep a house cool because the warm air from the house is able to move into the courtyard and escape. In the evening, when the relative temperatures are reversed, the cooler air of the courtyard is drawn back into the house to cool it.
- Look to the elements. Trees and other plants, pools and fountains add humidity to dry air.
- Insulate your home. This helps to stabilize the temperature of a house. Insulation is graded according to its ability to resist changes in temperature and the level you need will depend on your local climate.

SOUND

Another aspect of comfort at home is sound. Strange noises can keep you awake the first night in a new place: the nest of starlings in the roof gables sounds like they are inside, not just outside, your bedroom; the neighbours' music seems very loud; the traffic irritating. Quite often, once the sound is familiar and has been accepted as 'normal' you hardly notice it. But, when you want to keep the noise down, what can you do?

- Install double glazing. This helps to reduce background traffic noise on busy roads. Sealing gaps in windows and doors will also help. Be sure to compensate with other forms of ventilation.
- Create sound barriers. Trees and bushes absorb sound and planting mature trees or fast growers will speed up the solution. High walls, fences and earth mounds will also do the trick, and can be planted with climbers. The heavier and thicker the wall, the better it prevents noise transmission.
- Reduce impact noise. This is noise produced by something hitting a surface and it is transmitted through a structure, in much the same way as you can hear sounds passing along the ground better than through the air. In a house it could be noise transmitted from an exercise room, children's playroom or a refrigerator vibrating on the floor. Impact noise can be reduced by carpets and floating floors.
- Place appliances and white goods carefully. Refrigerators, washing machines and other household appliances should be kept away from partition walls.
- Select your rooms carefully. Consider switching rooms and using quieter rooms for sleeping if night-time noise is a problem. If you are renovating, you could consider moving bathrooms or laundry rooms to the noisiest areas of the house.

THE HOMEWORK OF HOUSEWORK

Before enlightenment, carrying water, chopping wood
After enlightenmment, carrying water, chopping wood

ZEN SAYING

The washing up never stops, so too the laundry. You wash the floor and an hour later it's splattered. A day spent spring-cleaning the sitting room gives it a civilized air for a while then the newspapers, toys, dropped socks and books pile up. It may be nice to walk into a sparkling, tidy house, but the housework required to keep your home that way can be a nightmare at times. It's no wonder that research confirms what we already suspected: housework increases depression.

As its name implies, it is work, but it offers less recognition, less thanks and less job fulfilment than paid work. While it's believed that exercise helps depression, and it's even been suggested that, as a light form of exercise, housework might help keep depression at bay, a study from the University of Glasgow found that even where housework involved exercise it did not boost morale but had the opposite effect.

Quentin Crisp, eccentric British actor and author of, among other works, *The Naked Civil Servant*, would hardly have been surprised. He claimed that housework was superfluous, as the dirt doesn't get any worse after four years. 'Women who clean are in a blind rage by half past ten in the morning,' a neighbour once told him, 'No wonder you're so nice to everybody.'

But what can you do to change housework for the better if you're not game to test Mr Crisp's four-year theory?

Lessen the load by sharing

This really is a case of the more the merrier. Whether it's because they care more about it, have higher standards or a domestic gene, women do more housework than men—even in a couple where both members work outside the home. And it's usually women whom you hear complaining about the dreariness of housework.

But a study of 1256 people aged between eighteen and 65 by Chloe E Bird of Brown University, Providence, Rhode Island, showed sharing was the issue that determined whether or not housework gets you down. In the rare cases of a couple where a man was doing more than his share, he was the one feeling depressed by housework.

In addition, the degree to which housework was shared has more to do with how depressed someone might be than the actual hours spent doing housework. For example, a city apartment that houses a couple with no pets or children takes fewer hours of work than a house that's also home to three children, a dog and has a big garden. However, depression does not necessarily go hand in hand with the bigger house and longer cleaning hours.

It's a balancing act

What's more depressing? A dirty untidy house or doing the housework? It's a question of finding your own balance. Jobs you can complete without feeling overwhelmed can lift your mood and give you a sense of satisfaction.

Set housework goals

Breaking down tasks into small, manageable ones can make housework seem more manageable. Decide to 'do the washing up and wash the kitchen floor,' rather than 'clean the kitchen'.

Prioritize

If life gets in the way of a pristine house, determine your priorities and concentrate on them rather than feel you have to do it all. When time is very tight, perhaps after the birth of a baby, you might only be able to keep on top of the bathroom and kitchen—the hygiene areas. Then as you adapt, you could add your living room or the next space that's important to your sanity.

VOX POP: How do you feel about housework?

'I regard it as a drudge and life would be fairly dreary if that was all there was. The irritating thing is that it never ends…but there is a certain satisfaction in drawing abreast of it, although you can never quite beat it!' PN

'At times trying to keep the house vaguely clean and in some sort of order is like fighting off a multi-headed monster. Sometimes it's all you can do to keep it back and beat one head down before another one appears.' AH

'When the children were little, it used to really get me down picking up their toys all the time. Then I decided I'd just tidy up once a week and not worry about it in between. I felt much better about it then.' EC

'It depends on your mood. When you're feeling lighthearted, housework can be fun but there are times when you don't feel like doing it and it's a drag because you really have to.' BA

'I've made a New Year's resolution not to do so much housework. It's such a waste of time.' JD

AN ELEMENT OF FUN

Mary Poppins said, 'In every job that must be done, there is an element of fun'—the hard thing is to find it! The jolly nanny approach might make you cringe, but it's an approach that can help with young children. The adult version might consist of putting on some music while you clean or watching a film while you iron. Alternatively, decide to put away ten items or put the kitchen timer on for ten or twenty minutes and see how much floor you can expose in that time in the kids' room, study or shed.

Home truths

Cheryl Mendelson—academic, lawyer and author of *Home Comforts: The Art and Science of Keeping House*—was raised on two diametrically opposite philosophies of housekeeping. Her maternal grandmother espoused light airy rooms, linen sheets and flowers on the windowsill, in the Italian way. Her paternal grandmother, with her British heritage, believed in sealing up a house against the sun and air, and keeping patchwork quilts and stores and tools at the ready for any emergency.

Cheryl experienced several false starts in domestic life as an adult before finding her domestic feet. She divorced a husband who let three wet dogs sleep on their bed, and lived another phase of her life as if in a hotel. Housekeeping is an art, she says, which uses your head, heart and hands to create a home that is comfortable, healthy, beautiful, orderly and safe.

Delegate

Get your flatmates, partner or kids to help you. It can take time to 'train' others to help, but it's worth making the effort in the long term. Even toddlers can pack away games, learn to put videos back in boxes and tidy up one toy before moving on to the next. School children can sort recycling, feed pets, set and clear the table. Older children can learn to iron and mend clothes. Adults are limited only by their motivation!

THE EFFICIENT HOUSE

Some houses seem to take more time to keep clean than others. Mess is a problem when there is no storage space, and a carpet on the floor of the first room you enter from a mud-prone garden can be a headache. The word 'efficiency' rolls off the tongue easily these days, even if putting it into practice is harder, but the idea that a house should be efficient is fairly recent.

Catherine Beecher, a schoolteacher who wrote *A Treatise on Domestic Economy for the Use of Young Ladies at Home and at*

School, in 1841, was one of the first proponents of efficiency in the home—for the sake of comfort and function. Her ideal home required adequate closet space and a comfortable kitchen—she advised her young ladies to consider where to put the stove and the sink, and to include drawers for towels and cleaners under the sink and a continuous work space with storage below and shelves above. Later, in 1869, with her sister, Harriet Beecher Stowe, she wrote The American Woman's Home. This included a ducted heating and ventilation system that supplied warm air to every room, without the need for fireplaces, and also provided for pressurized water thanks to a cistern under the roof. A room that in the contemporary conventional home might have been a dining room was converted to a bedroom by moving aside a larger closet on wheels. In the daytime, the closet divided the room into breakfast room and sitting room or—all change—to a large parlour and small sewing room. The model proposed that a small house not only cost less to build and maintain, but was also more comfortable to live in since it took less looking after—less housework.

A few decades later, American Christine Frederick learnt from her husband about the work of efficiency engineers who were introducing a new science to offices, foundries and factories. These engineers examined the height of work surfaces, the location of tools and the organization of work. Frederick studied, questioned and photographed her friends and other women at work, remodelling her kitchen as a result of her examinations. She found she could do her housework quicker and with less effort.

She published her findings in Household Engineering, in 1920. Among her advice to housewives was to plan what you are going to do in the day, do it, then rest.

Towards efficiency

Give your cleaning routine a workout and lessen your load by considering these practical solutions to housework's drudgery.

- Surfaces. Carpets need vacuuming and need swift action for spills while hard floors such as wood are easily cared for with a broom. If replacing kitchen worktops, consider patterned surfaces that won't stain easily. Pot stands and mats can help stop teapot stains and the like.

- Colours. Pale plain colours for upholstered furniture are usually unforgiving on stains and dirt, while patterned and/or dark colours offer good camouflage and may stay smart for longer.
- Quality. Well-designed and well-made items look better and cleaner for longer. They last longer too, saving money in the long run.
- Take to task. Analyze which jobs seem to take forever or are particularly irksome. Is there a better way? If you resent always picking up fridge magnets that your preschooler pulls off with glee, put them out of reach or in a cupboard for a year or so.
- Cover up. Use rugs in heavy-duty areas such as hallways and near the kitchen sink to catch dirt and spills. Throws

Kidszone

Small children are messy, curious and much more vulnerable to accidents than their adult carers. If you share your home with children—whether all or some of the time—consider the following:

- No pale colours. Cream carpets and white sofas are a disaster around anyone likely to have paint- or chocolate-smeared fingers, grass-stained trousers or dirty shoes.
- Breakables high. Glass and china are alluring. While many children can be taught to look only and not touch, it's easier for everyone if breakables are placed out of reach.
- Nasties out of reach. Even babies can open cupboards and drawers, so check they can't reach sharp knives or poisonous chemicals, including household cleaners.
- Teach independence. Conversely, make sure children can reach the things you want them to. It's no good expecting children to learn to dress themselves if they can't reach their school uniform or other clothes.

on armchairs and sofas can prolong their life or time between cleanings.

- Dust to dust. Tiny items take an aeon to move, dust and replace. If you love little things around you but hate the dusting, consider putting them behind glass—whether in small display boxes or larger scale cabinets—or on attractive trays which you can then lift up to dust around.

- Little and often. A wipe of the stove top after cooking, washing dishes after each meal, putting away a pile of laundry each time it comes off the line, a quick tidy of the family room before you go to bed…little and often stops big jobs from mounting up. In the case of spills and stains, it also saves time in the long run, as they are easier to deal with before they set in or have been walked around the house.

- House rules. If dirty shoes are creating too much work around the house, introduce a 'no shoes' or a 'house shoes only' policy for household members and guests alike. If dinners in front of the television or snacks in bedrooms increase the workload in clearing and cleaning up afterwards, reinforce eating at the table and make away-from-the-table eating an exception only.

CHANGING ROOMS

Buildings, the homes they contain, and the people who live in them continually change. We make additions, change rooflines, alter windows and strip back. Flatmates move out, married couples move in; babies move from a bassinet in the parents' room to a cot in their own; school children want a place to use a home computer; teenagers want a space of their own. Walls move within, doors disappear, new rooms are created in old spaces. Owner-occupiers constantly mould their homes—or do the buildings mould them?—steadily adapting the building as it annoys and limits them, viewing it as a canvas on which to play out their fluctuating ideas of utility, convenience, comfort and attractiveness.

The six changing layers of a building

Stewart Brand, author of *How Buildings Learn: What Happens After They're Built*, describes a building in terms of six layers, each of which experiences change in different ways. Brand attributes this idea to the architect Frank Duffy's four Ss—structure, services, space plan and stuff—and has added site and skin.

- Site. The geographical location, the building's boundaries and context, is the only element that does not change—although the surroundings can, especially in a city, where buildings rise and fall regularly.
- Structure. The foundation and load-bearing elements of a building are difficult and expensive to change, so rarely do.
- Skin. This is the exterior surface, which Brand says changes on average every twenty years.
- Services. The working parts of a building—electrical wiring, plumbing, a sprinkler system, communications wiring, and so on—are repaired and replaced as they wear out or become obsolete. How difficult this task is depends on how deeply embedded the services are.
- Space plan. The interior layout is highly changeable: walls and doors can move or vanish altogether; ceilings may be lowered for cosiness or removed for a cathedral feel.
- Stuff. This refers to all the contents of the removalist van on the day we move in to a building and all that we collect, shift and store in it from that day: furniture, appliances, bicycles, books and kitchenware. This is the most changeable element of any home.

Part of the fascination of old buildings is discovering how they have changed—and witnessed change—with time. Many much-loved buildings are old. We admire the weathering of their surfaces: downtrodden stairs, bricks muted with time, a sagging roof or bending beam. The sense of continuity through generations and a link to that other place, the past, is for many people a source of deep satisfaction and perhaps curiosity, too.

Fashions—whether style or utility driven—come and go. One of the drivers of small changes is the need for maintenance, without which buildings slowly crumble and dissolve. One story that illustrates this point beautifully concerns New College Oxford, England, which was founded in the fourteenth century. Around the end of the nineteenth century, its oak beams were discovered to be full of beetles and clearly needed replacing. The college forester was called; he revealed that a grove of oaks had been planted when the college was first built, specifically to replace the dining hall beams that the original builders knew would eventually become beetle-ridden. For 500 years it had been forbidden to cut down the oaks.

Keeping water out—whether from the skies or earth—is perhaps the most important task of maintenance. Water warps, swells, discolours, rusts, cracks, and invites mildew, mould and rotting. The habit in Greece of whitewashing houses every year does more than add sparkle—the whitewash also 'feeds' the walls of the houses, filling in tiny cracks before they have a chance to spread. The Japanese paint the ends of wooden exposed beams at temples to reduce water entry and slow rot.

The use of space changes with fashion as well as function. Take kitchens. When hired help or live-in help cooked the meals, the

Your essential maintenance book

A maintenance record book is a boon to the homeowner keen to protect his asset. It doesn't have to be anything fancy, just a place you record:

- Dates. When you replaced the roof/painted the dining room/added the playroom.
- Materials. The colour, brand, type, etc of paint/roofing material. The name of the oil finish used on your doors.
- Contractors. Their names and phone numbers can be useful for next time or for when problems arise.

kitchen was a mean room at the back of the house. As life upstairs and downstairs changed, the kitchen moved from the servants' domain towards the middle of the house—and with this move came improved refrigerators, state-of-the-art stoves, and new-style sinks.

Limited budgets, plot size and shape, rental agreements… there are always limits to what we can achieve in our homes. But we can borrow ideas from the past, from the houses of our friends and acquaintances, and from the beautiful homes featured in glossy magazines. Spaces in a home fulfil many functions, both material and spiritual: places to eat together; somewhere to go for an hour's peace; safe play places; somewhere for sewing, board games and other pursuits that require an undisturbed flat area; private and public realms. Here are some examples of the roles that rooms can fulfil.

For sleeping

Sleeping porches were common in American houses until the turn of the twentieth century. Clusters of beds in private alcoves provide children with both privacy and the promise of company not far off, while sleeping platforms are common in parts of the world. They could be one solution to space constraints when children come into the parents' bed in the early hours of the morning; however, bedding could be a problem!

For cooking

Should a kitchen hide everything behind smooth cupboard doors or should it be a more organic place with tools at the ready? A farmhouse kitchen welcomes everyone, from the person on cooking duty to children, visitors and diners. It's the 'heart and hearth of the family' and is in stark contrast to the tiny, barely functional kitchens found in so many inner city apartments.

For eating

Tea at the kitchen table; an after-school snack on a stool at the bench; family dinner around the dining room table; dinner in front of the television after a long day; or an indoor picnic in the sitting room for friends…different spaces create different moods and trigger different dynamics. Outdoors spaces—whether at a table in the shade of a tree or on an old cushion cooking potatoes in foil on the bonfire—provide proof that food eaten outside often tastes better.

For children

A typical middle class Victorian home was strictly zoned into areas for servants, children, the master and mistress. New smaller homes needed careful planning. For instance, Christine Frederick suggested in *Household Engineering* that children should be able to reach their rooms without necessarily disturbing adult activities.

While many suggestions from these ideal homes of the past are just not practical or possible in today's houses, you can still adapt them. Perhaps you could alter the location of a child's room to minimize disturbances while they sleep. Distinct kids' zones are ideal but not necessarily possible. If your house is in danger of being overrun by kids, consider creating an adult zone where children are welcome, but where toys are to be cleared away after play.

For looking out

Glazed or screened porches provide cool spots at the end of hot days. The old American front porch with its swing seat and sleeping dog; a space wide enough for a chair or two between house and street; windows that look out…these all provide links to the outside world.

For bringing the outside in

Decks, patios or terraces—the names vary over time—all provide firm ground next to the house that gives extra space for eating, entertaining or enjoying a quiet moment. Pavers, bricks and raised wooden boards are often the materials used. Awnings, shadecloths, umbrellas and trees provide extra shelter from wind, sun and even light rain.

Conservatories are traditional in temperate countries where some extra warmth is welcome, especially in winter. While the primary use is to grow plants, they are also somewhere to sit with

Stewart Brand (1938–)

When Stewart Brand, founder of, among numerous projects, The Whole Earth Catalog, needed more space in which to organize the chapters of his latest book, he had a shipping container delivered to his Californian home. He had the inside fitted out with long flat work surfaces on each side, installed metal sheeting above for attaching photographs and other graphics, and put up ample shelving and easy-to-access storage. Cheap carpet, an old sofa and lights added notes of comfort.

a cup of tea and a newspaper or a few friends and a bottle of wine. What used to be called a garden room is any ground floor room with big French windows looking out on to the garden. Balconies can be more than a viewing point to the outside world or a place for the cat to soak up winter sun; depending on their size, they can be an ideal place for alfresco dining. Roof gardens offer possibilities for unexpected greenery and open space. With some careful planning they can become highly individualized and private spots much treasured by residents. Window greenhouses and window boxes are other ways to link house and garden.

For storing

Attics, cellars, sheds and the garage are traditional storage spaces—although they are sometimes vulnerable to conversion to a new bedroom or study. Another option is built-in furniture. This can create individuality, convenience and efficiency and can come in a variety of shapes and styles: shelves to fit awkward spaces; kitchen cabinets (now commonplace); bookcases; fireside seats; and sideboards. The area under the stairs can be used for extra storage. Where access is awkward, pull-out cupboards on coasters can make more space usable.

Beecher's plans in *The American Woman's Home* included built-in closets for clothes, to replace wardrobes, cupboards and chests.

She recommended a coat closet near the front door, a broom closet near the kitchen, a linen closet in an upstairs hall and a medicine cabinet in the bathroom.

For washing

In the days of the portable bath, a maid (if you were lucky enough to have one) would fill it up in your dressing room. Bathrooms did not exist until it was suggested that dressing rooms might be fitted with a permanently plumbed bath. Eventually the idea of a dressing room was discarded from most homes and bedrooms became smaller.

The small standard bathroom follows a plan little changed since the 1850s. In some households, bathrooms are very busy places and house a toilet, shower, bath, washing machine and occasionally dryer too. Separate toilets avoid the necessity of queues for families and visitors alike.

Communal bathing has a long history: think of Roman baths, now a tourist attraction in the towns where their ruins persist. The Japanese have family-size bathing rooms. Jacuzzis and spa baths are usually large enough for several people to enjoy at the same time and outdoor ones offer starlight, too.

VOX POP: How did you make your home work for you?

'We live in a tiny two-storey terrace house. After a year abroad, we moved our sitting room upstairs to the best room in the house with French doors onto the balcony. We used the smallest rooms as bedrooms and I took what was previously an irritatingly small dining area as a home office. That left us with a dining room we could put a table in that we could all sit around and could have people round for dinner. It didn't matter that I couldn't close a door for privacy in my office as I only worked when the children were at school or day care. The result was we felt we'd gained a room.' MN

'My house sits lightly on the earth and was designed by a local Buddhist architect. It faces north to Mount Dromedary and is in a spotted gum forest overlooking the Bermagui River. The material is fibro, with quite a bit of corrugated iron. When it was being built the locals thought it looked like a cross between a chook shed and a shearing shed. In fact my daughter was a wool classer and she wanted a shearing shed content—we clearly succeeded! The house is full of light, the floors are polished and there are lots of windows. There is a long verandah with a wing at each end. One is my wing for the bedroom and bathroom. The other is a work wing with an office deliberately not attached to the house. This is a great idea because I feel I walk to work.' JS

For extra space
Granny flats—also known as secondary units, accessory apartments and mother-in-law units—are an international phenomenon, sometimes legal, sometimes illegal. Community pressure forced a local council in California a decade or so ago to change its mind over ordering granny flats to be pulled down where they'd been built without permits. The community maintained that the granny flats provided flexibility: allowing people to stay in their homes as their lives changed around them, incorporating space for an ageing parent, an au pair or a teenager. They were also affordable housing for the town's support population of nurses and shop employees while the rent from secondary units reduced the cost of primary homes by contributing to running costs or home loan repayments.

For moving from A to B
In a small house thoroughfares can become high-disturbance areas—the small kitchen that is also the only access to the back garden, the laundry room or bathroom can be dangerous as well as inconvenient. Understanding how a house is used can help you plan room changes as well as renovations and building works, both major and minor. In a small house an upstairs sitting room might have a better chance of staying civilized, as it's not on the way to

anywhere. On the other hand, the dining room that is the first point of entry is likely to become a dumping ground.

For creation
Studios, studies, workshops and other work spaces are often less than ideal, but no one seems to mind. When you're determined, even a tiny alleyway can become a pottery studio, or the garage may become a painter's hideout. A table in the bedroom or an alcove could be a sewing space or a mini home office, perhaps with a screen to hide works in progress.

For laundry
If you baulk at the thought of drying underwear in view of your neighbours, consider the drying room. This is a room, out of view, which can be opened by large French doors or a sliding wall to the outside, gaining ventilation and perhaps sunlight too if facing the right way.

For fun
Attics and attic rooms are fun. They don't necessarily even need proper stairs to reach them: Manning Clark spent three decades writing his classic six-volume *A History of Australia* in a tiny attic room reached only by a ladder. Platform beds, pull-down tables, and other ideas for living small can bring style to the compact space.

For transitions
Mud rooms—an apt name for any first entry room in the English countryside, the Australian farm or any place that gets muddy or dirty from time to time—are a useful transition space, whether an open porch or a utility room between a kitchen and back door. This is where children, gardeners or ramblers remove muddy boots and shoes and wet coats before proceeding into the nice clean house. It's also where wet dogs get a towelling and perhaps are left until they've dried off. Holiday houses and beach dwellers sometimes need sand rooms for a similar function—a quick hose down or brush off before coming inside prevents sand from taking over.

For being alone

Teenagers in particular like to be able to step away from the family from time to time. Architectural solutions to coping with teenagers vary. Some say you should make sure there's only one entrance to your home, with a passage to a teenage bedroom that brings them through the house—the idea being you know if they're in and if they're going out! The other viewpoint says let them come and go as they please, give them their own bedroom and a place they can have friends around, make it close to the rest of the family but separate too, a sort of 'teenager's cottage'. You can encourage them to join in family life by having them share the kitchen and bathroom.

AN INDIVIDUAL HOME: SMALL CHANGES FOR BIG DIFFERENCES

Most of us are magpies at heart, and the collecting instinct which stimulates toddlers to collect little piles of stones, shells and sticks and string, the child to collect stamps or dolls and the teenager to collect gramophone records, stimulates the adult to collect whatever he or she can afford and finds pleasing.

SUZANNE BEEDELL, *RESTORING JUNK* (1970)

Your favourite items—whether they are a painting your son did when he was three, a trio of family photos or a battered old chair you inherited from your grandmother—cheer and individualize a space. Grouping similar items together increases their visual impact and marks the territory as your own: jugs from around the world; framed, worn and used maps of places you've been; even shells and driftwood. The extension or major renovation may not always be possible, but there's much you can do to make yourself feel at home.

Havens

A chair in an alleyway garden invites you to pause for coffee, to read or to enjoy a glass of wine at the end of the day. Even a small table on a balcony sets the scene for breakfast alfresco. Children love little havens, but so do adults—think of window seats, hammocks, a rug by the fire.

A shady spot

Sunny gardens invite snoozes and relaxed basking but, especially in hot climates, a little shade reduces skin burning and adds comfort. Small trees, a canvas screen, umbrellas and shadecloths are ways of creating shady spots.

Plant power

Indoor plants bring greenery and life into the home, beauty and a way of personalizing a space. They help create dappled light and are natural sculptures which can be moved around frequently. Plants may also be good for health. Researchers at the University of Technology, Sydney (UTS), report that common indoor potted plants like peace lilies and kentia palms clean indoor air. Micro-organisms in the soil mix that share a symbiotic relationship with the plant metabolize pollutants. In addition, plants turn carbon dioxide into oxygen, and researchers in England found that homes with a number of pot plants had a third less nitrogen oxide than those without. While you don't need a rainforest in your home to make a difference, the more plants and the more variety, the better.

Your plants will last longer if you undertake a little research and choose them according to how much light they need and where you intend putting them. Make sure the pots have adequate drainage and that the plants are fertilized and watered as recommended.

As a change to cut flowers, consider flowering plants you can take outside once the blooms have faded. Orchids will keep their flowers for months, hyacinths sweeten the air with their fresh smell,

Michael Mobbs (1950–)

It started out as an ordinary inner city bathroom and kitchen renovation, triggered by the needs of a growing family. But as environmental lawyer Michael Mobbs was increasingly angered and depressed about the growing waste and pollution he saw around him—especially what he saw as government's lack of will to do anything about it—he and his wife decided that at least one home in inner city Sydney would be different. Their house would 'make' all its own water, ensure no storm water left the site, manage all its own waste water and be a net exporter of solar energy to the main electricity grid.

The Mobbs family moved out while tradesmen transformed their ordinary terrace house according to detailed specifications. They moved back in, in 1996, to a house that looked normal but operated in a very different way. The family gained so much more than a new kitchen and bathroom, and it also liberated Mobbs from the anger that had come to dominate his life. He says, 'It is enough to stand under the shower and know the water is not running into the Pacific Ocean.' The project required research, clear goal setting, the desire to do something and the belief it could be done. Anyone can do this, Mobbs believes. Another outcome was the confidence and knowledge to design and build sustainable houses, and with that, a career change.

Mobbs now runs his own company, Michael Mobbs Sustainable Projects and Design. 'I want to make sustainable housing mainstream,' he says.

cyclamens and chrysanthemums brighten while they bloom. And don't forget about your windows. Flowers, greenery or herbs in window boxes improve your view as well as displaying your efforts to passers-by, while plants on shelves fixed across windows can create beautiful effects without cutting out too much light.

A blackboard paint wall

Blackboard paint is now available for a permanent mat, art space or communication space. Place a box of chalk nearby so that household members and visitors alike can leave their mark.

An individual piece

Painting an old chair, table or chest of drawers you've salvaged from the junk shop can be enormously satisfying. Stripping back to the original wood can also be rewarding, but is time consuming and won't bring good results if the wood was never intended to be exposed. After cleaning and making good small repairs, a light sanding makes new paint adhere better to old. Leaving, rather than filling in, cracks and holes creates a rustic look if that's what you're after. While traditionalists recommend oil-based paint for wood, water-based emulsions work too. Cupboards can be painted to blend in with or contrast walls; a collection of odd chairs can be painted to match. Further decorating possibilities include the following:

- Distressing. A decorator's treatment to imitate the soft lines and textures of ageing, at its simplest it involves sanding back the paint in several key spots—such as corners or the edges of chair backs—to reveal the layer underneath. For a rich effect, try experimenting with several layers of colour and sanding back to expose a new patina of colour.

- Stencilling. You can make your own to fit in with themes already in place in your home or choose from the many available commercially. Many books contain template designs that could be used on furniture, walls and doors alike.

- Free painting. The contrast of a solid, finished piece of furniture decorated with free hand painting can be surprisingly attractive. More controlled work includes folk designs, while abstract patterning ranges from splattering to sponging.

COLOURING OUR LIVES

One of the easiest ways to change your home is with colour—on walls, in curtains, and for your upholstered furnishings.

Before you get started, remember that choosing colours from postage-stamp-size colour charts is hard. Identifying colours you like on a bigger scale will bring the end result closer to your expectations: open your eyes to friends' and others' homes and spaces, identify what you like and what doesn't work for you.

Pinning down the characteristics of the rooms in your home helps too. In a dark room or a dark corner, a colour will appear many shades deeper. In addition, colours don't act independently; on the contrary, they change each other. Red next to white will reflect and warm up the white, while a deep blue will tend to look more purple next to terracotta, and so on.

THE COLOUR WHEEL

A scientific approach to colour makes use of the colour wheel. This is a series of circular bands, divided into wedges of different colours. At its simplest the wheel consists of the three primary colours (red, yellow and blue), the secondary colours (orange, green and violet), and three tertiary colours (for example, turquoise), which are the result of mixing a primary and a secondary colour together. Crimsons and reds through to oranges and yellows are usually referred to as warm colours. Lime green, through greens and blues to violet are referred to as cool.

Complementary colours are those that are opposite each other on the colour wheel: red-orange and turquoise; yellow and violet; blue and orange; blue-violet and yellow-orange. Used together complementary colours can produce a domineering, rather heavy effect, but neutrals or highlights of other colours from other parts of the wheel can lighten the effect. While complementary colours are not generally a relaxing combination, they might work well in rooms where this is not called for, such as a kitchen or hall.

Colour harmonies, on the other hand, sit together on the wheel; for example, orange and orange-red, or turquoise and blue.

People who work with colour describe its characteristics in terms of hue, intensity and tone. The hue is the actual colour—whether it is a lemon yellow or a greeny blue. The intensity, or saturation, refers to the colour's brightness and density—a strong clean intensity at one end of the scale fading to what is sometimes called a 'knocked back' colour, with the addition of duller hues at the other. Tone refers to how dark or light a colour is.

Strong colours can be tiring in large quantities but might work in a small room that's not often used or for a feature wall. Contrasts often relieve: bright orange flowers in a predominantly blue room, for instance, or fresh green plants and cushions in a red room.

THE PALETTE

How you use colour can have a surprising effect on your own mood as well as on the atmosphere of a room. Below is a brief outline of the various colours, including what each is said to symbolize and the effect you can create with it.

Neutrals and naturals

Texture is paramount when neutrals and natural colours are used; consider coir and sisal flooring, wooden floorboards, garden trugs of pine cones, beach treasures such as bleached driftwood, shells, and basketry. The earliest artists' pigments were the neutral colours of ochre, raw and burnt umber, and sienna.

If you take a close look at nature, you'll often find that seemingly neutral or natural colours actually contain many hues—shells may have touches of pink or blue, garden finds have hints of green. Used together, neutrals and naturals are calming, while gold adds exciting highlights to a neutral scheme (for instance, in a picture frame, or crockery).

Beiges and browns need not be dull. Think of tortoiseshell, mahogany and parquet flooring, unbleached linen or patterned veneer or a variety of textures or shades of colour—like tweed.

White

Symbolizes: purity, perfection, the absolute. While in the West brides often wear white, it is the colour of mourning in Asia.

White comes in many shades and tones. Wool 'whites' tend to be creamy, while cotton and linen are sharp, cool whites. White textiles offer many traditional opportunities for pattern without added colour: think of lace, quilting, appliqué. As white reflects other colours so ably, its shades vary subtly according to its neighbour. The blue of a carpet will create blue reflections on white walls; red curtains will leave a warm glow, and so on. If painting with white, differences in finish—matt, gloss, rough—will also affect the final result. White-painted wooden floors give off a clean, bright feel and as the paint wears off, produce a soft, warm effect that is no less attractive. White kitchens—rooms and crockery—give pride of place to food. White partners and complements other colours, enhancing the freshness of green, contrasting with reds, showing off the brilliance of deep blue. It provides a dramatic backdrop for paintings and other artworks and is also a popular choice for making small spaces seem larger.

Blue

Symbolizes: calm, reflection, the intellect, and both the infinite and the void from which all life develops. The blue of lapis lazuli symbolizes divine favour. Ramu, an incarnation of the Hindu god Vishnu, is usually depicted with blue skin, so too Krishna. In both cases, the blue represents the enormity of the heavens.

We live on a blue planet so it's not surprising that we're fond of the colour of its skies, lakes, rivers and seas, in all their moods. Many traditional fabrics are a combination of blues: the ticking of mattresses, the indigo blue of Japanese batik prints, the blue water-resistant guernsey sweater of fishermen. The same applies to crockery: blue and white delftware from Holland; blue stencilled fish on mass-produced plates and bowls from China. Blue is refreshing, uplifting and peaceful. It tends to create calm rather than excitement and is a natural choice for a restful bedroom, although it can work all around the house.

Purple

Symbolizes: pride, grandeur and justice. In the West, purple signifies royalty and majesty—which it also did in ancient South America. It came to symbolize wealth as the ancient Greeks used a purple dye extracted from molluscs, which only the rich could afford.

Lavender, lilac, heather, black hollyhock and pansies, plums, grapes and blackcurrants...the plant world offers a garden of delicate shades within the spectrum of purple and violet. The sea offers another—think of the sheen of mother of pearl or the gloss of seaweed. Purple in a room, especially on large expanses like walls, can take on a Gothic look, and the Victorians were fond of it in a gloomy way. Some people find it cosy in bedrooms and dining rooms used primarily at night. Used sparingly it adds a note of luxury and it is useful as a dark shade when you would prefer not to use black.

Green

Symbolizes: life, spring and youth. It represents hope and joy and is the sacred colour of Islam. In Christianity it is the colour of the Holy Trinity. The 'green' movement is concerned with ecology, but green is also the colour of jealousy and decay.

Sweeping fields, leaves of every colour, moss, lichen and a wintry sea: green too is a much loved colour of nature. From Europe's oaks and America's pines to the palms of the tropics, green reminds us of plants and, because of that, many people find it restful. Some decorators say it is a difficult colour to use in several shades within the same room, others say it can never clash. Green successfully complements blue, white, wood shades, and red highlights. It is infinitely variable, ranging from lime green, pea green, British racing green, mint and moss to malachite, sage, olive and celadon. Green lends elegance to formal rooms in shades such as jade or emerald. In paler shades it aids contemplation in studios and libraries. More yellow hues, such as pistachio, are cheerful while the cooler shades make for a peaceful place to sleep.

Yellow

Symbolizes: gold, light and the sun. In Islam golden-yellow represents wisdom and good advice, while pale yellow is the colour of deceit and betrayal. In Egypt it's the colour of envy and disgrace. In Europe it has connotations of cowardice, while in China it used to be the royal colour and in India, it is used at the festivals of Somavati Amavasya to denote the power of the sun. Yellow is also the most visible of the colours and is used internationally for warning.

One of the three primary colours, yellow brings instant sunshine to any room. It is said to be the friendliest and warmest of colours. Always cheery, never dark, it works well in small spaces such as stairways and halls as well as large, cluttered or busy rooms.

Orange

Symbolizes: flames, luxury and splendour. In both China and Japan it's a colour of love and happiness, while the saffron robes of Buddhist monks show they have taken vows of humility and renunciation.

The tones of orange range from earthy terracotta and muted cornelian to delicate coral. A colour found naturally in their landscapes, it is often used in Morocco, Sicily and Tuscany. Orange is a dramatic colour and works well in conjunction with brass and inlaid wooden ornaments. The soft earthy tones radiate warmth and are found both inside and outside houses in almost every culture around the world. In various shades it's at home in kitchens, dining rooms and living rooms, and combines well with furnishings in neutral shades and rustic textures.

Red

Symbolizes: life, blood, fire, passion and war. It is the bridal colour in India and China as it is associated with fertility and good luck. Holy days in the Christian calendar used to be marked with red (hence 'red-letter days'). It's often been used as a symbol of revolution. Associated with virility and danger, red is a popular colour for sports cars.

Though generally warm and lively, towards the oxblood tones it can also be gloomy and claustrophobic. Red tends to bounce back from walls, making rooms seem smaller, but used well it creates drama. As it seems to 'pull together' a wall, it can work well in rooms with lots of shelving. An attention grabber, red is hard to mix with other colours—wood tones work well, as do subdued modest tones such as silver-grey.

Black

Symbolizes: the colour of death and mourning in the West, also 'black magic'. In China it is the colour of north and winter, while Kali, the Hindu goddess of destruction, is black.

A theatrical choice for interior design, black is often used in nightclubs as a contrast to glitter and sparkle. Most people would find a room with walls of unrelieved black heavy going, but a single black wall creates drama and definition for a collection of pictures and other art objects. Slate, ebony and dark furnishings with brown and grey tones are some of the ways black shades find their way into a range of colour schemes.

USING COLOUR

The extent to which colour can affect mood or be therapeutic is debatable, especially as it seems we perceive colours subjectively—what's green to one person is blue to another. But there's no doubt colour has power and energy: it can camouflage, harmonize, vitalize, make things stand out, or shock. Colours are a useful decorating tool and can be used to a variety of effects, to create the atmosphere you desire, to give a place your own individual stamp or simply to please the eye.

For liveliness

To enliven a room, use complementary colours, such as orange flowers in a predominantly blue room, a painting with strong greens in a red room, violet details in a yellow room, and so on.

For serenity

Avoid contrasts and choose a palette of related shades instead. Serenity is often created by using pale soft shades of blue or green, together with shades of white. Combine this with uncluttered spaces to induce a feeling of calm, light and pleasure.

To increase space

Pale colours, including pale floors, reduce the feelings of change, crowding and clutter in a room and increase space and light.

The effect of light

Colours change mood and shade in different light.

- Neon is harsh and creates bluer hues.
- Ordinary light bulbs are warmer and friendlier.
- Candlelight is even warmer.
- In a yellowish artificial light, yellows become more intense, reds become more orange, whites turn creamy and purple moves towards brown.
- Lots of light can make blue and white look stark.
- Dark colours such as black, magenta and violet hardly change in strong sunlight.
- Primary colours are intensified and glow in strong light.

Dark rooms

By painting dark rooms in light tones such as white or cream you will increase the feeling of space. But by painting a small dark room in a dark colour, you can create a sense of drama.

Sun-drenched rooms

These are adaptable. If you use neutral colours, you will still have the sunlight to create liveliness, but bright colours can work well too.

To maximize light

Especially in small corners, consider painting the immediate surround of a window in a light colour. Walls that receive the most light can be painted brightly or lightly, or hung with mirrors for maximum reflection. Sheer curtains, of muslin or voile, can also help create a feeling of light—especially when the impression of a view (dappled leaves or rows of chimney pots) is better than the real in-the-raw view.

To zone and define space

Lowered ceilings, part walls, arches, and the like help to define spaces within larger spaces, especially in open-plan living. Paint can exaggerate the effect—by using contrasting colours on different parts of a space, for instance, on the walls—or minimize it by using the same colour or similar colours along a stretch of wall that encompasses several living spaces. One strong-coloured wall in an otherwise neutral scheme—for instance an orange wall in a predominantly white room—can increase the feeling of space.

To create intimacy

A dark colour will appear to lower the ceiling, making the room seem cosier. Dark colours on the walls will also reduce the apparent size of the room.

To highlight

A highlight is a noticeable, but relatively small sample of a colour—plant pots, a bunch of flowers, a row of ornaments—that draws the eye, creates interest, but doesn't dominate. Some schemes cry out for them. A dining room with wooden dining table and chairs and a wooden floor, for example, needs colours, perhaps in the form of pictures or curtains. A touch of coral in a pale combination of blues and whites warms up the whole effect. Overmatching is tiresome and boring—rather like the over-coordinated job interview suit.

For drama

Use deep colours. Think of the plush velvet of the theatre.

THE BLANK ROOM

We often inherit a colour scheme which, if we can live with, we use as a starting point for our redecorating. The blue kitchen cupboards or a pale yellow wall we don't intend to repaint for a while, a green sofa…sometimes a painting or an embroidered cushion gives us the next move. Rooms that evolve usually work better than ones that have been planned from scratch on day one. Like home renovations, decoration is better when you've lived in a place for a little while and observed how it changes in the day, and how you and your family are using it.

Gather, pinpoint and collect inspiration: the colour schemes you covet, the textures you admire. Find a scrapbook, noticeboard, box file or similar and gradually fill it with postcards, magazine cuttings, and so on. To fully appreciate your selection, take a look at the combination in full sunlight, artificial light and on a dull day. Try putting a vase of flowers in front as well.

Before you take anyone's advice have a look at their colour schemes—this goes for interior decorating writers' as well as friends' rooms. The photograph of the all red room hailed in a decorating book as bold and stylish might not be what you want to live with. Sometimes it pays to observe how the locals colour their houses—what works well in the light quality of one climate can look overdressed in another.

When you're sure of your scheme, a colour board can help focus your ideas: pin fabric remnants, paint colour charts and play around until you get the effect you think will work.

Small is beautiful

Bigger is not always better and living 'smaller' certainly has several benefits.

- Less cleaning. This is especially important for the working woman who finds that, while she shares the bills, the housework still falls to her.
- Cheaper to build. Using fewer materials enables more of the budget to be allocated towards quality considerations. If a house is well designed, it will be a nicer place to live in as a result.
- Cosier. Large rooms and houses might impress, but small places can be homely and have character.
- Nooks for one. Christopher Alexander's classic book *A Pattern Language* looks at how people use architectural and urban space. A place for one person, he says, need only be one central room, with nooks around it. The nooks replace what are rooms in larger houses: a nook for bed, bath, kitchen, workshop and entrance. Nooks offer more continuity of space than a division into rooms, he says.

Colour in the house can be changed most easily by working with two elements: paint and soft furnishings. Paint is adaptable, transforms, cleans and sets a new scene. It is available in all shades and from chalky textures to lacquer shine. You can use it on virtually anything: walls, doors, window frames, wooden staircases, floors, wooden chairs, tables, chests, etc.

Paint finishes are virtually an industry in themselves: ragging, dragging, rolling, scumbling, washing, stencilling…the home decorating section of the bookshop is overflowing with them. Be careful what you try: the fashion victim could be kept very busy trying out the latest hot scheme and covering up the latest no-no.

Curtains, around windows or across doors, introduce colour, texture and climate control—they keep the warm in and the cold out in winter, and the heat out on the hottest of days. Upholstered furniture and cushions add spots and layers of colour and hue, while tablecloths, bedspreads and blankets can be changed according to mood, season and use. An otherwise neutral room can take on an entirely different feel by switching deep orange and red cushions and throws to citrus green ones.

SPACE

Only the lucky few can afford to live in a house with all the space and storage they want. If you have growing children, space-taking hobbies or work at home, every scrap of space seems to fill up. Here are some possible solutions to consider.

One extreme to another

If you yearn for space in a small house with lots of possessions, consider leaving some rooms freer and others more cluttered so you can at least enjoy a feeling of space somewhere in the house.

Double up on room function

The kitchen of the 1700s was family room, office and the place where visitors were received as well as the place to prepare and consume meals. Anyone with a big enough kitchen, especially a farmhouse kitchen, no doubt uses it like that now. Guestrooms might also be sewing spaces. A study by day can be a dining room by night. Many rooms are called on to be storage rooms too— built-in cupboards in the bedroom, bookcases in the living room, and so on. Sofa beds allow you to put up a guest in the sitting room. With a few alterations for comfort, a garden shed or workshop can become a home office.

Link outdoors with indoors

Rooms that open up into an outside space—whether garden, courtyard or balcony—give a feeling of space. Bringing plants up close to a window also gives an illusion of space outside, as does placing a mirror inside to reflect and double the size of a view.

Open up

Knocking down walls to open up rooms increases the feeling of space, but consider whether open-plan living is for you first. Although it's been a trend in the last few decades, there's a lot to be said for the privacy and separation of activities that individual rooms offer. Open plans are said to allow space to flow from one room to another, but the trouble is that sight, sound and belongings flow too.

Continuous colour

Using a limited palette of colours throughout a room or using a continuous colour on walls and floors helps to create the illusion of space by simplifying the outlook. If you are painting the whole home in one go, you might even consider creating a more in-tune environment by sticking to and repeating just a few colours throughout.

The lowdown

Low-lying furniture can save a really small space from seeming unbearably cluttered. For instance, a double futon bed can just squeeze onto the floor of a small room and the room will remain light and airy because of all the space still above the bed. A formal high bed would look cramped and out of place. Similarly, large cushions or bean bags are a good option for extra seating in a living room.

Daring diagonals

Tables don't have to align with the walls; chairs do not have to sit in corners. The diagonal is the longest line in a rectangular room and by creating some with furniture and in design features such as built-in platforms and shelves, you can make rooms seem bigger and more spacious.

Build in storage

Wall-to-wall shelving and floor to ceiling built-in wardrobes make the most of available space while creating pleasing, uncluttered lines. Unusual spaces, such as those under the stairs, can often be used effectively for storage. Well planned storage also makes it easier to live in small spaces as you can have what you need at hand—whether it's books or brooms—without falling over it.

Lighting up

Wall-mounted rather than tabletop lamps, even light rather than patchy, make a room seem larger. Mirrors, especially those that reflect a window or glass door leading to a garden, help create a feeling of space.

MOVING HOUSE

Moving house can be expensive; it's inconvenient and stressful, but it's nonetheless a frequent—if not exactly popular—pursuit.

You may move because your current house is just too small to accommodate a growing family or a growing need for space; because the lawn has got too unwieldy to manage and the house too big to keep up with maintenance; because you don't like the way a neighbourhood has changed; or because you want to move closer to family. You may move nearer work, into the catchment

Moving: the figures

Fires, floods, into an owned house, for cheaper rent...the reasons for moving are many. Data from the American Housing Survey of 2001 undertaken by the US Census Bureau shows that the top five reasons for moving were:

- to establish own household (2.0*)
- a new job or transfer (1.9*)
- needed a larger home (1.9*)
- to be closer to work or school (1.7*)
- wanted a better home (1.4*).

The top five reasons for choosing a neighbourhood were:

- convenient for job (3.8*)
- house was most important consideration (2.6*)
- convenient to friends or relatives (2.5*)
- looks/design of the neighbourhood (2.5*)
- good schools (1.1*).

The three most important reasons for choosing the home were:

- financial (5.2*)
- room layout/design (2.9*)
- size (2.4*).

Most people felt they had moved to a better home (53 per cent), but 17 per cent reported moving to a worse home. Three per cent of respondents had moved within the same neighbourhood and most of the rest said they'd moved up a neighbourhood (43 per cent) or to a neighbourhood about the same standard (37 per cent).

* Figures given above are in millions.

area of better schools, to chase a different lifestyle or to find a house closer to your dream home.

A study from the Institute of Social and Economic Research at the University of Essex in the United Kingdom found a link between moving house and income. Their research showed that moving house eventually lifts your earnings; that individuals and households who move house have higher incomes than those who remain at the same address. They also found that those who moved between regions, as opposed to just locally, had the greatest gains, but sometimes it took a while for a positive impact to kick in.

VOX POP: On moving

'I went to four primary schools and we spent spells in three countries before I was six. My parents travelled again once I was at university and, as all of these experiences were positive, it was an easy decision to emigrate to Australia. But now that I'm here with a husband who's from New Zealand, with two young children and no family on either side, I think there's a lot to be said for staying in one place.' AH

'I moved from the city because although life was pleasant, it was awfully predictable. I had a lovely garden with Altissima roses scrambling up the wall. One day I was looking at them and I thought, "My life is going to be like this for the next twenty years." When I moved from the city to the country, I didn't know what to expect except a huge difference. The move has been a very rich one in both a personal and financial sense. I have made varied and interesting friends, seen alternatives in health treatments, now go to yoga regularly and generally have a much fuller life. I'm fitter. There are no takeaway places, so healthier, and $20 lasts a long time in your pocket.' JS

THINKING OF MOVING

Before making any decisions, you should create your own checklist for what's important to you in a location as well as a home. This will help speed up decisions and ensure you don't overlook something that in hindsight should have been a priority. Possible inclusions:

- Lifestyle changes. Will the move bring with it changes in your lifestyle? Will you have opportunities for different activities?
- Transport/mobility. Is a car essential? Can you enjoy a walk from your front door? What public transport is available? Can visitors reach you without a car?
- Shopping. Where would you do a weekly or monthly shop? How far would you have to go for emergency milk/newspaper/chocolate?
- Family, friends and neighbours. How far away are they? Can you entertain/put people up?
- Services. Where is the nearest hospital/doctor/ dentist/ pharmacy/ swimming pool/cinema/other amenities that are important to you and your family?
- Climate. Look at the seasonal variations in minimum and maximum temperatures and rainfall if you are moving to a different part of the country. Look at a house's exposure to wind and sun.
- Location. How close are roads, rivers and bush? Are floods or fires a potential hazard?
- Future change. Are there new developments/roads/train links planned? The zoning—commercial, residential, rural—of an area will give you an idea of potential change.
- Noise. How much noise pollution will you be exposed to from roads/local pubs/other industries?
- Upkeep. Are there aspects to a house that would make it more or less expensive or difficult to maintain? This could depend on whether there's a garden, the size and age of a dwelling etc.
- Renovating versus moving. There is much to weigh up: what exactly does your current house lack that you think you'll find elsewhere? Is it only by moving that you can achieve this? The cost of moving—removalists' fees, setting up costs, real estate fees and stamp duty—mounts up to quite a renovating budget if you decide to stay put instead. If you yearn for more space but live in a plot that is the shape of a pencil no amount of clever extensions will give you a wide, open living

area. On the other hand, a house that you are generally happy in as far as the street it's on, its proximity to amenities, and so on may be worth adapting.

- Country versus city living. City dwellers usually imagine the country life to be healthier. Statistics, however, often paint a different picture. Depending on the city and your lifestyle, it can be surprisingly easy to get sufficient exercise there: places you might need to go are often near enough to consider reaching under your own steam, and walking and cycling can even be quicker than public transport. In the country you can find yourself jumping in the car for almost every trip because of the distances involved. Rural health services are often spread thin and under-funded. In rural Australia, for instance, family doctors are in short supply, so too are specialists in psychiatry, obstetrics and anaesthesia. Unemployment may also be higher than in the city, leading potentially to financial worries.

Whether you're staying put or moving out, a home reflects so much about your life: how you balance your need for space with your financial wherewithal, your need for belongings with your need to get rid of clutter, the desire for a sparkling home with the desire for and availability of time to clean and tidy, your urge to live in the country with the need to be near city-based work. But even small changes can make a place more comfortable, healthier, less of a burden on the environment—and more of a place that you're happy to call 'home'.

TAKING STOCK

Take a pen and paper and run through the following questions to help you clarify any problems with your home and come up with solutions. It may help you throw light on how you use the different parts of your home and what you like about it, despite your misgivings. By putting pen to paper you may also identify themes you hadn't previously realized were so important to you.

1   The basics
(a) Who lives in your home? List all the members of your household, including pets.
(b) What do they get up to? List each household member's activities and space needs, particularly challenges not entirely met: maybe you still can't find the right way to store tools or quite where to put out the sewing machine.
(c) Do they need a quiet, private space or will a corner in a communal room do?
(d) What furniture do they need? Can any do double duty (eg. desk and storage, sewing table and dining table)?
(e) What would make each activity easier, more comfortable and more convenient? Are any of your possessions awkward to store (eg. bikes, craft equipment)?
(f) Are there activities that you'd like to be able to do at home which, with a little adaptation, could be incorporated?
(g) How do the rooms work? Think about each room, how often it is used, by whom and with what level of satisfaction.
(h) Where do the following activities take place: sleeping, cooking, eating, watching television, homework and study, writing of letters and paying bills, using the computer, art and craft, sewing, laundry, bathing and work? Consider changing the function of a room that's barely used.

2   **Cooking, entertaining and eating**

(a) Who cooks? Does s/he prefer to be left alone or chat with friends and family while creating? Do you have joint efforts?

(b) What are meal times like? Do you like to sit at a kitchen table or eat from a tray on the sofa?

(c) How do you like to entertain? Just with casual callers and a cup of tea? Large formal cocktail parties? Seated around a dining table or lounging in the garden?

3   **Family or household group time**

(a) Where do you group?

(b) Can you all sit outside together?

4   **A sense of home**

(a) What do you like about where you currently live? What are its drawbacks? What would you improve, if anything, if you had the time and budget?

(b) Are you planning/would you like to move?

(c) If so, what are you seeking? How important are the following in choosing where to live?

- location
- local amenities
- attractiveness/appeal of surroundings
- cost of living
- being near family
- availability of work
- the house itself
- fate/the way things work out.

5 **A sense of belonging**

(a) What events led you to this home?

(b) Is it like other places you have lived? How different or similar is it to other homes you've had?

(c) Is it far from where you grew up?

(d) If you have made a dramatic move (eg. migration, city to country) what was the motivation and has the experience matched expectations?

6 **Changing homes**

(a) Have you made any changes to your home?

(b) What difference have these changes made to the experience of day-to-day living?

(c) What changes, if any, are you planning?

(d) What does this involve?

7 **Flow-on effect**

(a) What aspects of where you live affect your lifestyle?

(b) Does where you live affect other aspects of your life (eg. your health, contentment, financial situation or relationships)?

8 **An individual home**

(a) What inspires you in terms of objects and ideas about the past and present local history or the natural environment of where you live?

(b) Where have you lived in the past? What inspires you about other places you've lived?

(c) What sort of architecture appeals to you? Do you tend to be attracted to older styles or do you prefer new buildings?

(d) What sort of space do you feel most comfortable in? Cosy spots? Open spaces? Bright and breezy? Minimalist or lived in? How do your current living spaces compare with your ideal?

(e) What are your favourite furnishings and why do you like them?

(f) Which of your worldly goods do you treasure most and feel you could not do without (eg. books, clothes, kitchen appliances, a specific collection)?

(g) What places that you've visited inspire you (eg. other people's homes, holiday spots)? Did they have a mood you'd like to transport to your home if at all possible?

*I like work: it fascinates me.
I can sit and look at it for hours.*

JEROME K JEROME,
THREE MEN IN A BOAT (1889)

6. WORK

'WORK AND LOVE' WAS SIGMUND FREUD'S
ANSWER TO HAPPINESS. AND IF YOU LOVE
YOUR WORK, SO MUCH THE BETTER—
WORK SHOULD BE ABOUT MORE THAN
SIMPLY GETTING YOUR DAILY BREAD.
IDEALLY IT GIVES YOU A SENSE OF SELF-
VALUE, INTEREST, CHALLENGE, LEARNING,
MAYBE A SENSE OF STRETCHING
YOURSELF. IT MAY GIVE A SENSE OF
COMMUNITY TOO, BY BRINGING YOU INTO
CONTACT WITH PEOPLE YOU WOULD NOT
OTHERWISE MEET.

AT WORK IN THE 21ST CENTURY

The words used to describe how people earn a living have various connotations. 'Work' usually means labour, while a 'job' can be a task for money or a particular defined task. A 'career', on the other hand, carries with it a sense of progression throughout life. Ironically, another meaning of 'career' is to rush in an uncontrolled fashion—perhaps what happens when you feel your work life is out of control.

In the past few decades technology has revolutionized both the workplace and the types of work carried out there. A generation ago, it was not unusual to expect to stay with a company for several decades, in the reassuring knowledge that a pension would provide for you comfortably when you retired. Now recruitment agents advise young people to gain broad experience by switching jobs every few years—and many people are left much to their own devices to work out how to support themselves when wages dry up. The place work occupies in our lives has changed too: many mothers work, even when their children are young, as many households now need both adults to work in order to remain solvent.

Standard working hours are also changing. By 2000, in Britain, the idea of the nine to five job was fast becoming obsolete. A study by the Institute of Social and Economic Research found that well over half of men (59 per cent) and women (52 per cent) employed were in non-standard jobs. That is the jobs were either temporary, involved working away from the employer's premises, were for less than 30 hours a week or more than 48 hours a week, or were not during the regular working day. Almost 1 in 5 British workers worked more than 48 hours a week, while around 1 in 10 worked less than sixteen hours a week. As many work opportunities have become shorter term in nature so people's fear of losing a job has become greater.

Changes in employment trends reflect a complexity of social change. A society that increasingly seeks legal redress needs more paralegals and legal assistants. A growing and ageing population can feed an increase in health care and social services, for instance, in occupations such as emergency medical technicians and paramedics. More leisure time and higher wages mean more jobs for actors, directors, producers, lobby attendants and ticket takers. These are just a few recent examples from the Bureau of Labor Statistics in the United States. Technology has elbowed out workers in the textile industry—including garment sewing machine operators—as well as those in railroad brake, signal and switch operators, where computer controlled cars have become the norm.

Predictions for the decade 2000–2010 emphasize the need for training and education. 'Air traffic controllers and nuclear power reactor operators are the only occupations of the 50 highest paying that do not require a college degree,' points out the *2003 Occupational Outlook Handbook* of the US Department of Labor.

WORKING IN THE GLOBAL VILLAGE

Work can be a blinkering experience. Look up from the desk (if you are one of the millions of workers worldwide with an office job) and take a broader view.

- By far the world's largest work force is in farming: half of the labour force according to the International Labour Organization (ILO). Only a third of these works for wages and over half of all agricultural workers are women.

- Of the estimated 100 million enterprises in the world, by far the majority are small. More than one billion of the three billion workers in the world are self-employed in agriculture or work in small facilities.

- More than 200 million adults work in tourism and travel, representing around 8 per cent of global employment. Women account for 70 per cent of these workers and half the work force is aged 25 or under. The ILO estimated that nine million workers lost their jobs in the industry because of the downturn in tourism and travel after the September 11 attacks on New York.

- Senior managers in Hong Kong, Switzerland and Ecuador are the best off financially, according to Mercer Human Resources Consulting. It looked at average salaries in 50 countries and

A snapshot of Europe

An analysis by the Economic and Social Research Council of 73,000 households across fifteen European countries, published in 2002, found a diverse employment picture:

- In Denmark, 67 per cent of mothers of children under sixteen are in full-time employment. At the other end of the scale, the figure for the Netherlands is 11 per cent.
- In Greece, 1 in 6 people works in agriculture—compared to 1 in 60 people in the United Kingdom.
- An average of 11 per cent of working-age adults across Europe live in households where no one works. The United Kingdom had the highest proportion of non-working households, at 15 per cent.
- Spain had the highest unemployment rate at 14.1 per cent, compared to Luxembourg with 2.4 per cent, and 5.5 per cent in the United Kingdom.
- In Scandinavia two-thirds of women have full-time jobs. In Italy, Spain and Greece, 40 per cent of women without children are in full-time employment, and around 1 in 3 mothers has a full-time job. Similarly, less than a third of British mothers work full time, whereas two-thirds of women without children have full-time jobs.

calculated their purchasing power based on tax and social security deductions and the cost of living. Germany and the United States were also in the top five. Despite low salaries, many South American countries offer workers greater purchasing power than in European countries. Senior managers in Vietnam, Bulgaria and India are the worst off, with low salaries and relatively high taxes. Australian senior managers ranked 25th; New Zealand, 13th; and those in the UK, 11th. Quality of life—combining issues such as housing, political stability and schooling—was not taken into account.

- The International Labour Organization estimates there were 180 million unemployed people worldwide at the end of 2002, up twenty million on the previous year. Some of the job losses stem from what's been labelled the bursting of the information and communication technology bubble in 2001, and economic shock waves following the September 11 terrorism attacks.

● By 2010, the International Labour Organization estimates nearly 60 per cent of the world's labour force will be in Asia. A quarter of the global labour force will be in China.

A JOB FOR ALL REASONS

Jobs come with a range of conditions, expectations, responsibilities and benefits—whether picking fruit in school holidays; heading a worldwide charity; doing work experience during a gap year between study; or committing to a mediocre administration job because it allows you to also fit in a burgeoning catering business.

The vocational job

Many jobs requiring specialized training and study fit into this category: medicine, dentistry and others in the health professions. Some courses of study lead to a profession—such as law—but by no means do all graduates continue on to practise what they studied.

The stopgap job

When the money's run out and the ideal job is not in sight, it's time for the pioneer spirit in you to do what you can to pay the bills. Migrants and those just starting out do it all the time. The doctor whose qualifications are not recognized in a new country takes a cleaning job. The science graduate works in a factory filling orders. Typical stopgaps include working in food preparation or service, market research, and leisure-centred jobs in cinemas or tourist spots.

The toe-in-the-door job

The secretary who becomes a television producer, the editor who started as mail boy...examples are everywhere. Taking a low paying, even menial, job in an industry or organization you aspire to work in can give you valuable experience and contacts.

The temporary job

Is temp work a dead end or a stepping stone? A UK study published in 2002 in *The Economic Journal* found that temporary workers—accounting for between 7 and 10 per cent of workers in the United Kingdom—have lower levels of job satisfaction, receive less training and are less well-paid than permanent equivalents. But fixed-term contracts are more likely to lead to permanent jobs and any gap in payment is then quickly closed. Temp work opportunities range from secretarial and accounting to medical or financial services, and there are many specialized temping agencies, especially in large cities. This can be a way of making good contact with agency staff, demonstrating that you are reliable and professional, as well as gaining experience in your field.

Part-time work

Part-time work tends to bring with it less status, less responsibility, fewer opportunities for promotion, less job security, and less training. But despite the drawbacks there are times when it suits because you have other responsibilities, whether it's doing the books for a spouse's home business or caring for a sick or young family member. Alternatively, it might be possible to balance two part-time jobs so that in combination they satisfy your needs for enough income, creative outlet or companionship.

Self-employed/freelance/consultant work

This is a common option for the newly redundant. Going freelance allows you to gain new fields of experience, stay afloat (possibly!) and keep up your contacts. It's not for the fainthearted, but can suit those who hate working in a bureaucratic organization.

VOX POP: How important is work?

'It's very important. It makes me feel useful and skilled. It's also an opportunity to meet people and make a difference in their lives.

Vocabulary of the new economy

- Workaholic. The term was coined in 1971 by the US author Wayne Oates, and means someone obsessively addicted to work. In a UK survey in 1999 over half the respondents reported feeling they had become workaholics in response to the demands of their jobs.
- The clear desk fantasy. Wouldn't it be nice to clear your desk once in a while and have every task completed? Sadly, in a world where tasks overlap and there is a constant flow of demands, interruptions and revised plans, it's just not going to happen.
- Looking busy. The body is going through the motions—tapping the keyboard, flicking the report page, jotting down a plan— but the mind is not on the job. It is a hazard of many workplaces, especially ones where the boss works late and others feel they should 'show' willing, if not 'be' willing. Says Margot Cairnes, a futurist and keynote speaker, in her book *Staying Sane in a Changing World*, 'Someone described it as musical chairs. If you weren't looking busy when the music stopped, you mightn't get a seat.'
- Work ethic. A belief in the moral value of work per se.

Money is OK. It's intellectually and physically challenging.' Mental health nurse

'I've reached the point where I absolutely love what I do, and only do what I love. I've managed to close the gap between what I do and who I am. I am very lucky.' Freelance management consultant

'Work is reasonably satisfying. If I could, I would stop work to concentrate on projects that really interest me—something bigger, bolder and riskier—but which would take time and research. At the moment, commercial considerations dictate most of what I write and the need to pay bills clips my wings. I can't figure out how to pay this week's rent with next year's royalties.' Travel and tourism writer

- Parkinson's law. Work expands so as to fill the time available, first stated by Professor C Northcote Parkinson in 1955.
- Peter's principle. In a hierarchical system, the drive for promotion as a reward results in every employee being promoted to his own level of incompetence. That is, you are promoted each time you do a job well until you are in a position just beyond your abilities, where you remain—doing a job badly.
- e-thrombosis. This occurs when a blood clot forms due to prolonged inactivity—such as sitting for long periods while using a computer—and travels to the lungs. The term was coined in 2003 following the recent case of a New Zealander who spent up to eighteen hours a day at his computer and nearly died after a massive blood clot formed in his leg veins. The condition is well known in the travel industry, where it tends to be referred to as DVT, or deep vein thrombosis.
- e-world. While the machine age of the nineteenth and twentieth centuries was characterized by automation and mass education, the e-world is distinguished by businesses on the world-wide web, corporations in positions of political power, and services (rather than manual labour) being paramount to the economy.

'I get great satisfaction in giving my best in my work. I give 100 per cent when assisting clients in workshops, my part-time regular work is a great balance.' Spiritual kinesiologist and part-time receptionist

'Work is important and I take pride in it. A job well done, especially if it requires specialist skills, gives me great satisfaction.' Accountant

'Work is too important, sadly. A bad working life always affects other aspects of your life. For some reason a happy working life doesn't always do the same in reverse.' Public relations manager

'It's very significant. Work takes up a lot of my time. I enjoy it but it can be stressful (sales pressure, arrogant people). It's the best of a bad bunch. Anything else I've tried is worse, and I can't earn this sort of money doing anything else.' Sales manager

'It gives me something useful to do, something to contribute to society. I get more out of it than money—there's learning new skills, using existing skills, new experiences, achievements, self-expression, and so on. I wouldn't completely stop work if I could.' Computer programmer

Job sharing

Job sharing—where two people share one position—is seen as a way of working part-time hours in positions that usually require full-time commitment. While it can suit parents with young children, it's also a viable option for people studying, attending courses, caring for other family members or simply wanting to work fewer hours. In the United Kingdom, job sharing almost doubled in the 1990s, reaching 1 per cent of the work force by 2000. Job sharing exists at

Enid Blyton (1897–1963)

Children's author Enid Blyton made a handsome living from her writing, but her father's ambition was for her to become a concert pianist. She dropped her piano studies after he left the family home to live with another woman, and began training to be a teacher. Her studies included Montessori methods and, on completion, she became nursery governess to a family of four. Her first book, a collection of poems under the title *Child Whispers*, was published in 1922, and by 1925 her earnings from her writing were enough for her to give up teaching. In 1935 Enid Blyton published six titles, and in 1940, thirteen. She regularly wrote 10,000 words a day on her portable typewriter on the verandah of her Buckinghamshire home. By the early 1950s, Enid Blyton had had almost 40 publishers and by the end of her writing career, in 1965, she had published over 400 titles. Among her creations were Noddy and the Famous Five.

professional and managerial levels, but more typically it involves clerical and administrative jobs. It's generally up to those who want to job share to ask for it in the first place, make a good case for it, and then make it work in practice.

Telecommuting

Companies large and small are increasingly open to the idea that some jobs can be completed at home just as efficiently as at the office. Removing the need to come into the office every day may provide an employee with much appreciated flexibility. The American Telecommuting Association says it's the fastest growing work pattern in the United States, second only to casual dress days. A good way to make it work, it says, is for employees to 'drop in' to the workplace at least once or twice a week. While employees are glad to save time on commuting back and forth, companies report extra productivity.

Work experience

This is often a valuable way of encouraging a company to give you the 'break' you've been looking for. The fact that you've had some experience on an organic farm or in an advertising agency may help persuade potential employers that you are serious, especially if you are new to the field.

Voluntary work

Volunteers are needed close to home—to shop for old people or accompany a disabled person to a study group—and far away—a country recovering from war or with ecological challenges—so there's always an opportunity for your skills and experience to make a difference. Margot Cairnes says there is the equivalent of 29 million full-time jobs in the not-for-profit sector, and for every paid staff member there may be many more giving their time and energy without pay. Some companies allow staff time off for voluntary activities such as mentoring, helping at events or working on sustainable projects. Many people volunteer their time as a way to give back to the community. Others, like PD who hosts a Sunday morning radio show on community radio, do it because it gives them an opportunity they'd otherwise miss out on.

In 2000, VSO—Voluntary Service Overseas—reported an increase in applications from professionals, especially managers wanting a break from mainstream careers. Another factor in the increase, it says, is the fact that people are becoming fed up with their work—whether they're in construction, the health professions or teaching—and want a better deal from a job. They see volunteering as both professionally and personally rewarding. Volunteering is also a way to build skills in a challenging environment: ME left a job in the NHS (the UK's National Health Service) as an accident and emergency nurse because of rising levels of aggression and violence from patients. She took a volunteer job as a clinical nurse tutor in Greece. Chartered civil engineer PK felt he was pushing paper around his desk in his UK job so applied for a more creative post in Pakistan.

The 'this will pay the bills' job

After making a reasonable living in a rock band, JB sorted mail at the post office while he studied for a degree in communications and led a few yoga classes. Following a spell of trying for communication-based jobs but getting nowhere, he decided to take unpaid leave from the post office and take the plunge to teach yoga full time. Within a few months he managed to build up enough classes to allow him to resign from his mail sorting altogether.

While different life stages may call for a different approach to a job or work, it may also be that we have a need for work that fulfils in different ways. In *The Age of Unreason*, Charles Handy presents the idea of 'the work portfolio' where different bits of work in our lives can fit together to form a balanced whole. It's an interesting perspective, and the opposite of the idea of the one, secure, all-fulfilling job. However, as that looks like becoming more and more of a rarity, the portfolio approach may well be worth cultivating. It can also represent a way to balance a variety of needs, whether they are creative outlets or a regular cash flow. In Handy's portfolio, paid work includes:

- Wage work. Taken to mean 'money paid for time given', this covers salary work undertaken by employees.
- Fee work. This is money paid for results delivered and is the way many freelancers and craftspeople work.

Free work includes the following:

- Homework. This would include all the work at home, from cooking and cleaning to maintenance and child minding.
- Gift work. Work done without pay for the community, charities and neighbours comes under this category.
- Study work. Serious study or training can enhance other aspects of the work portfolio as well as being fulfilling in itself.

JOB SATISFACTION

How satisfied are we with work? It depends who you ask. In a poll commissioned by VSO in the United Kingdom in 1999, 1 in 4 said work was taking over their lives and almost two-thirds said they'd switch to a job they enjoyed more even if paid less. VSO concluded that people were fed up with work. Yet, another survey undertaken around the same time said most workers were satisfied with their work. Further research reveals a number of other conclusions:

- 'I don't like Mondays.' It's official. We like our work more at weekends and on Fridays—when we're either not doing it or it's soon to be finished. These were the findings by Dr Mark Taylor of the Institute of Social and Economic Research (ISER). In the same study, he found that overwork was the major contributor to low levels of job satisfaction for both men and women.
- Women are happier at work than men, according to other research from ISER: 22 per cent of British female workers said they were completely satisfied at work against 13 per cent of British men. Researchers speculate that one possible explanation is women's lower expectations.

- Shorter working hours mean greater job satisfaction. One study found that people working up to fifteen hours a week reported higher levels of job satisfaction than full-timers.
- Seasonal and casual contracts can cause less satisfaction and more mental distress than regular employment.

Many practical issues underlie job satisfaction. Complaints may seem trivial when considered individually but when added to extra work they can snowball.

Work environment
Sick building syndrome, issues of air conditioning, and battling with old technology and noise can all erode the sense of job satisfaction.

Opportunity
Generally, employees are more satisfied with work when it presents challenging opportunities—like the chance to participate in interesting projects or to take on extra responsibility.

Esteem
Employees want and need to be recognized for putting in extra.

Pride
A workplace where standards are high is much more likely to have satisfied employees.

Salary
A survey by the Oregon Employment Department in the United States found a distinct correlation between job satisfaction and hourly wage. Only 30 per cent of those on a rate between the legal minimum and $10 said they were very satisfied with their job, compared with more than 60 per cent of those earning more than $35 per hour.

Freedom to make decisions

When you can make decisions or have input into them job satisfaction is greater. Nobody likes to feel they are only ever told what to do without any say.

Stress

When the stress gauge is continuously on 'high' your job satisfaction takes a plunge, particularly when work interferes with your personal life or is a continuing source of worry.

Flexibility of working hours

As life feels more and more of a juggle, the offer of flexible working hours enhances job satisfaction.

The boss

When employees feel that managers are good leaders—good at motivating, striving for excellence, and taking action when needed—they are more likely to be satisfied with their job.

Vocations

Some surveys show that teachers and others working in local government and not-for-profit organizations report a high level of job satisfaction.

Personal development

As management structures flatten and promotions are less easy to come by, issues of personal development and fulfilment become more important. Employees now desire variety and learning opportunities as well as career development.

Are some jobs more inherently satisfying than others? In the Oregon Employment Department survey, business owners reported being most satisfied with their jobs. Perhaps this was due to a feeling of control. Workers in the fishing, forestry, ranch and logging sectors ranked second. Among those least satisfied were labourers and equipment cleaners.

BRINGING ABOUT CHANGE AT WORK

The ability to deal with problems at work calmly and even cheerfully is a talent worth cultivating. Schedules and systems rarely go to plan and it's how you deal with these everyday problems—dealing with delays, communicating setbacks, appeasing an angry customer—that can set you apart.

Apart from inherent task-related problems in a job, there are bosses to deal with, pay issues—the sting when you find out someone doing a similar job to you is paid more—or times when a staff vacancy means that you're literally doing two jobs at once. Some things you can attempt to change directly: you can ask for a salary increase giving reasons why you believe it should be awarded or you can suggest a temp be employed until a permanent solution is found. And while you can't change personalities or, without quitting, job location, you might be able to alter dynamics and small things within your control.

The domino effect

Small changes can bring about big changes, as consultant David Dibble describes in his book *The New Agreements in the Workplace*. He tells of a visit to a software company in trouble. The warehousing and shipping area was in turmoil, with rubbish lying around. The employees explained they'd asked for garbage bins for two years but no one listened. Dibble took the matter in his own hands and purchased $69-worth of bins. While it was a small action, it had a big effect on morale and within months the warehousing section was redesigned, repainted and efficiency had soared.

Relationships

When faced with a frustrating or even hurtful relationship at work it helps to remember that relationships take two. They are also the result of a subtle combination of dynamics, personality and circumstance. If you are able to change your 50 per cent input to a relationship, you'll see a change in the relationship as a whole.

Research by the Canadian Policy Research Network's JobQuality.ca has revealed that, in Canada at least, it's in the education sector that relationships with a supervisor are more likely to be good. Health care and social assistance are the industries where workers are least likely to say they have a good relationship with their supervisor. Not surprisingly, workers who do not get along with their boss are less satisfied with their job, less motivated, and more likely to quit and seek work elsewhere.

Beating boredom

When initiative and creativity are crushed to the extent that you give up, that's a breeding ground for depression. Especially in a large organization, a repressed sense of self-expression and a feeling that your talents are not used can be the price you pay for job security and the perks that go with the job.

In his *How to Stop Worrying and Start Living*, first published in 1953, Dale Carnegie describes how a stenographer made her work more interesting by setting herself the goal of beating her own records of filling out oil lease forms. She counted how many she'd filled in before lunch and aimed to surpass that in the afternoon, and then to beat the previous day's number the next day. 'Result?' asks Carnegie. Neither promotion, praise, thanks nor increased pay, but 'it did help to prevent the fatigue that is spawned by boredom.' The anecdote has an old-fashioned ring to it—in today's more 'go-getting' world, you can't help thinking maybe she should have tried to get a more interesting job! But there's also a ring of truth about it: sometimes, when you at least aim to give a job your best, you find it more interesting.

Do your best

'If a job's worth doing, it's worth doing well', you may have been told as a child. This ideal is common to a wide range of philosophical and religious thinking: the Protestant work ethic, the Buddhist ideal of mindfulness—paying attention to the task at hand with all your mind—and teachings of the lesser known Toltecs (from the ancient city of Teotihuacan, near Mexico City).

Always doing your best, whether you are a checkout assistant or art gallery manager, gives you pride in your work, fuels a desire to constantly improve and find interest in your work, and can often open up opportunities.

STARTING THE CHANGE PROCESS

When you want to bring about change at work there are a few steps you can take to get things moving.

- Help yourself. Whatever is in your control, you can change. It may only be small things like improving your own work environment, asking for some help in research or reviewing 'the way we do things' in a system that's part of your job, but it can all help.
- Timing. Sometimes it is best to do nothing, but simply observe and see how things unravel. During this time, documenting a problem—whether it's the cumulative hours of wasted time an old computer system causes you or the times a superior humiliates you in meetings—can help you grasp the true extent of the problem. It can also provide you with hard facts to back up your case later on.
- Change the view. Changing the way you look at a problem can sometimes help, as can talking it over with colleagues. Do they also perceive certain behaviour as a problem? How do they deal with the fact they're expected to be at breakfast meetings (maybe they've found an acceptable way of saying no)?
- Out in the open. Where possible, keep confrontations low key and as pleasant as possible. Avoid entering into them when you're feeling angry.
- Step into others' shoes. Trying to understand someone else's behaviour or a certain situation can help you feel more positive about it. Step back and try to work out if it is a particular set of circumstances that triggers offensive behaviour. Is there a way of avoiding the triggers?
- Offer solutions. If when you discuss the problem with your boss or your team you also present them with a solution, you've turned a potential conflict into something positive.

Handling the information workload

The technology of communication at the office threatens to turn into a torrent: phone calls to your land line, mobile phone, emails, faxes, voice mail, inter-office memos, pagers...let alone the morning post. You are bombarded with facts, reports, surveys, announcements and invitations. There is more to respond to, more contacts to keep up with, more information to digest. How do you stem the flow?

- The ground rules have changed. First, you have to acknowledge that information availability and communication accessibility have changed dramatically over a matter of decades. Data is available all too easily, so the survival skill becomes not that of seeking information, but rather discerning between useful and useless information. You need to know when to read further and when to move on.

- Fine-tune your filters. Make sure you are giving your time to what matters in your job, not getting swamped by details you don't need now. The form a filter takes depends on what the problem is: a freelance journalist who receives a mailbox of mostly irrelevant correspondence might open mail at the post office and throw away the unwanted stuff straight away. Message systems let you return calls when it suits rather than be interrupted throughout the day. You can read your emails at set times of the day rather than being distracted from other work.

- Perfect your planning. Planning ahead, anticipating problems or flagging 'think about' scenarios, identifying what information you need and being proactive about getting it will get your job done better.

- Refine your research. Be precise about what you need, and creative and thorough about finding it.

- Organize better. Create systems, tracking tools and checklists for complex tasks so the routine aspects go smoothly, leaving you more time to handle obstacles and unexpected problems as they arise.

GETTING MORE FROM YOUR JOB

In a scene from the Australian Broadcasting Corporation's television drama 'SeaChange', magistrate Laura is called on to find community work as a punishment for Dan's fishing without a licence. Knowing that he'll find pleasure in anything that's out of doors, she sets him the task of filing an unfathomable mountain of documents in her office. To her dismay, he sets to the task with bulldog tenacity, coming up with the perfect, cross-referenced system in alphabetical order. 'You actually enjoyed that! Didn't you?' snarls Laura in defeat.

Clearly Dan has an ability to throw himself into any situation and take pleasure in small victories. How can you implement this technique in your work?

- Be clear about what you are not satisfied with in your job.
- Ask for more responsibility.
- Ask for other tasks.
- Think of ways of making your workplace more enjoyable.
- Learn new skills.
- Take an active role in meetings and in the decision-making process.
- Steer clear of sticky situations that could end up embroiling you in office politics.
- Always behave ethically. Don't blame others for your mistakes; Don't take credit for others' successes.

Helpful habits

Commonsense practices help you to make the most of your time in the office. Making them part of your daily routine is even better.

- Give yourself five minutes at the beginning and end of each working day to take stock and plan.
- When attacking the tasks that need a clear head, clear some desk space too—leave on your desk only the documents you need for that task.
- Deal with tasks in order of importance.
- Learn to delegate.

Beatrice Wood (1893–1998)

Beatrice Wood was born in San Francisco. Her adventurous spirit took her to Paris in her late teens, where she enjoyed the company of surreal artists such as Marcel Duchamp and Man Ray and acted in the Comédie Française. She discovered ceramics when aged 40 after buying six lustre-glazed plates and wanting a teapot to match. Beatrice enrolled in pottery classes and was soon hooked.

In her autobiography, *I Shocked Myself*, she describes how she learnt the hard way about running her own ceramics business. Her first profits were wiped out by a fine for not having a social security number and Board of Equalization permit. When she delivered goods to a store she was stunned to be asked for an invoice. Beatrice soon realized she'd have to change 'from a dreamy girl into a business-minded person, meticulous and accurate'.

Businesswoman she became, and an acclaimed ceramicist too, admired for her lustre glazes, footed bowls, chalices and mischievous figurines. She was awarded numerous honours—including being made a living treasure of California in 1983—took part in hundreds of exhibitions and continued to work until shortly before her death. The American Craft Museum in New York planned to honour her 100th birthday with a tribute exhibition but, as it was delayed, she had to wait for her 104th. The curator thanked her for her patience and stamina—as well as her longevity.

WORKING SMARTER

Being busy is not necessarily being productive. If you suspect you could be working more efficiently and leaving work on time a few evenings a week, take a look at your work practices. If you discover invoices are being paid the old-fashioned time-consuming way, simply because 'this is how we've always done it', maybe it's time to get up to date. Reviewing systems can be very rewarding if everyone involved is enthusiastic and determined to find a better way. There are many other ways of working smarter.

Structure the day to suit

If you think best in the morning and tend to get interrupted all afternoon, plan to do the work that requires most concentration—whether it's finishing a report or coming up with new ideas—before lunch. If you suffer an energy-low mid afternoon, make this the time to return calls or catch up on filing.

Plan

Planning is an essential part of all work, whether it's planning a circus act or the launch of a new washing machine. Diaries, timetables, schedules, tracking systems and lists can help to avoid delays and disasters, and help you meet deadlines and expectations.

Don't panic—focus

The bigger the task and the tighter the time, the more honed your focus needs to be. This rarely means simply working longer hours; in fact, there are times when this will be counterproductive. Instead it means giving 100 per cent of your attention to the key tasks in hand and not letting yourself be distracted by less important issues.

Making the most of meetings

'He's in a meeting' is the common catchcry at work. While meetings are essential to exchange ideas, communicate information, discuss options and come to an agreement, rambling, unfocused meetings can really be frustrating. They eat into the day, making it harder to achieve the work you'd like to, and can be energy draining. Rules can help refocus and make meetings productive again. Consider:

- A time limit. Not only does this keep people on the ball and moving through the agenda, it also eases that sense of frustration people experience when they don't know when they're going to get out. If lively discussion or unexpected news means time blows out, agree whether to continue for another half-hour or arrange a follow up.
- A goal. What is the main aim of the meeting?

- Action. Some people swear by minutes. Others prefer an agreed action plan, brief and to the point. Speed things up by writing it during the meeting, photocopying it and distributing it right away.
- Best time. If a meeting's more administrative than creative, schedule it for the afternoon, rather than take up everyone's most productive, pre-lunch time (if you agree on when you all feel lowest, that is).

Crunch time

Many people find that when working hours are radically reduced, their efficiency reaches for the stars: their determination to finish a task before the day's end makes it happen. With extra focus, you find you work faster and more productively. The pressure of less time makes it easier to prioritize and delegate—because you have to. Somehow, again, because you have to, you often find your organizational skills soar.

The office move

In order to combat the negative physical effects of sitting at a desk all day, try the following:

- Stretch every hour or so by reaching your arms up over your head and to the side.
- Take a walk at lunchtime or do an exercise or yoga class.
- Use the stairs whenever possible and get off your chair every now and then to file, fetch a glass of water or drop a report in to a colleague.
- Move your legs and feet frequently.

A HEALTHY WORKING LIFE

'It is not work that kills, but worry', states the English proverb. Unfortunately, it's not true. According to the ILO two million adults die every year from occupational accidents and work-related diseases. Added to that, there are 270 million occupational accidents every year and 160 million workers with occupational diseases. In Australia, 16 per cent of all deaths between 1989 and 1992 were because of work-related accidents.

RISKY BUSINESS

In his book *Working People Talk About What They Do All Day and How They Feel About What They Do*, American writer Studs Terkel makes no bones about the price we pay for work and the wages it brings: 'This book, being about work, is, by its very nature, about violence,' he says. This includes violence to the spirit as well as to the body, ulcers, accidents, shouting matches, fist fights, nervous breakdowns and daily humiliation. Just how risky is work and what are the most dangerous occupations in this risky business?

For the office worker, one of the greatest threats to health is simply the sedentary nature of the job. In the short term this can mean backache, joint pain, neck strain, and so on. In the longer term, if you don't make up for a sedentary job by moving at other times of the day, you are at an increased risk of developing many of the health problems associated with lack of exercise. That list is growing, but currently includes heart disease, diabetes and obesity.

The big outdoors is where danger lurks for the world's workers. Farming, fishing and forestry are among the most dangerous occupations; commercial pilots are up there too, so to speak, topping the most dangerous occupations list in Australia and in the top ten of many other countries.

Farmers are exposed to mechanical and chemical risks as well as unpredictable weather. Machinery such as tractors can roll over on operators; farm equipment may catch loose clothing or long hair. Crop and manure storage can create toxic gases and there are pesticides to deal with too.

In the United States, the fishing fatality rate was sixteen times higher than for fire fighting or police work, and 40 times higher than the national average. It's a similar picture in Britain, where trawler men are reported to be 50 times more likely to have a fatal accident at work than the average worker. As well as bad weather, the hazards they face include running aground, collisions and falling overboard while hauling in nets.

According to US figures, workers most at risk from homicide are those that work at night, work alone, and handle money. This makes taxicab drivers most susceptible, with a homicide risk ten times the average. Police and guards also have a higher than average risk.

When you look at non-fatal injuries, it's overexertion that's the problem: lifting objects or, in the case of nursing aides, moving patients. Training in good lifting techniques could help here.

A third of work-related accidents in Australia happen on public roads and one-fifth occur on farms.

However, possibly the riskiest occupation is that of elephant trainer. It's a small work force, with only an estimated 600 trainers in the United States. But with two fatalities occurring in some years, this represents a rate of 333 per 100,000—68 times the national average.

STRESS

Injuries and fatalities aside, according to research by UK private health fund BUPA, the biggest health problem in the workplace after back pain is stress. It affects an estimated five million workers in the United Kingdom alone. While stress is hard to define—and combatting it may call for different action in different workplaces—it is among the top causes of long-term sick leave for UK employers. The ILO estimates that stress is the reason for more than half of all lost working days in Europe.

Taking a big picture approach, stress at work—like stress generally—has to do with feeling out of control. There are some factors that are particularly likely to cause stress:

● Deadlines. When a job has to be done by a certain time, it puts the pressure on like nothing else.

- Work overload. Too much work, especially when it is categorically unmanageable, leads to enormous stress. In an era of cost cuts and downsizing, work overload can reflect a lack of resources.
- Long hours. A survey by social policy researchers CPRN's JobQuality.ca found a direct correlation between hours worked and the feeling of being stressed. The self-employed male working more than 50 hours a week was the most likely to cite demands and hours as a source of work stress. Conversely, women were more likely to feel the stress of long hours in employment rather than self-employment, but this could reflect the move to self-employment as a way for women to achieve flexibility and a balance of family and work commitments.
- Nature of the work. Some people find the very core of their job has emotional aspects that are very demanding—teaching, for instance. Research from Canada found 50 per cent of professionals and managers said they were stressed by long

---

Top ten work stressors for management

The Net Futures Institute of the United States surveyed 600 executives and managers about the stressful aspects of their jobs. It found that the top ten stressors were:

1 Deadlines
2 Budget constraints
3 Financial stress/earnings
4 Constant change
5 Email overload
6 Poor organizational communication
7 Impact of layoffs and reduced staff
8 Pressure from upper management in terms of performance expectations
9 Urgent but unimportant tasks
10 Conflicts with co-workers.

hours or work demands compared with 35 per cent of clerical staff—the Canadian national average for any job—and 28 per cent of blue-collar workers.

- Boredom. Mind-numbingly boring jobs, with little opportunity for social contact, initiative or stimulation, cause stress.

- Technostress. The tyranny of technology allows communication to flow at an unmanageable level. In addition, once you rely on computers in soft and hardware forms, the effect of a crash or even slow response time coupled with a deadline is stressful. According to a survey, which labelled the problem 'brownout' as opposed to blackout, 70 per cent of network managers suffer from BOSS (brownout stress syndrome). This occurs because the brownout removes the employees' sense of control and reduces their freedom to make decisions.

- Fly in, fly out. Research from the Edith Cowan University in Perth, Western Australia, released in 2002, showed that families who deal with the 'fly to work, work for an extended period, fly back home for a rest' scenario faced increased domestic stress. The pattern, common in mining jobs, was particularly disruptive for mothers, who reported communication problems and isolation. The good news is that children seemed unaffected.

Signs of stress

There are several signs that all may not be well at work.

- Heavy drinking. Alcohol is used as a quick way to relax and masks the adrenaline produced by stress. But it's no long-term answer.

- Skipping meals. Too busy for lunch? No energy to cook a meal in the evening? Tucking into biscuits and chocolate for comfort? Good nutrition is something you can do for yourself. It will also give you increased energy and a stronger immune system.

- Insomnia. Stress can disturb sleeping patterns, making it harder to get to sleep and preventing deep, refreshing sleep.

- Too tired to exercise. Just when you need the benefits of exercise—it can invigorate as well as help keep you in tip-top health—you feel too lethargic.

- Irritability. Stress can send your sense of humour packing as well as make you more irritable and anxious.

If you recognize one or more of these symptoms in your own behaviour you should refer to Chapter 2 for ways to break the cycle, reduce stress and keep your mental health in trim.

THE BALANCING ACT

Once work was life and life was work: tending animals, fetching water and fuel, or mending clothes. They were inter-linked so closely that we didn't think of balancing work with leisure—holidays were special because any time off work or with the family was rare. If the children were old enough they helped out; if they were too young, they played in the background. Now the catchcry is for a balance between life and work. And figures like ones from the American Medical Association which state that 28 per cent of executives die within 24 to 30 months of their retirement because they have suffered burnout seem to prove that something's wrong. Too much work and not enough 'other' is one way of looking at it.

Another argument runs that balance is an illusory pursuit. Adult education and training expert Sandra Kerka writes in a US Department of Education digest, 'balance implies either/or'—investing in one role requires taking from another. Yet, she argues, 'creative people use their brains and deploy their gifts whenever and wherever they feel the urge.' Integration is what we should be seeking, she says, 'the happy confluence and merging of all the activities in our lives'. It sounds perfect but may be hard to achieve. The standard office job—unlike manual farm work, for example—is sedentary, and if you are to remain healthy you need to balance that fact with exercise in another segment of your life. If you walk a substantial distance to work, you will have integrated the two successfully, but this is often not possible.

The idea of integration is echoed in psychologist Mihaly Csikszentmihalyi's book *Flow*. In a chapter on work, he describes a number of people who have achieved what he calls 'autotelic' work—or flow in their work. Their lives, work and personalities are intertwined in a fulfilled and happy way so that they barely delineate between work and leisure. One of his examples is a hard-working 76 year old, Serafina. She lives in an Italian Alpine village and rises at 5 am to milk her cows. She cleans the house after cooking breakfast then, depending on the season, takes the herd to the meadows, tends her orchards or cards wool. Alternatively she cuts hay and carries the bales back to the barn on her head. While this is her work, these are also her favourite activities. Csikszentmihalyi believes many of us can learn from people like Serafina. Any job can, in theory, be made more enjoyable—and therefore less of a problem to balance. It's partly about turning it into a sort of game where possible, and partly about incorporating flexible challenges, immediate feedback and variety.

Maybe it's not a question of either balance or integration but of vocabulary: 'balance' has a myriad meanings. To the upwardly mobile executive who's not sure he likes the direction his work is taking him, it might mean less golf with visiting clients and more time messing around in boats with mates he's losing touch with. To a factory worker with irregular shifts at unsociable hours, a balance of work and leisure would be a luxury. All she wants is some ordinary time with her family—a couple of days a week—even some sort of predictability would be a step forward.

Whatever the reason, many people agree that the life–work balance has got out of kilter. In 2003, 68 per cent of executives and managers surveyed in the United States by NFI Research said the work–life situation of people in business was unbalanced. 'More and more people feel they have to make a choice between their job and their family,' said one respondent. Aaron Ross, chairman of a UK organization called the Work Life Balance Trust, explains the source of tension: 'Britain needs to move away from a workplace designed in the 19th century, when most workers had a home-support system based on family and neighbours.'

Whether you subscribe to the balance, integration, or plain survival school, many people seem to feel that managing life and the constraints of earning a living seems to have got harder. There are several key issues that most people consider when faced with questions of 'balance'.

VOX POP: Do you think work is something you need to keep in balance with other aspects of your life?

'Balance work with non-work. Don't just live for work or your life will stop when work does—be it through retirement or ill health.' TS

'A full-time job really eats into the week. Without other interests, there is little to life. My work is not my life, nor who I am.' HB

'I'm a painter with a home studio—so family life can encroach on my work. There's always so much to do around the house. But I've worked out that for each painting I need one hour of painting to two hours of looking, so I cover a canvas as quickly as I can while I've got the enthusiasm then move on to the next one. That pattern seems to fit in with home life too.' MW

'My children get heaps of my time and attention as I only work when they are at school or day care, and that's not full-time. So the family–work balance is fine. But when work mounts up, it's the creative pursuits that go. And I miss out on extra exercise like morning stretches or runs because I'm trying to grab scraps of time while the children are asleep.' AH

'My job means I travel every week. I'm upset that I can't do ordinary things like join other friends on a Friday for a coffee. I wanted to play hockey this winter but I've not had one Wednesday night at home. Also I miss out on thinking time, and time to get out my patchwork fabrics.' MH

Family

Do both parents try to work while they have young children or even older children (who may need ferrying around)? Does one work part-time or freelance and take on the role of Mr or Mrs Flexible, covering in times of sickness and school holidays?

If they choose to continue to work mothers often report preferring part-time work, and some social research seems to support this as a good option for children too. One study in Britain found a link between full-time work for mothers with preschoolers and the children's later success. The study, funded by the Joseph Rowntree Foundation, followed the fortunes of more than 1200 people born in the 1970s and, interestingly, compared siblings. It

Tell the children

Ellen Galinsky, president of the US-based Families and Work Institute, a non-profit research centre, spent fifteen years researching and writing her book *Ask the Children: The Breakthrough Study That Reveals How to Succeed at Work and Parenting*. The book is brimming with comments from children with working parents ('Work if you want to work,' said an eleven-year-old girl); tips about communicating better with children (such as ways to help them think beyond the here and now); and statistics comparing how non-working and working parents spend time with their children (in some cases, very similarly).

Galinksy recommends that you teach your children about the world of work by:

- arranging an office visit
- telling them about your work, how your working day's been and lessons you've learnt
- letting them play out work scenarios, whether as a pilot, chef or personal assistant
- taking the time to explain the full spectrum of reasons you work, not just the financial ones.

found, among other things, that children with mothers who worked full-time for longer periods (2.5 years compared to 1.5 years) during their early years were less likely to achieve A-level qualifications. They were also more likely to be unemployed and more likely to experience psychological stress.

Health

When long hours or a physically demanding job start to impinge on health it's time to rethink the way you earn money. The stress of setting up new businesses and schemes may be stimulating, but some people decide they've had enough.

In 2003 almost half the respondents in a survey of News Limited staff across Australia said their workload was damaging their health and wellbeing. More than half said the pressure of work was disturbing their sleep and leading to regular headaches; more than a third said the workload meant they were chronically irritable. They also felt pressured to work when ill: 55 per cent said they felt pressure from management, while 22 per cent said they pressured themselves. Half the work force took work home and three-quarters worked an extra 7.6 hours on top of the standard 38-hour week.

Romance

Couples who both work long hours may find the romance squeezed out of their lives. It takes time to keep in touch, even when you live together. In an Australian Job Futures/Saulwick study released in 2003, which surveyed 1000 men and women, 33 per cent of women said the sheer effort of work and the stress involved with it left them uninterested in sex. The male libido is not so easily crushed by overwork—only 13 per cent of the men reported a similar decline.

Work away from work

Work doesn't stop when you leave the office, factory or store. There's the work at home too: the house to clean and the chores to see to. With less family support, it's harder to get it all done.

DOWNSHIFTING

One way people find a better balance is by 'downshifting'—also called voluntary simplicity, old-fashioned economizing or simply 'getting a life'. It's a trend seen in developed countries such as the United States, the United Kingdom and Australia, where those with enough have decided they don't need any more and perhaps can even survive on a little less. While this may leave them with less cash, it gives them more of that other precious commodity: time.

'Slowing down', 'getting out of the rat race' are all part of the vocabulary. So too are values—a decrease in the perceived value of money and possessions, and an increased value placed on time, health and peace of mind. Often the idea of downshifting goes hand in hand with ideas of sustainability and self-sufficiency and a healthier lifestyle.

A study released in 2003 by think tank The Australia Institute, *Downshifting in Australia, A Sea-Change in the Pursuit of Happiness*, labelled those that sought a lifestyle change 'sea-changers' after the popular ABC television drama 'SeaChange'. This program centred on a corporate lawyer and high-flier who turned her back on city life when her marriage fell apart. The researchers found that 23 per cent of Australians had in the last ten years voluntarily made a long-term change in lifestyle that resulted in earning less money. An additional group of people opted to earn less when returning to study or starting their own business. A US survey reflected similar figures, showing that almost 1 in 5 adult Americans have at some point in their lives made the decision to reduce income and consumption and manage on less.

The downshifters say they are pursuing balance, fulfilment and—the most important reason—more time with their families. Those on low incomes are more likely to be seeking a healthier lifestyle, whereas those on a higher income state personal fulfilment as a major reason. Some make the change following severe illness, the death of someone close, a marriage breakdown or a prolonged period of self-questioning.

Advances in technology can help you downshift as long as you remain in control. If you don't, you could find yourself working longer hours than before as laptops, networks, faxes and emails make it possible, in theory, to work anywhere with communication lines at any time of the day or night.

People downshift in a variety of ways. Some of the options include:

- Reduce working hours (this is the most popular means).
- Take a reduction in perks to work less and spend less.
- Change career to a lower paying one (this route is more popular with men than women).
- Stop paid work altogether (women are more likely than men to do this).
- Get away from it all and chase a dream—whether it's a hobby farm, running a pub or selling their own ceramics.
- Change to a less demanding job.
- Take a sabbatical. Taking a year out of the rat race, maybe moving overseas, to the country, taking a voluntary post and living off savings. There are short-term ways to downshift that can enrich your mainstream activities too.
- Selling up. For example, in the United Kingdom a house in the capital city might be worth five times more than a similar place in a different county away from the commuter belt. People have the option of selling the London house, buying a delightful house a few hundred miles away and then using the difference to 'upshift' their lifestyle.

Do downshifters feel the pinch? The Australian study showed a small proportion of downshifters regret the change—less than 1 in 10. Around a third are quite happy, thank you, and don't even miss the money. But for some (around 15 per cent), the loss of income is felt very hard even though they still describe themselves as happy; while the highest proportion—a little over a third—say they're happy but, yes, they miss the money.

Allowing employees to downshift can be of benefit to employers too if a UK Department for Education and Employment survey is to be believed. Conducted by the Institute of Employment Studies (IES) in 1999, it found that allowing workers to downshift their hours:

The freelancer's safety net

Going freelance can be one way of controlling your own working hours and environment, although feast or famine is often the freelancer's lot and managing the workload can be difficult. It's hard to say no, so if you are lucky enough to get lots of work offers, you may find yourself with too much on your plate. On the other hand, you might have a few months of minimal income. Being prepared is half the battle. If at all possible:

- Set aside six months' living expenses
- Explore different ways of earning a living
- Make a detailed plan of attack
- Get your financial records straight from day one and see an accountant if in doubt about tax and other administrative details.

- reduced casual sickness absences
- made employees more honest about absences
- improved staff retention
- made employees more productive
- attracted more job recruits
- improved morale and commitment.

The options offered by employers ranged from flexible hours, part-time work, job sharing, and emergency flexibility to home working and tele-working arrangements. There was also an easy transition from full-time to part-time and back to full-time work.

THINKING OF DOWNSHIFTING?

Are you tempted to reduce your working hours but not sure how you'd manage? A successful downshift needs some research. There are several key areas you will need to consider.

Your spending

How much do you live on now? What proportion of that is basic living expenses and what part luxury or discernible? Where are your major expenses? How much of that is tied to your job? Where could you save if you put your mind to it? Is the money you have working for you as hard as it could? A detailed look at the financial side of life could highlight a range of areas where you could cut back without sacrifice. You might save money in the long run by buying fruit and vegetables from a large market or growing your own rather than shopping at the corner store. You could make your money work harder by shifting your savings from a low interest account to a higher interest Internet account.

Your work

How do you feel about your work? What sort of a kick do you get out of it? Does it stretch you too much or too little? In what ways does work make it harder to find balance in your life? What are your options for cutting back your hours? Would your current employer consider a part-time position for you? Is there another role in the organization you'd be happy with but that you feel would not spread into your personal life the way your current job does?

Do you have a realistic business idea or one you'd like to explore? What are your passions? Do you have interests that could involve earning opportunities too, albeit at a lower rate than you've been used to?

Your lifestyle

Explore your options. Do you secretly nurture a desire to make a radical change but need to think out some sort of safety net, or is what you're thinking about more along the lines of making small changes—like going interstate for a camping holiday instead of an overseas trip? Are you prepared to spend less on smart clothes, eating out, the supermarket bill…?

Your skills

Other downshifting talents that might be called on include bartering (there may be a barter scheme in your area where people can swap babysitting for carpentry or apples for oranges), budgeting, basic DIY, kitchen gardening and home cooking.

CHANGING CAREERS

The teacher turned human resources consultant, the salesperson turned winemaker, or the ambulance officer turned translator… changing careers is at times in answer to a necessity, at others a happy brush with chance. The demands of a young family may mean the shift work associated with being an ambulance officer is too inconvenient, while the person selling wine may uncover a deep interest in it, decide to study winemaking, then find she has a real talent for it.

Changing careers is more common than it used to be, and career management—whether you stay in the same environment or move around—falls largely to the individual. The days of working your way up the company career ladder are all but gone.

When you want or need a career change, how can you go about it? It is certainly a decision that requires much soul searching.

Direction

Where do you want your career to go? First think high: what would you do if there was nothing to stop you? Then think low: what are the obvious jobs open to you? Which aspects of various work have you enjoyed and which have got you down? Richard N Bolles, author of the best-selling *What Color Is Your Parachute?*, says almost half—45 per cent—of Americans say they would change their career if they could. One way to explore new areas would be to consider your interests and see what job opportunities you can identify there.

Skills

What are your working skills? Take time to create a long list of your qualifications, the skills you've developed and used at work, and the various jobs you've held—whether a stint at door-to-door selling as a student or assistant manager at an oil company. Some of these skills will be transferable to other fields.

Learning

Where would new skills or qualifications take you? Could a course in bee- or bookkeeping open new doors for you? Do you feel slightly defensive about your computer skills or has working for a poorly resourced organization meant you've become out of date with the latest software in your industry?

Research

Finding out about your own industry—whether it's publishing or prison management—and others you might be interested in gives you information to work with. What are the employment trends? Which skills are in short supply? Who are the main operators? What are the pay levels? You may say you are fed up with working with computers and want to work in the arts but are you prepared for the often-low pay? Research takes many forms—hunts in the library, on the Internet, keeping an eye or ear out when reading the newspaper or listening to the radio, talking to as many people as you can—each method brings a different quality of information.

Take stock

Taking stock of your work situation involves looking objectively at your past and present then stepping back while you consider the future. How do you feel about work? What hopes and ambitions are you nurturing? Ask yourself the following:

- How well do my skills, values and job match?
- Which of my skills do I value most and take the most pride in?
- What are my strengths and weaknesses?
- What sort of work culture do I thrive in?
- What fields do I find fascinating?

A trio of working skills

One way of looking at skills is to think of them in three groups: data, people and things. Within each group is a range of skills: from recording to analyzing data; serving, supervising or mentoring people to handling things and setting up systems.

The advantage of late starts

According to research published in 2003 by the US-based Personality and Social Psychology Bulletin, it may not be such a bad thing to achieve later on in life. A study of early achievers—those who were acclaimed young—in the field of politics, science and literature found that early success was linked with early death. The study, by Professor Stewart McCann, a psychology researcher at University College of Cape Bretonin Nova Scotia, Canada, analyzed the lives of 1672 male US state governors who had died before 1978.

Other research has found a distinct correlation between the age of receiving a PhD and the length of life: the earlier the doctorate, the shorter the life. A small study of women who won an Academy Award for Best Supporting Actress also supports the idea that early success may lead to a shorter life. While no explanation has been found, speculation focuses on a few theories.

- Strains, challenges and obligations accompanying outstanding achievements may accelerate physical and mental declines in some people, which could lead to premature death.
- Early achievers may have tendencies towards unhealthy behaviour.
- People who peak early on in life may become less motivated to stay successful and healthy.

- Is my work challenging?
- Are there other areas of the organization I could move to?

Side stepping

There are many kinds of career changes. Some involve side stepping to a new occupation in the same field: from nurse to doctor, dancer to choreographer, bricklayer to building consultant. Another side step takes you to the same occupation in a different field: hospital cook to restaurant chef or taxi driver to chauffeur. Finding a brand new occupation in a brand new field is the most difficult type of change to pull off. Instead, aim for a series of stepping stones along the path, by changing either your occupation or your field as you progress. For example, a salesman in radio who wants to become a reporter in environmental issues could attempt the path of salesman in environmental issues (using selling skills to find sponsors perhaps) to reporter in environmental issues, or reporter in radio (with perhaps some volunteer radio experience along the way) to reporter in environmental issues. Clearly, there would be many skills to learn and no guarantee of easy success, but it's a more likely way to switch than straight from one job to another.

LOOKING FOR WORK

There are always jobs out there. (People get injured, or sick, quit, retire or die.)
RICHARD NELSON BOLLES, *WHAT COLOR IS YOUR PARACHUTE?* (1972)

Whether we've just emerged newly qualified from a course of study, are seeking a career change or have just lost a job, at some time the mature adult needs to find employment. According to Bolles, we find ourselves on the job trail on average eight times in our lives. The way things are moving, that figure looks like it will increase; in which case, you'd better keep your job-hunting skills well honed.

FIRST FIND THAT VACANCY

There are two main ways of identifying potential jobs. One involves identifying places you know have vacancies, that is, that have let it be known by advertisements. The other is to identify places you'd like to work and approach them—a surprisingly successful way of getting a job, as it saves companies the hassle of advertising or going through a recruitment agency.

Research published in 2001, using data from the British Household Panel Survey, scrutinized the success rate of various methods of securing a job. Applying directly to an employer was the most successful strategy, while replying to advertisements and using government and other employment agencies was the most common method. It also confirmed that the more methods you use to look for a job, the greater your chances of finding one. The persistent bird may also catch the worm: in areas of higher unemployment and for those who have been unemployed longer, the intensity of searching decreases. Other methods of identifying potential jobs include:

- Network. Let everyone you know that you're looking for work. Spread the word by contacting former bosses, colleagues, family friends and professional acquaintances.
- Read job advertisements. Scan the newspapers and specialized press every day.
- Use the Internet. The Internet is a useful tool, but don't let it run your search. Explore web-based recruitment opportunities such as ones where you can set up a profile and receive information about vacancies in the fields you nominate; look at corporate sites, both as part of research about a company and to view its vacancies. Some sites allow you to post a résumé for companies to consider; many will allow you to apply for a position by email and send an already prepared résumé.

Job matching for 'abled' and 'less-abled'
According to the US National Center on Workforce and Disability, looking for a job when you are disabled is no different from the rest of the population. You need to have a clear idea of the type of work you want to pursue, consider what type of environment suits you best, and use your personal and professional network as part of your job-seeking strategy. 'Job matching' is the phrase used to refer to fitting a job environment and description to the individual in terms of interests, support needs, personality and skills.

- Get out and about. You never know when you might meet someone or see something that leads to that perfect job. If nothing else, getting out and about in the real world can open up your ideas.
- Meet face to face with employers. Setting up informal meetings over a coffee is a great way to obtain valuable information about what's going on in the market.
- Be flexible. If your job-seeking methods are not working, you may need to change your tactics. It pays to look for different kinds of work: part-time, contract, filling in for maternity leave, and so on. Even if these are not ideal, you never know where they might lead. Gaining more experience in the right direction will also help you the next time you're job hunting.
- Be persistent. The more hours you put into job hunting and the more methods you use, the more likely you are to find work.
- Take it seriously. Treating job hunting like a full-time job will speed up the time it takes to find a new position. Give the search structure by developing a routine and make a point of calling contacts on a regular basis.
- Think small as well as big. With research, you may be able to identify small companies within your field as well as larger ones.
- Telephone talk. Directly talking to someone in the hiring position can help—some US job-hunting programs recommend calling 200 potential employers a day. In some lines of work you'd be hard pushed to keep up that frequency or even achieve it! Working out and even writing down what you are going to say can help you to sound professional. How do you plan to introduce yourself? Remember to name the colleague who suggested you call. Perhaps include an open-ended suggestion such as calling in for a coffee or sending in your résumé. Prepare one sentence that describes you and highlights your best relevant skill—it will help to reduce the 'ums' and 'ers'.
- Plan B. While working on plan A, have in your mind plans B, C and D. If you have plenty of job-seeking ideas up your sleeve you are less likely to find yourself psychologically relying on the one application or the one industry.

WHEN YOU FIND A VACANCY

You've identified a job vacancy that suits, whether it's a great career move or has the perfect hours for your current situation. How can you increase your odds of securing it?

The application: quality counts

Your chances of success are enhanced if you spend more time on fewer applications. Treat each application as if you really want the job but at the same time resolve not to be devastated by rejection. A good application increases your chance of employment, whereas a shoddily put-together one is a waste of time.

Research

Pre-application research is as important as pre-interview investigation. Be sure to look at the company website; dig out any annual reports; scan newspapers for relevant stories; talk to former employees if possible; find out who the clients are and who the major players in the industry are. If feasible, deliver your application by hand; it will give you an idea of the feel of a place and the people who work there.

Show; don't tell

Wherever possible, you need to give evidence of your skills and work record. This could be in the form of a report you've written, graphics you've produced, or sales figures you've improved. Coupled with this is the 'evidence principle': give at least three points of evidence to prove any skills you claim.

The résumé (curriculum vitae)

There are many different approaches to résumés. For advice approach a careers advisory service or read up on ways to prepare one. Whatever personal style you opt for, a résumé should be:

- succinct
- easy to read and understand
- relevant to the job
- up to date.

It should also look impeccable. For many employers, looking at résumés is a screening method so don't give them any reason to throw yours straight in the 'no' pile. Make it look as good as you can and do the obvious: run it through a spell check; make sure you have all your contact details; and, if your grammar is dodgy, get a friend to check it for you.

The covering letter

A letter to accompany an application or résumé should be short and to the point. It should address the requirements of the job if you are responding to an advertisement, and point out your most relevant qualifications and experience. Highlighting 'soft skills'—such as experience in negotiation, counselling or presentation—may give you the edge over someone with similar qualifications.

The interview

Interviews can take the form of a seemingly relaxed chat over a cup of coffee, being faced with a panel of interviewers, taking competency or personality tests, or being thrown 'killer questions' for shock value. Proper preparation will help to quell your nerves and give you the sense that you've done all that's possible.

On the day of the interview, plan to arrive early and leave lots of margin for delay if you are travelling far. It's not always necessary to get your best suit out for a job interview—appropriate dress is the key, although it's better to be over- than under-dressed for an interview. Making sure you look clean and tidy and don't smell of garlic or alcohol is a start.

The more you know about a company, the better you'll come across, so have some questions ready to ask your interviewer that show you've done some research. You'll feel more at ease if you prepare some ready answers to standard questions and any possible tricky questions about your résumé, gaps, career U-turns, etc. Basic questions might include the following:

- Where do you see yourself in five years?
- What is your highest achievement?
- What do you know about this organization?

Location, location, location!

People have always moved for work opportunities—think of the great influx into cities during the Industrial Revolution. Does where you work still affect your earnings? The answer is maybe.

The Occupational Employment Survey of Employers—a survey of 800 jobs and earnings in almost 400 locations undertaken between 1998 and 2000 by the US Bureau of Labor (BLS)—found scientists to be the top earners, no matter where they worked. Similarly, chief executives were among the highest earners, while those who worked in food preparation and serving were the lowest. The earnings of musicians and singers varied substantially according to location—they were top earners in Denver, Colorado, Cincinnati and Ohio but in the lowest group in Kansas City, Missouri and San Jose, California. Chefs and head cooks were also variously rewarded according to location: they ranked second to bottom in earning groups nationally, but second from the top in Miami, Florida. Electricians, radio announcers, couriers and messengers were also cited as having widely varying pay levels. Some locations might demand additional duties or qualifications, explained the BLS. Other factors affecting earnings are:

- level of experience
- level of education—higher education qualifies you for higher pay and increases the likelihood of on-the-job training and promotion
- number of years on the job
- choice of industry
- skill and motivation
- complexity of tasks performed and responsibility assumed.

But before you move in search of higher earnings, take into account the idiosyncrasies of the job market there. Earnings might be higher, but openings might be fewer. The cost of living, including rent and the purchase cost of housing, could be higher. Other factors to consider include training requirements as well as intangibles like the culture of a place, the availability of activities, the weather, school system and local government, and proximity to friends and family.

- Why did you leave your last job?
- What are your strengths (and weaknesses)?
- What sort of management style do you work best with?
- Why are you applying for this job?

The interviewer might ask some 'killer' questions. These are designed to knock you off balance and give the interviewer a chance to see how you think on your feet. Take a few seconds to absorb the question. You may not feel comfortable answering it, but remember, above all, to remain courteous and calm, diplomatic and positive. Try not to show that you're panicking— even if you are!

Some possible killer questions might be:

- Would you lie to me?
- What about yourself have you never told anyone before?
- Do you think you are intelligent?
- Who would you most like to sit next to on a plane?

Follow up

Always follow up with the person who interviewed you. A brief and personal letter following your meeting is an ideal opportunity to add more weight to your case.

DEALING WITH REJECTION

The 'I regret to inform you...' letters can become disheartening and, if you're not careful, counterproductive to your job search.

Long-term unemployment can drain you of energy and enthusiasm which, in turn, keeps you trapped in a vicious cycle: when you're down, you're less likely to come across at your best in an interview. What can you do to break the cycle?

- Use your emotions. Some therapists encourage tapping into your anger—if it's there—and using it creatively to give you extra energy and persistence in your job search.
- Be useful. Give yourself the chance to feel useful in other ways. Remind yourself of ways you help others. While you have extra time on your hands, use it wisely: try to lift your fitness level or

take on a small job around the house you've been putting off, whether it's sorting the family photos or making a curtain.

- Fake enthusiasm. Practise looking and sounding like you are enthusiastic with friends and family. Sometimes the pretence can break through into real enthusiasm.
- Boost your confidence through preparation. Research the company as much as possible and prepare for an interview by going through stock questions. Have ready-made 'explanations' for aspects of your work record you feel defensive about.
- Keep trying. Make sure you investigate every possible way of getting work.
- Think laterally. Consider jobs other than the obvious ones or consider voluntary and community work as a way of keeping in touch with other people and stemming feelings of self-pity.
- Keep your options open. If you're not feeling confident enough to go self-employed yet, at least start taking notes about any opportunities you notice.
- Keep learning. Consider further education or classes for interest. ND took a course in floristry, thinking she would enjoy it now and perhaps might like to work a couple of days a week in a flower shop when she retired from her self-employed position as a marketing consultant. But when her marketing work dried up she found herself doing some work experience in a florist's one afternoon a week. After a few months, this turned into a virtually full-time job. Although the pay was a fraction of what she'd charged in marketing, and her fingers were cut and callused, she was thoroughly enjoying the challenges of learning a new business and was happy with the way things had worked out.

LIFELONG LEARNING

Lifelong skills development must become one of the central pillars of the new economy.

21ST CENTURY SKILLS FOR 21ST CENTURY JOBS, A REPORT OF THE US DEPARTMENT OF COMMERCE, US DEPARTMENT OF EDUCATION, US DEPARTMENT OF LABOR, NATIONAL INSTITUTE OF LITERACY AND THE SMALL BUSINESS ADMINISTRATION (1999)

It is generally accepted that better education brings a working life with better benefits, less unemployment and greater pay. But learning, we are increasingly told, is not something you do at school, maybe university and then stop. The concept of lifelong learning—whether it's keeping up with the graphics programs in a design job or fine-tuning public speaking skills as a CEO—is now as much a part of keeping up with work requirements as it is about retired people joining the University of the Third Age. Rather than a job for life or even one profession, people are now more likely to switch jobs frequently and have several careers. Retraining, taking professional exams, and keeping up with new trends within your field are all part of expanding your areas of expertise and knowledge.

But attaining skills is not just about qualifications. 'Soft skills'—such as the ability to work in a team, the ability to analyze and communicate information—are also increasingly valued.

Some learning opportunities are handed to us on a plate. Some employers encourage their employees to stay on the learning track by paying for course fees and allowing some time out for study or management conferences, but others with tight budgets or a different view of their role leave employees on their own when it comes to self-improvement. Not all learning has to be in the form of formal degrees and diplomas, however. Other ways include:

- Professional associations. These might offer seminars, workshops, a newsletter or e-bulletin.
- Sharing with peers. Not everyone is prepared to help or share

knowledge about the practicalities of a new promotion or insights into the challenges of a particular position. But many are. You can only ask.

- Workplace seminars. Corporate videos that cover a problem or stagnant area can be rented; speakers can be invited; workshops can be organized.
- Trading information. A group of people in the same field can agree to divvy up reading trade or professional journals and share the knowledge over a meeting, perhaps once a month.
- Internet updates. Many journals, broadcasting services and organizations offer free information in web-based bulletins and articles. This can be an easy way to keep abreast of developments.
- Distance learning. Increasingly universities offer part-time courses for professionals with Internet support.

STARTING A BUSINESS OR SELF-EMPLOYMENT

Self-employment runs the gamut of dog walking and cleaning to starting up a transport operation or property development company. It provides an income and interest but, while it could be argued that the 'job security' is no less than that of the sackable salary worker, you will miss out on retirement payments from an employer, paid sick leave, paid annual leave, long service leave, expenses and benefits.

ESTABLISHING A BUSINESS

Sometimes a business can keep your lifestyle afloat, providing you with a reasonable cash flow and allowing you to live where you want. But there are many hurdles to jump over before you can say a small business is successful: paying bills, paying staff (if any), putting aside money to update equipment, paying tax, and setting up a contingency fund for lean times and emergencies.

A tough task master

Starting a business yourself often means putting in much longer hours than an employer would dare to pressure you to do. It may even pay you less as the economies of scale often mean an employer can afford to pay you more in salary than you'll pocket yourself in your own business. And even businesses that have gone on to make their owners wealthy probably had lean beginnings. Then again, stories of millionaire entrepreneurs abound…

Success rates

For one reason or another, businesses can close in a disappointingly short time. Poor management (which can cover a multitude of sins), poor accounting, inadequate financing, excessive debt, lack of market knowledge, and overwhelming competition are among the many reasons businesses can fail. Small businesses that operate on the brink of closure are hardly a recipe for stress control. Few are what people would consider hugely successful, but many bring satisfaction and employment.

Preparation is all

If your proposed business will represent a major investment in your time and/or money, you'll need to research your idea as much as you can—are there enough potential customers, for a start? You should also look for other expert advice, whether in the form of small business seminars, courses, government agencies or professional consultants. A course in small business management could be an eye opener; it will touch on skills such as marketing, financing, market research, tax and insurance planning. Industry associations may be another valuable source of hard-to-come-by information.

The business plan

A business plan is a blueprint for business. It's a useful tool when preparing or considering a business and a vital one if you intend seeking financial support. It should address all the factors needed to run a viable business, including defining your business and product, analyzing the market—particularly its trends so that you can work out your ongoing costs—and predicting when you'll go into profit and how you'll repay debt. It will need to cover cash flow statements, balance sheets and much, much more.

BUYING A BUSINESS

Buying a business means, in theory, that you are taking on an established customer base, a supplier network, and all the equipment and staff needed to keep business flowing. As well as taking sufficient time to assess information you are given, you should be on the lookout for information that may be withheld (eg. disgruntled customers or staff, wornout equipment, current favourable supplier contracts that are unlikely to be renewed). The golden question in buying a business is what its future holds. While to a certain extent this depends on your own skills, you'll also want to know about:

- Sales. What is the trend, on the up or declining? Who are the customers and suppliers?
- Costs. Will yours be the same?
- Profits. What is the profit trend over the last few years? What will happen if sales decrease?
- Assets. Have a written list so you know what equipment you are buying. Have an independent valuer check it if in doubt.

There is much personal questioning to cover too: whether the business is right for you; whether you could build it if desired; whether the price is fair, especially where goodwill is included and staff loyalty expected. According to investment manager and author Paul Clitheroe, there are three golden rules for buying a business:

- Always seek the advice of someone you trust who has relevant business experience before agreeing to a purchase.
- Never commit to a purchase without having an accountant examine all the figures.
- Seek advice from a solicitor before signing a contract.

Jeff Bezos (1964–)

Amazon.com, the online store that reported sales of US$1.13 billion in the third quarter of 2003 alone, started life in a garage in Seattle. Founder Jeff Bezos, a computer science and electrical engineering graduate, decided to open an online bookstore after reading about the growth rate of the Internet. Real estate gets more expensive each year while technology gets cheaper, he reasoned; books are easy and low risk to ship. He'd recently quit his job as senior vice president of a Wall Street investment bank but had no previous experience of retailing. The first team built desks out of doors and held meetings in the local Barnes & Noble bookstore. The company went on line in 1995, and went public in 1997. That year sales were $147 million. It now sells music, DVDs, software and much more. While the company received negative press about substantial losses in the early days, Bezos says a long-term vision helped everyone stay heads down and not get distracted by outside views.

BUYING A FRANCHISE

Franchises range from internationally recognized fast food chains to local mowing services. For a fee you buy a business idea with an image and system already in place. It is less risky than starting up your own business, but the downside is less individuality—you have to operate within a tight framework laid down by the franchisor. Buying a franchise is a major investment so you need to do plenty of research. Ask these and many more questions:

- What does the purchase include?
- What benefits are you entitled to? Is there national advertising? Are you party to the savings of bulk buying?
- What assistance or advice can you expect should you run into problems or wish to expand?
- What training is offered?
- Are there other fees to be paid? (Ongoing royalty and service fees are the norm so you need to be clear about these from the start.)

You also need to take a close look at the franchise and the industry it's operating within. Is it growing? What are the trends? What is the track record like? Where possible, seek out other franchisees and find out what it's like dealing with the franchisor.

WORKING AT HOME

For some it's ideal. They love where they live and there are no local job opportunities. Others find the distractions of housework too great to concentrate on work usefully. Whether it saves you childcare fees—something often suggested by financial advisors— depends on your working habits and the habits of your children. More often than not, working from home simply means a switch of location not a solution to the demands of working and caring for children at the same time. In this case you'll be paying childcare fees just as if you worked in someone else's office not your own home one.

The pros

- Flexibility. If the sun calls you out for a walk, perhaps you can put in extra hours when it's gone down for the day. If the cat turns up in the morning with a walnut-sized eye, you can take it to the vet without having to apologize to anyone, and can hope to make up time later.
- Technology. With many jobs technology means you can work as effectively at home as in the office—at least in theory.
- No commuting costs, and perhaps a reduced clothing budget too.
- No rental of an office, shop or studio, if they were alternatives.

The cons

- Capital. You need to set up a home office including, depending on your work, a computer, fax machine and printer. An employer might be persuaded to fund your set-up. If you are self-employed, the repair and maintenance is yours to arrange and pay for—and it's up to you to work out how to meet your deadline while your equipment is in for repairs.

- Isolation. If you thrive on coffee machine chatter, you might find working from home lonely. On the other hand, you can structure your day, depending on your work, by making sure some part of it is out of your home office. You could meet friends or colleagues for lunch, attend some meetings at an employer's, and so on.
- Continuous. Some people find it hard to switch off from their work when they operate from home, but a room with a door you can shut might be all you need to create cut-off.

Work is perhaps one of the fastest changing aspects of life today. The work itself, the way we do it, our expectations of it—especially our expectations of what will happen when, and if, we stop working—are all subject to change. Thinking outside the 'nine to five' and seeing work as encompassing a range of situations—volunteer, freelance, home—brings dignity back to all sorts of work. It also means you are more likely to have work when you want it.

TAKING STOCK

These questions will help you to explore your feelings and aspirations about your working life.

1 Current job or work

Answer each of the following questions in a few words.

(a) How near is your current job to what you'd ideally like to be doing?

(b) What are its good points?

(c) What do you dislike most about it? If you could change one aspect, what would it be?

(d) Some people say if two of these three are right, you'll stick at a job: money, colleagues, the job itself. Would you agree?

(e) How does your job rate? Give yourself 1 point for each of the three areas mentioned above that you're happy with.

2 Past jobs
(a) What are some of the jobs you've done in the past?
(b) Have you ever freelanced or been self-employed?
(c) What were the best and worst aspects of other jobs?
(d) Have you recently changed career?
If so:
(e) What were the main reasons?
(f) Did you have a clear idea of what job/career you wanted to move into?
(g) Has the change lived up to your expectations?
(h) What have you lost?
(i) What have you gained?

3 Future jobs
(a) Are you thinking of changing career or evolving your job?
If so:
(b) Is this to a related field or a different area altogether?
(c) Will you need new qualifications?
(d) What would be the main reason for the change? What would you hope to gain?

4 A working life
(a) Where does work fit in your life? Would you stop if you could?
(b) Do you need to balance your work with other interests?

He who knows he has enough is rich enough.

LAO TSU, *TAO TE CHING*
(SIXTH CENTURY BC)

7. MONEY

MONEY MAKES THE WORLD GO ROUND. IT CONCERNS US ALL: RICH, POOR AND IN BETWEEN. WORKING OUT HOW YOUR HOUSEHOLD CAN MAKE THE MOST OF YOUR EARNINGS CAN BRING PEACE OF MIND AS WELL AS MORE VALUE FOR MONEY. WITH RESEARCH AND SOME ADVICE FROM A QUALIFIED FINANCIAL ADVISOR, A REVIEW OF YOUR FINANCES MIGHT ENABLE YOU TO REALIZE A LONG-HELD DREAM OF OVERSEAS TRAVEL OR PUT ASIDE THE MONEY YOU NEED FOR A RENOVATION THAT WILL MAKE A DIFFERENCE AT HOME.

MONEY AND HAPPINESS

Does having more money make you happier? Up to a point, yes. Grinding poverty is miserable and financial hardship has both psychological and material consequences. When the Titanic sank, the first class passengers had a higher rate of survival than those in third class. A total of 60 per cent of first class passengers survived compared with 25 per cent of steerage class; although these figures are slightly skewed by the fact that more women survived overall and a higher percentage of first class passengers were women. The deterioration of your financial situation that tends to accompany unemployment is also a major source of high-level stress.

At any one time, in any one country, rich people are on average happier than poorer ones, says Richard Layard, professor of economics at London University, in a lecture entitled 'Income and Happiness: Rethinking Economic Policy'. But societies do not grow happier as they grow richer. The underlying reason for this is that we start off with one set of expectations; then, as we become richer, our expectations increase along with our wealth—even overtaking it—so we remain as unsatisfied as before. Psychologists call this exhausting phenomenon 'the hedonic treadmill'. Layard explains this ever upwardly mobile 'norm' with reference to two terms: habituation and rivalry.

Habituation is also referred to as 'adaptation' in psychology. Put bluntly, when you experience an increase in your standard of living, you think it's great to begin with, then you get used to it and it fails to give you a thrill anymore. 'I had no central heating at home until I was 40,' says Layard in his lecture by way of illustration. 'But now I can barely imagine living without it.' We are particularly good, research shows, at becoming used to and taking for granted our creature comforts. It's similar with big winnings: lottery winners report feeling happier for a while, then life goes back to normal.

Rivalry, on the other hand, is about what happens in your reference group. If everyone receives a pay cut, it's not so bad. If everyone gets a pay rise except you, you feel mad. Relative earnings are more important than absolute ones: it's all about keeping up with the Joneses, and preferably outdoing them.

At a more individual level, research shows that whether more money makes you happier depends on your values. If you value money highly, it makes you happy. PhD candidate Ariel Malka and business professor Jennifer Chatman at the University of California, Berkeley, who looked at money, happiness and work values, called such an attitude an 'extrinsic' orientation, in a report published in the *Personality and Social Psychology Bulletin* in June 2003. For 'intrinsic' orientated people, however, money had a negative effect on wellbeing. Those of an intrinsic orientation, who worked because they enjoyed it or found it fulfilling, were less happy when their earnings increased. This could be because accepting a higher paid job had taken them away from what they liked doing.

Choie Sew Hoy (1837–1901)

Dunedin merchant, Otago gold dredger and benefactor Choie Sew Hoy came to the South Island of New Zealand via California and Australia, from his home village near Canton, China. Like many others from Poon Yue, as his region was known, he was willing to work, and believed in helping others in the same clan. He arrived in Dunedin in 1869, and soon after was supplying Chinese stores throughout Central Otago. During the 1880s he established the Sew Mining Company and backed a special steam bucket gold dredger. His machine began work in 1889, uncovering 40 pounds of gold a day and triggering a dredging rage across the island, with his dredger the prototype. Throughout his life in New Zealand he helped friends and relatives to migrate and give themselves a chance to work themselves out of poverty. He even helped ship back their bodies to their homeland when they died—the belief at the time was that Chinese bodies should return home so their spirits could rest among kith and kin. Sew Hoy's body was exhumed a year after his death for a final journey on the Ventor, but it struck a reef and sank, taking all but ten coffins with it. 'My poor father died twice,' said his son on hearing the news. The House of Sew Hoy still stands in Stafford Street, Dunedin.

Alternatively, making more money could have made them question why they were doing it, the researchers said, drawing on research that shows that, in some cases, being paid for doing something fun makes it less enjoyable.

As a result of the hedonic treadmill, or the human traits of habituation and rivalry—whichever explanation you prefer—we always think we need more, no matter how much we already have. In a 2002 report, 'Overconsumption in Australia', author Clive Hamilton of think tank The Australia Institute, says 62 per cent of Australians believe they cannot afford to buy everything they really need. And almost half of those with a household income of $70,000 plus—'the suffering rich', as Hamilton dubs them, tongue in cheek—said they couldn't afford all they needed. A quarter of these said they spent nearly all their money on the basic necessities of life.

Part of the reason relatively well-off people may feel they are doing it tough could be explained by 'luxury fever'. This is a term coined in the United States to describe a growing desire to emulate lives of the rich and famous—with all the 'trophy' homes, luxury cars and cosmetic surgery that goes with it. (Quite a few commentators blame television for letting us peep into these privileged lives, when before we were quite happy to compare ourselves with our peers.) Others call it 'affluenza': the bloated, sluggish and unfulfilled feeling that results from efforts to keep up with the Joneses. Symptoms include a four-fold increase in credit card debt in Australia over eight years, and a sharp rise in personal bankruptcies. Personal savings in the United States have fallen by around 40 per cent in two decades.

MANAGING YOUR MONEY

Happiness is less a matter of getting what we want than of wanting what we have.

ED MYERS, QUOTED IN CLIVE HAMILTON, *GROWTH FETISH* (2003)

More money won't make you happy for long, but there's little doubt money problems bring stress and unhappiness. Getting on top of your finances can be the incentive you need to make real life changes: to plan a life with less work, start a business or save for an overseas sabbatical.

Good financial management means you get the most out of your money as well as a better night's sleep. Many of us may feel we don't want to fill our minds with finance and figures, but it pays for everyone once in a while to review their financial situation. Spend a little time with a notepad and calculator, and check you are not wasting hard-earned cash or missing opportunities for financial growth. Credit cards, for example, are notorious for their high interest rates. If you are having difficulty paying yours off, it may make sense for you to consolidate your debts into a personal loan with a lower interest rate—while stopping your credit card use at the same time.

Discuss your options with someone qualified to give financial advice before you make any decisions.

KEY FINANCIAL CONCEPTS: A BEGINNER'S GUIDE

A new set of vocabulary entered the English language in 2003 after a Cambridge University report claimed that nine million people in Britain had a morbid fear of coping with their financial affairs. 'Financial phobia' or 'fiscal phobia' was most common among sixteen to 24 year olds, with 30 per cent being diagnosed as 'financial phobes'. 'The sufferers are otherwise sane and well-adjusted, but become seized with anxiety, guilt or boredom when confronted with the need to manage their money,' explained *The Guardian*. A lack of confidence in their ability to deal with financial

The language of money

Money talks but people are not always willing to listen. Inhabitants of a village in Switzerland were asked in 1993 if they would be willing to have a radioactive waste repository built in their village. Just over half said yes.

When money came into the equation and the villagers were asked whether they would agree to the proposal if they were offered a specified amount of compensation, only a quarter said yes. Clearly they knew 'money isn't everything'. And most, it seems, would not have fallen into Oscar Wilde's definition of a cynic as someone who, 'knows the price of everything and the value of nothing'.

matters combined with the increasing complexity of financial products is thought to explain the attitude.

If you have an aversion to bank statements and bills, you are certainly not alone. But knowledge is power in the money game and the key to successful money management. Many of the money basics owe a lot to common sense and there are a few concepts it pays to get your head around. If you consider yourself financially illiterate, here's a brief guide to get you started.

Interest

This is the cost of borrowing. It works in two ways: when you are borrowing—on a credit card or on a home loan—it represents the speed at which your debt will grow. High-risk loans—for example, by companies to people with poor credit ratings—usually carry high interest. Home loans, or mortgages—which offer the added security of the property itself—usually carry lower interest rates than what is sometimes called 'consumer credit' (such as credit cards or personal loans). Some mortgages are structured so that you pay off interest on the loan first, then start chipping away at the capital— the initial sum that was lent.

When you have investments, interest is what you receive for allowing your money to work for the borrower.

Dips in official state-set interest rates are generally good for borrowers but bad for investors who may be relying on interest to provide income.

Compounding

Compound interest is when the interest earned on money in a bank account or in an investment scheme is ploughed back into the original sum. It's like serious snowballing—the next time interest is calculated it is based on the larger sum (the principal as well as the interest already earned), so it will be greater again. Compound interest accelerates the growth of an investment. The greater the time of investment, the more dramatic the difference between compound interest and ordinary or 'simple' interest. With an interest rate of 10 per cent over 40 years, an investment of $1000 will grow to $5000. But with compound interest, that principal investment of $1000 will become $45,258 over the same period.

Investment

Put very simply, an investment means putting your money where your hopes are—you acquire an asset in the hope of it producing income and/or capital gains. Here are the main types of investment:

- Interest-bearing deposits. These are available from a range of financial institutions including banks and building societies. Individual accounts may vary in detail, but generally they include: term deposits (where you agree to 'park' your cash for a fixed period at an interest rate fixed for the duration of the deposit); cash management trusts (where money is pooled with that of other investors and you are free to dip in and out as needs arise); debentures (a type of debt security backed by the general credit of the issuer and not by a specific security); government bonds (a debt security issued by the government at a fixed rate and term); and bank bills (bills of exchange drawn by one bank on another, issued for a set number of days at a fixed interest rate).

- Unit trusts. This is a type of managed fund where pooled money is invested in a wide range of investments such as property, cash, local and international shares.
- Shares. By buying part ownership of a company, you hope for dividends (profits), capital growth (an increase in share price, so that if you sell your shares, you gain), bonus shares (extra free shares) and offers of rights to buy more shares. Shares come in different forms, such as ordinary shares or preference shares. Ordinary shares are the most common traded, and give voting rights and the right to attend an annual general meeting. Preference shares may earn higher dividends than ordinary shares, but may be associated with limited voting rights.
- Real estate. Whether it's your own home or an investment property that you rent out, many people like the tangible nature of bricks and mortar as an investment.

Whatever the investment, always look closely at the fees involved. These can come in the form of establishment fees, exit fees, account keeping charges, and commissions.

Risk and return

Investments vary in their level of risk. A term deposit is 100 per cent secure: you know what your profit will be as you place the investment. Investing in emerging market shares overseas, on the other hand, might be considered quite risky, as you can't predict whether your punts will prove profitable. If high-risk ventures succeed, however, they can be highly profitable or, in investment speak, give a good return.

The key to spreading risk is not to put your eggs in one basket. The golden rule of investment, according to the experts, is 'diversify'. This translates as putting your money in different kinds of investments: property, shares, cash and bonds, for instance, and, where possible diversifying within those. Shares might be spread across sectors such as finance, retail, construction and health services, and again, among a range of companies within each sector. Yet another diversification would be investing both locally and internationally, and the latter across different countries. Diversification takes some of the sting out of riskier, higher-return investments by balancing them with lower risk, lower-return ones. It also provides a further cushion by evening out the normal fluctuation in share value across a portfolio. In a varied group of investments, it's unlikely that all share prices will take a nosedive at the same time.

Time

Most investments need time to outrun normal fluctuations in the market (also referred to as 'volatility') and grow—that is the attraction of most retirement plans. Regular contributions over the long term can result in a significant sum to draw on when wages run dry. If you have money you'll need sooner rather than later you need to consider how best to invest it. As a general guide, short term in the financial world means around three years; medium term, four to nine; and long term, over ten years. Some investment options are not usually recommended over the short term. Shares, for example, have a good track record over the long term, but crashes can bring serious losses over a year. However, if you don't need to cash in your shares for ten or even twenty years, that one-year loss will be insignificant. Buying property is usually considered a long-term venture, particularly as there are many fees involved in a purchase—solicitor's fees, loan fees, stamp duty, and so on—that add to the initial expense.

A roof over your head

Renting brings with it flexibility and less responsibility than owning your own home. But many consider rent 'dead' money that's simply lining a landlord's pocket. In addition, as rent continues to increase along with inflation, it can become more expensive than a mortgage payment that has remained the same and so decreased in real terms over the years. 'If we had to rent our house, it would cost $420 a week, and we couldn't afford it. But our mortgage payment is only $175 a week,' says AM. Many people find mortgages the only way they can save. In theory, a renter could

Gearing up

Borrowing money to invest is common with real estate. But is it a safe option for other investments such as shares? If you are thinking of 'gearing'— a term that means to borrow money to invest based on the equity you hold in your assets—ask yourself the following:

- Could you manage if interest rates suddenly soared and your repayments increased accordingly?
- What would happen if you lost your job?
- What would happen and how would you feel if the investment lost money for a while?

If you are tempted because you see advantages in speeding up the growth of your money so that you improve your financial situation at retirement, but are worried about the risks, you should consider putting a ceiling on the amount you borrow. For example, A and PN were advised not to borrow more than 20 per cent of the value of their assets as they were both self-employed, with a family and not at ease with debt.

invest a certain amount a week but, without the 'convenient' discipline of a mortgage, very few do. As house prices soar, an increasingly attractive approach is to get a foot in the property market by buying an investment property, perhaps in a suburb you wouldn't consider living in, but which you can afford.

A few simple principles can bring huge savings over the term of a mortgage. Paying weekly rather than fortnightly or monthly saves on interest. Paying in extra—even small amounts—helps to pay it off more quickly. An account that lets you pay extra when you want and accumulates these advance payments, and then allows you to redraw on them when you need, can provide an efficient way of saving an emergency fund as well as help to reduce interest. If you are seeking a mortgage or considering refinancing one make sure you do your research. Find out what features are available, their advantages and disadvantages, and work out which ones will

What sort of an investor are you?

Financial planners describe people in terms such as conservative, cautious, prudent, assertive or aggressive. How much of a risk you can afford to take or are comfortable with depends on a number of factors:

- Comfort zone. If you are very comfortable financially and losing the money invested in a particular scheme or fund would not be disastrous, your risk tolerance is greater than if the amount you can put aside represents savings out of a tight, perhaps scarce budget.

- Dependants. The family man or woman usually feels more conservative about investment risk than a single person in their late twenties on a good salary.

- Strategy. Some strategies are simply more risky than others. Borrowing against your house to invest, for example, carries a higher risk than using savings. Diversification and the long-term view tend to bring down the risk factor.

- What buffer do you need? Are you the sort of person who likes the feeling of a comfortable buffer between earnings and spending or do you sleep easy even when you are sailing close to the wind?

- Volatility. How often and by how much the value of an investment moves up and down—its volatility—is often confused with risk. Whether volatile investments are a risky option usually depends on how long you're prepared to keep them before cashing in. Shares are highly volatile, but usually increase in value over the long term (at least seven years). Then again, very stable investments such as cash deposits run a different 'risk'. They may not keep up with inflation and could offer a poor return over time. These very stable kinds of investments may suit in the short term but are rarely advisable for longer.

work for you and your time frame (the way some mortgages are structured, for instance, makes them unsuitable for buyers who'll be moving on in three years or so).

Debt

There's good debt, bad debt, and ugly debt that's simply out of control. Good debt is money you owe on an asset that will (or should) increase in value, such as property or a small business. Bad debt is incurred for consumption, whether it's a car, Caribbean holiday or clothing. It is usually high interest, eats into future earnings and your purchases decrease in value, often to nothing—these are known as diminishing assets. When bad debt approaches the danger zone, high-interest debts can snowball to an unmanageable amount and cause you serious financial problems.

Tax

Most people—not all—want to minimize tax. You can do this by claiming all the deductible expenses you can and keeping good records. Educate yourself about all the items you can claim, perhaps sunscreen if you are an outside worker or a briefcase for an office job. The self-employed can make substantial claims, some on home office expenses, but you should be aware of the long-term implications of making some claims. For instance, in Australia, making claims against your home expenses for items other than running costs (such as rates, for example) can have capital gains tax implications.

While some investments have significant tax savings, most advisors recommend investing for investment reasons first and tax benefits second. At the same time, it pays to be aware of how certain investments will affect your tax or, for instance, what tax will be paid on the profits that are made. Most governments offer tax incentives for retirement planning schemes that can bring you significant tax savings.

VOX POP: How do you feel about money?

'I love it! I've had lots in the past and barely any. Lots is definitely easier to live with. I've got a few property investments and a decent cash buffer should work dry up. I believe state pensions will be gone by the time I come to collect so I find it easy to save and invest for the future.' DL

'I dislike having to deal with financial matters because I find it profoundly boring and have no natural aptitude for it. That doesn't mean I'm fiscally irresponsible. I keep my eye on finances, pay my bills and avoid getting into debt. I think it's important to have enough money to pay for the essentials and a little bit over to have some fun. I've had times when I earned more than friends and colleagues, and times where it was a stretch. When I look back on "the good times" I can't remember if they occurred during times of more or less money, what made them memorable was the people I was with and my relationships with them.' PN

'I find bank statements rather interesting and enjoy tracking down where the money went, making plans, even if I don't keep to them. When the money runs out, I stop spending. I like the adage "make the last cheque bounce"—but you have to get the timing right or you might end up with ten years in penury!' EB

'I'm well paid for someone at my stage in my new career, but not for a 41-year-old graduate. However, I'm heavily indebted from an unsuccessful business I had, so money is a bit tight. I still do the things I want to do, but less often than I would like to. But it does mean it's hard to save for the future while my debts eat up so much of my income.' HB

'I resisted the idea for a long time, but now believe money can contribute to feeling good, though in a limited way.' ML

'Stress city! It never, ever ends, but it is a reality so there's no point pretending it doesn't matter. You need to deal with it because it ain't going to change!' CT

'At various times in my life I've turned my back on higher earning opportunities but what money I do have I like to be working for me: when necessary I'll spend time researching, for instance, the best mortgage, and calculate our monthly expenses, but then I want to forget about it. I don't like money matters filling my head too much of the time.' MH

Goals

Flexible, realistic goals you review regularly bolster motivation when it comes to saving. You need short- to medium-term and long-term goals. They can be simple: saving for a trip, or paying off the home loan in five years; or complex: investing a small inheritance or modest redundancy package in a range of managed funds that you've researched. If you haven't reviewed your financial situation for a while, a detailed budget (working out where your money goes) might throw light on some areas where you could easily cut back. (See Appendix B, 'The money check-up', on page 390 for more pointers.) If you feel things have got out of control, you might need to make some cool-headed decisions: consolidate credit and store card loans, for example, or drop the idea of a new car and work out how you are going to climb back into the black.

Retirement

If your idea of retirement is to stop work at 60 and live pretty much as you do now, you need to work out how you'll do that. Where will the money come from to give you even 70 per cent of your current earnings for twenty years? If, with a few calculations, you work out that the best you can do falls far short, then at least you can adjust your expectations. An old age that's dependent on state aid can be tough.

Some strategies to make up for lost time are:
● cutting back spending

> ## Retirement: the figures
> In Australia, at age 65:
> - 20 per cent of people are still working because they have to
> - 5 per cent have enough to be comfortable
> - 1 per cent have enough to do exactly what they want.

- retiring at a later age
- tapping into home equity by downgrading in order to release cash for investment
- considering a reverse mortgage (where you receive income and at the same time a loan balance develops against your house, which is deducted when it is sold)
- working investments harder (research and check for every extra percentage interest)
- getting tax wise
- looking for extra income, perhaps from an interest or hobby
- considering retirement plans on offer when job hunting.

Insurance

Insurance is enormous business. Eric Tyson, American author and financial counsellor, estimates that 1 in 12 dollars in the American economy goes to pay for insurance. The insurance industry centres on the idea of protecting what you have now and what you would like to have in the future. Here are the main types to consider:

- Home contents. This is an important consideration for both renters and homeowners. Insuring for replacement value rather than what's known as an 'indemnity policy' ensures you can go out and buy the things you need to set up home again if, for instance, you lose your home contents in a fire. If you particularly want a specific item covered, such as a bicycle, computer or piece of jewellery, you should check the policy before signing.
- Building. This should be considered for both your home and any investment property. It generally compensates you for damage by fire, wind or hail but often excludes flood.

- Life. With a life insurance policy, if you die, your nominated dependants will receive a lump sum. Many advisors recommend both parents in a family have life insurance even if one does not work. The calculations involved in working out how much to insure for may seem a little daunting: you need to consider what loan payments would need to be covered, funeral expenses, an emergency fund, and more. The intricacies of policies also vary; for example, renewable life insurance allows for full cover for a shorter time.

- Income. One of the least popular forms of insurance, this protects what some would say is your greatest asset—your ability to earn an income. According to the Consumers' Association, you are twenty times more likely to be off work for six months because of sickness or injury than to die before reaching retirement. Yet people are far more likely to insure for the latter, not the former: only 1 in 10 workers in the United Kingdom has income protection. It's a particularly important consideration for the self-employed whose earnings may dry up immediately while the bills keep flooding in. In some countries, such as Australia, the premium is tax deductible. Types of policies you might come across include accident and sickness, critical illness, disability, and income protection.

- Small business. Factors covered by insurance may include fire, business interruption or loss of profit, burglary, machinery breakdown, product liability, and so on. Some aspects, such as workers' compensation, may be compulsory.

- Health. Assessing your health risks and finding out exactly what you can expect from the state and what not should form part of your decision whether to take out health insurance. If you decide to go ahead, you need to be very clear about what's covered and what is not in your policy. Some new mothers have been shocked to find that while pregnancy care was covered by their health insurance policy, the costs of newborn intensive care were not.

Shop around, talk to insurance agents and brokers, read the fine print and look at the details of protection offered, exclusion clauses and so on before signing up. Some points to consider:

- Make sure you understand the policy. A plain English policy will make it simpler.
- What excesses or waiting periods apply? In the case of income insurance, for example, you may be able to reduce a premium if it's possible to wait for a few months before claiming. Many experts advise taking the highest deductible excess you can afford. So, if the first $1000 in a home contents claim wouldn't hurt, opt to pay that yourself and reduce your premium.
- How are claims calculated? Is it based on replacement value or actual value? Will you be covered for 50 per cent of your lost income or 75 per cent?
- Are benefits in the case of income insurance indexed to inflation? Will they rise along with the cost of living or, should you find yourself disabled and unable to work, will your income be stuck in the stone age?
- Check what cover you have through any of your pension or superannuation plans.
- Make sure you understand all duties of disclosure, and exactly what aspects of your life the insurer wants to know about. If an insurer believes that you've withheld information, it may not agree to a claim.

COMMON FINANCIAL MISTAKES

If it's any consolation, few people have the tidy set of affairs often showcased in financial books or magazines. While lack of expertise is certainly a contributing factor, many common problems are the result of a few very simple mistakes. A review of the way you handle money can put you back on the right track.

Lack of planning

Procrastination costs you money, especially when it results in cash sitting in low-interest-earning bank accounts, high-interest debts on credit cards, or delaying a savings plan that you could afford with a little adaptation.

Rainy days
Financial experts strongly advise protecting yourself against potential illness, unexpected financial challenges and the death of a spouse. A first goal, whatever stage of life you're at, is an emergency fund of some sort (consider, too, how 'liquid' it is, i.e. how quickly you can draw on it in the form of cash), and at least giving the various forms of insurance some consideration.

Overspending
According to *Personal Finance for Dummies* author Eric Tyson, the average American saves 5 per cent of his earnings. Australians save around 4 per cent. This is simply not enough—experts say we should aim for at least 10 per cent. Consumer debt is soaring as attitudes relax and loans become more widely available.

Credit balance
A credit card balance carried from month to month is expensive debt. Buying on credit means that you are spending your future earnings and often encourages you to spend more than you can really afford.

The hard sell
Beware of high-pressure salespeople pushing financial products you don't fully understand—whether it's a newly structured mortgage or a type of life insurance—and aren't given the time to consider. A bad decision can backfire and see a reversal of fortunes. You may not only never see the returns you were promised, but you could also lose your initial investment.

Research, research, research
The bigger the decision—and the more money involved—the more you need to shop around. Obtain as much objective advice as you can before taking the plunge. The more educated you are, the

better the choices you'll make, whether with the aid of a financial advisor or on your own.

Head over heart

Emotions cloud the financial picture, so it's best not to make strategic decisions when your emotions are flying high, in a period of grieving or following a divorce, for instance.

Andrew Carnegie (1835–1918)

The son of a weaver, Andrew Carnegie was born in Dunfermline, Scotland. His father emigrated to Pittsburgh in 1848. Carnegie worked at several jobs, including factory hand, telegraphist and railway clerk. He invested his savings in oil fields and later in his own business, which grew to become the largest iron and steel works in America. He donated millions to a variety of causes, including public libraries across the United States and Britain. The Free Public Library in Hokitika on New Zealand's South Island was one of eighteen built in New Zealand with his assistance. In 1911 he founded the Carnegie Corporation of New York to promote the advancement and diffusion of knowledge and understanding.

The corporation's capital fund, originally donated at a value of $135 million, was worth $1.6 billion in 2002. It continues the themes of Carnegie's work, focusing on education, international peace and security, international development, and strengthening the US economy. Carnegie believed it was the duty of a man of wealth to set the example of modest unostentatious living and to consider surplus revenues as trust funds to be administered for the best results for the community.

CLIMBING THE FINANCIAL SECURITY LADDER

Authors of financial books are fond of pigeonholing people according to their age and/or life stage. While this can be useful as a benchmark of where you could be financially, it may also be quite depressing. It is of little help to you to read that, at age 50, at your peak earning capacity, with your children gone and your house paid off, you should be looking at a second or third investment property; when in fact you started late in the family-planning stakes and still have preschoolers, chose self-employment over a nine to five job and are still chasing the mortgage down a dark tunnel. The overly neat packaging is also at odds with the fact that, financially, few people approaching retirement age are where they'd like to be or could have been with better planning. In addition, the ground rules can change. Education is a prime example: new graduates are entering the job market already saddled with debts in the form of student loans. In many areas, house prices are now so prohibitive that the idea of buying one is for many people nothing more than wishful thinking. Despite this, it can be useful to consider a 'ladder' of wealth growth or goals even if you're temporarily stuck on a lower rung.

GETTING STARTED

If you're just getting going, there are a few goals and issues you should consider:

- Build an emergency fund. Some people recommend that you aim to save enough money to cover six months' expenses. If you feel you have little left over after the basics, this can seem an impossible task, but a little by little approach will gradually get you nearer the goal—and if you never start, you're guaranteed never to reach it. To be really comfortable, the self-employed person might need to put aside a year's expenses. Unfortunately, many in this category feel too financially squeezed to have much left to put aside.
- Protect your income against illness or, particularly if you have dependants, disability or death.

- Draw up a savings plan. This should cover goals for both the short term (holiday, Christmas shopping) and long term (house deposit, investment portfolio).

THE NEXT RUNG ON THE LADDER

When life feels a little more established, you'll probably find you have to revise your financial strategy to take into account both present and future needs. Typical aims might include the following:

- Retirement planning. Depending on which country you live in, this can range from looking into options concerning superannuation in Australia, pension schemes in the United Kingdom or retirement accounts in the United States.
- Property acquisition. Owning your own home makes sense financially. You could look at borrowing to buy property or making inroads into a mortgage if you already have one.
- Education. If you have children, think about education costs as early as possible. This will help you build the funds to pay for university or private school fees if you choose that option.

MOVING ONWARDS AND UPWARDS

When your financial situation is fairly comfortable, and you find you have surplus funds, you might consider looking at:

- Long-term care planning. Will you be able to afford nursing home fees or a home nurse should you need extra care?
- Serious investment. With a comfortable disposable income and many of your goals already reached, you can afford to take more investment risks with a portion of your money.
- Inheritance planning. Researching the tax and legal implications of what you'd like to leave children, charities or friends might enable you to leave them more and/or save them heartache later on if complications arise.

SAVING

Annual income twenty pounds, annual expenditure nineteen nineteen six, result happiness. Annual income twenty pounds, annual expenditure twenty pounds ought and six, result misery.

MR MICAWBER IN CHARLES DICKENS, *DAVID COPPERFIELD* (1850)

The piggy bank's easy to raid; the cash in your wallet too easy to spend. When bills are paid and shopping done there's nothing left over.

Not only do we find it hard to save, we also tend to spend 110 per cent of our earnings—whatever they are, high or low. As you earn more, your expectations change. As a student you might have been happy with the occasional cheap and cheerful pizza meal out. But now that you have your 'serious' job, you expect to eat at nicer places more often. Once you never dreamed of using taxis, but you haven't taken a bus for years. Some of the ideas below may not seem significant, but if together they bring your spending back to 100 per cent of your income, rather than 110 per cent, you may be nearer to Dickens' definition of happiness.

Don't save cash

Experts like Paul Clitheroe, who presents an Australian television show on money, publishes a money magazine and is director of ipac securities, advise you not even to try to save cash. The ideal way to save is to have part of your wage packet diverted directly into a 'no touch' savings account such as your mortgage or similar. That way you can't get your hands on the money even if you want to.

Needs versus wants

Remind yourself every now and then of the difference between 'needs' and 'wants'. If you are tempted to buy something you don't have the cash for, ask yourself which category it falls into. If it's only a 'want', put your cash away.

Money drainers

Some spending is like pouring money down the drain:

- Gambling. The odds are not on the gambler's side.
- Unnecessary bank fees. Check out your bank fees and consider switching accounts.
- Fines. Parking tickets, late video return penalties, and late payment fines are a waste of money.
- High interest on credit card balances. If you cannot pay off your balance, check how the interest rate compares to other cards and how it is calculated. You may be able to make savings simply by cancelling one card and switching to another. Some cards will let you start with a balance from another.
- Clothes you don't wear. When shopping for clothes, err on the side of caution. Don't buy the designer trousers that are only a little too tight or the shirt that's a bargain only you're not entirely sure about the colour. If you're trying to lose weight, promise yourself a spending spree when you've lost weight, not before.
- Inflation. Without careful planning, money sitting in a bank account that pays low interest loses its buying power. The effect is quite dramatic over a couple of decades. For instance, at 4 per cent inflation, the buying power of $100,000 in 2001 will be reduced to around $46,000 by 2020.

Little and often

The best savings plans allow you to put a little, affordable amount of money aside regularly, such as every week or month. Over time, even the small amounts will add up and, once compounding sets in (see page 263), your savings will grow significantly. A dollar a day saved between the ages of eighteen and 65 with an average interest of 10 per cent would amount to $400,000, says Clitheroe.

Cut financial flab

Are you paying unnecessary fees on your bank accounts?
Do you leave money in a savings account with poor interest

when you'd be better off paying extra on your mortgage and redrawing it as and when you need to? There are many ways you can make money work harder for you without any difference to your lifestyle. Try talking to your bank about simple ways to save.

Hold the purse strings

It's not what you earn that counts in the saving stakes, it's what you spend. Curbing spending is half the battle. Knowing where the money goes is the first step—otherwise known as the budget.

Shop smart

Bulk buying, buying at sales, finding out about seconds and warehouse stores can all save you significant amounts throughout the year. Buying quality that will last also makes more sense than buying badly made goods that will fall apart and need replacing after just a few years.

Become a cash king

The sooner you get into the habit of buying only when you have the money in your hand or in your account, the less you'll be forking out on interest and other fees related to credit.

Look after your assets

Maintaining your home and keeping it leak free and sound saves money in the long run. Extend this practice to all your possessions—from business suits to appliances—and you'll find yourself replacing them less often.

A clever house

Household bills are easy to reduce. Don't heat every room, just one. Turn off appliances when they're not in use. Try washing clothes in cold water and use the clothesline not the dryer whenever possible. Get into the habit of using every scrap of a product before opening the next box or bottle. A little frugality goes a long way.

Communications

Phone packages, Internet servers and mobile phone deals range significantly in price and service. A regular review of whether you've got the right deal for you can save you a considerable amount.

TEN WAYS TO SAVE $100 OR MORE

Working out what you can trim from a budget can be hard when you feel you are not leading a life of luxury, even if you are by world standards. Here are ten examples of how an Australian family of four found they could cut at least $100—often much more—from their budget. Not all of these ideas may apply to you, your situation or location, but they could help you spot where you might be able to make a few savings.

1   The milky way. Consuming 1.5 litres of milk a day means that if the Jones family buys 3-litre, not 1-litre bottles, they save about 20 cents a litre. This adds up to $2.10 a week, or $109 a year.

2   Better deal insurance. Shopping around for home contents insurance resulted in a new policy costing $100 less.

3   The coffee bill. Mrs Jones found she'd slipped into a coffee habit at work, nipping out for a latte three times a day at $2.50 each. She decided one strong coffee a day was ample, saving $5 three days a week. That adds up to $720 over 48 weeks a year.

4   Sweet deals. Reining in the after-school sweets to three times a week rather than every day saved around $8 a week, or around $400 a year.

5   Joining up. Paying swimming pool entry in advance for a multi-visit pass, joining a favourite museum for free entry, and paying for an art class early when a discount was offered all added up to savings of over $100.

6   A little less. With a discount liquor store across the road, a $7 bottle of wine most nights did not seem extravagant, but by deciding to halve wine consumption to two bottles a week, most weeks, Mr and Mrs Jones save $14 a week, or $728 a year.

7   The video wait. Renting the newly released kids films costs $6 a night—and the kids usually want to watch it several times so that

Financial tips for the self-employed

One of the hardest aspects of being self-employed is the irregular flow of money. At best it makes it hard to plan; at worst, a shortfall at the wrong time can make paying a hefty phone bill a challenge. What should you be aiming for?

- A cash buffer. An emergency fund can help smooth out the rough times. Your buffer could take the form of advance payments on a home loan that you can redraw immediately or money in a high-interest-paying Internet account.

- Take cover. Explore options for income protection. Think about your needs—mortgage payments or a payment to a spouse in the case of your death—and see what you can afford to protect.

- Check out your options. Ensure that any savings or investments are earning the best possible interest and make sure that any loans, including mortgages, are the best possible for your situation. (If you consider refinancing, do your sums first to include penalties for exiting your current loan early, establishment fees for a new loan, and so on.)

- Look ahead. Start forming some plans for a future with less work. Planning late is better than never. Read up, research, maybe see a financial counsellor, and explore your options.

- Avoid bad debt wherever possible—such as credit cards and car loans. If your debt is riding high, make reducing it a top priority.

attracts late fees too. Waiting until they hit the $4 a week mark saves at least $2 a week (more if both children choose a video).

8 Transport tips. A multi-trip bus pass keeps the cost of rainy-day bus trips down for Mr Jones.

9 Weekly shopping. Shopping at the weekend market for fruit and vegetables rather than topping up at the local store throughout the week saves at least $15 each shop—that's nearly $800 a year.

10 Discount days. Seeing a film on a bargain night saves $5 per ticket. The Joneses go to the cinema every couple of months, saving $10 a time for two adult tickets.

RISING OUT OF A FINANCIAL CRISIS

Emotions run high in times of crisis. A financial crisis is particularly worrying and can often affect relationships too. Charities and government agencies may have financial counsellors who can help you take an objective look at your financial problems and form a plan of attack. Running through a money check-up (see Appendix B) will help but here are a few other suggestions. Remember to discuss all options with a qualified financial advisor who fully understands your specific situation before taking any action.

Identify your debts

The first step is to identify all your debts and then prioritize them. Once this has been accomplished, contact your creditors (the people to whom you owe money). Some may agree to an initial part payment or they may agree to you paying off the debt in regular instalments. Speak to those creditors you cannot pay immediately as well as the ones you can. Being upfront and proactive is a far better option than ignoring their demands.

Consolidate

Consider consolidating all your debts into one, at the lowest possible interest rate. This will make the debt more manageable and could save money if some of the debt is currently high interest.

Look for support

Make sure you are not missing out on allowances or grants that could ease your budget.

Cut up the credit cards

If you continue to use your credit cards, you will make your debts worse. Credit cards are also high interest and therefore the worst kind of debt. By cutting your cards up, you'll remove temptation.

Take a radical review

Identify areas you can cut back and save on at home, in transport, entertainment, and so on. Emergency action could include

Eudora Moore (1848?–1943)

Eudora Moore lived in the coastal town of Indianola, Texas, during the Civil War when Federal troops occupied it in 1863. With money and goods in short supply, Eudora and her family exemplified the saying 'necessity is the mother of invention'. Her father made shoe soles out of a side of tanned leather, using an old black cloak of a very heavy material for the uppers. Her mother made pants from a wool parlour table cover and dyed it with pomegranates. Eudora made hats for the boys out of shucks (like a husk) or palmetto (a tropical palm). When the Yankees left town, they left behind much clothing. Eudora's mother boiled it in lye water, rinsed it thoroughly and dyed it with pomegranate rinds or pecan hulls before making it into clothes for the boys. They made bread out of cornmeal when flour was short. Eudora did not suffer from lack of food and clothing during the war, but she lost many childhood friends who did. Eudora's story is one of many described in *Texas Tears and Texas Sunshine: Voices of Frontier Women*, edited by Jo Ella Powell Exley.

measures such as having your phone blocked so that it takes incoming calls but does not allow you to dial out.

Identify problematic money behaviour

If a gambling habit has got out of control, seek help. Continued major budget blowouts may require a serious rethink about your lifestyle and how you support it.

FINDING THE RIGHT ADVICE

If your financial appetite's been whetted, there are many organizations and resource centres that will be able to give you more information about financial planning and investment matters:

- Consumer associations. Increasingly, money matters form an important aspect of the research and lobbying these independent organizations carry out. Some publish specialized money magazines, while all cover financial issues from time to time in their general publications. Many publish their own books covering finances and sell others they consider useful. In addition, you might approach them for general advice about sources of information and financial planners.

- Government authorities. To encourage as many people as possible to become financially independent, many government authorities have information to give out, run seminars or offer financial counselling for debt management and wealth creation.
- The financial industry. While this is not an independent source of information, it can be a useful one nonetheless. Some institutions will offer a free initial consultation that can help get you started on a financial review.
- Financial advisors. These have the distinct advantage of knowing about a lot of different products in the industry but some have taken a battering in recent times for the quality of their advice. Before arranging an interview, talk to a few and try to get a feel for their approach and how they conduct sessions, what they feel their strong points are, how they charge, and particularly if they receive a commission for products they sell you.

Money matters can seem way too difficult to deal with at times. But, taken in a step-by-step manner, looking at the facts, researching and considering options, it is possible to change old habits, untangle problems and get back in charge of your financial life.

TAKING STOCK

How do you feel about money? Are you financially phobic (hate opening bank statements/dealing with tax, etc) or pragmatic? Does it bore you or fascinate you? Do you worry about it or believe it will arrive when needed? Now's the time to take stock.

1 Saving and investing
(a) Do you find it hard to save and/or invest for the future?

(b) If you don't, what is your motivation to save?

(c) If you do, what makes it hard?

(d) What works for you (eg. a regular saving plan, a piggy bank, frugal living)?

(e) In what ways do you try to make the most of the money you have (eg. have no car or credit card, are careful with purchases)?

(f) Do you worry about or plan for retirement or do you assume you'll either work till you drop or scrape by on a pension?

(g) If you are already retired, do you feel you were well prepared financially and/or have you had to significantly adapt because of changed financial circumstances?

2 Work and home

(a) It's said that however rich we are, we never feel we have enough money. Do you agree?

(b) Has lack of funds prevented you doing things you'd really like to or do you feel your life would be pretty much the same whatever your income or wealth?

(c) Do you seek work opportunities for their financial rewards or other benefits?

(d) Have you spurned a better-earning career for creative or adventurous pursuits? Have you discarded work or jobs you liked because they didn't pay enough?

3 Financial institutions

(a) Do you consider yourself financially literate?

(b) Are you at ease dealing with banks, loans, etc?

(c) Do you regularly review your accounts to check they are the best for you, and can you confidently assess them?

If you can't be good, be careful

ENGLISH PROVERB

8. HEALTHY BODY, HEALTHY MIND

GOOD HEALTH IS A TREASURE WE OFTEN ONLY RECOGNIZE WHEN WE LOSE IT. EATING WELL, FEELING FIT AND STRONG, SLEEPING WELL...THESE ARE SOME OF LIFE'S SIMPLEST YET MOST FUNDAMENTAL PLEASURES. MANY OF THE STEPS TO MAXIMIZING HEALTH ARE ONES YOU CAN TAKE YOURSELF—TODAY.

THE COMMON COLD

Exercise makes you feel good about yourself. Healthy eating keeps weight down and cuts your chances of developing cancer and heart disease. Learning to relax helps you cope with stress and anxiety and may help to keep headaches at bay; there are many reasons to bother about your health. Although many infectious diseases are under control in the West, so-called 'lifestyle' diseases—including diabetes, which has serious health implications—are rampant. Many of these can be prevented with the simple measures of sufficient exercise and better eating—consuming more fruit, vegetables and other fibre-rich foods, for instance. Stress is known to reduce the efficiency of the immune system so an all-round approach to health might also mean that you suffer less from the common cold.

All-expenses-paid holidays in the English countryside near Salisbury were a feature of medical research in Britain for 44 years, starting in 1946. The price for the volunteer holiday makers: being exposed to one or more of the 200 viruses that cause the common cold, then being subject to daily routine checks. 'Holiday makers' were housed at the Common Cold Unit at Harvard Hospital under the auspices of the Medical Research Council. Walks on Salisbury Plain were allowed, but Salisbury city was out of bounds. Participants could reapply every six months—and many did. One couple attended the unit 21 times. The quest: to understand the common cold, the most prevalent illness that we suffer, and one of the most frequent reasons for a visit to the doctor.

A cold is defined as a minor infection of the nose and throat caused by several different viruses. Around a third are caused by rhinoviruses (from the Greek rhin, meaning 'nose'), of which there are more than 110 types. Then there's coronaviruses and a group that also cause more serious illnesses, as well the cold, and which includes adenoviruses, the Coxsackie virus, the ECHO virus, and orthomyxsoviruses.

Despite the work of the Common Cold Unit, and other study centres around the world, a cure is not yet in sight, although symptoms can be alleviated. Plenty of theories abound as to the best way to treat a cold and its accompanying symptoms: the feeling of being stuffed up with a runny nose, sneezing, a sore or scratchy throat, a cough and a reduced sense of taste and smell. While they are usually mild, colds can exacerbate asthma and chronic ear problems in children and pave the way for more serious infections, for instance, a sinus infection with a cough.

FIGHTING COLDS AND FLU

Much of the advice for keeping colds and flu at bay is the same as that recommended for staying healthy generally.

A healthy lifestyle

- Eat plenty of fruit and vegetables. While the belief that increased vitamin C (more than usually needed) is beneficial to a cold is controversial, not having enough is considered likely to increase the severity of respiratory tract infections according to the UK's Cold & Flu Council.
- Keep active. Thirty minutes of moderate exercise five times a week is recommended.
- Manage stress. High stress levels reduce the production of the natural 'killer' cells of the immune system. This in turn reduces your resistance to viral infections and your ability to fight foreign bodies.
- Be prepared if you're 'at risk'. Doctors consider the following to be among those at higher risk of colds and flu than the general population: the over 65s; residents of nursing homes; asthma sufferers; those with chronic metabolic diseases such as diabetes; and women who will be in the second or third trimester of pregnancy during the flu season.
- Consider flu shots.
- Avoid high infection places such as hospitals.
- Wash your hands. Cold and flu viruses are spread in droplets of mucus when you cough or sneeze. Some of this remains on an infected person's hand, and can be spread by hand to hand contact or by touching an object that's infected—such as handrails and door handles. Touching your eyes or nose with an infected hand is one of the easiest ways to catch a cold.

The cold facts

- Children suffer eight to ten colds a year; adults usually have two a year.
- Most people will suffer around 200 colds in a 75-year lifetime.
- Colds and flus can only be differentiated by isolating the virus. Most people distinguish them by severity: Dr Chris Steele, a GP from south Manchester, England, recommends taking the Ten Pound Note Test. If you see a £10 note on the ground and pick it up, you have a cold; if you're too ill to bother, it's the flu!
- Most colds are caught at home from partners and children.
- Colds usually last around a week but can last longer.
- Symptoms develop between one and three days after a cold virus enters the body.
- The National Center for Health Statistics estimates that colds cause around 45 million days of restricted activity in the United States and 22 million days lost from school each year.
- Cold viruses arrive at the front of the nasal passages—just a few particles are enough to cause an infection—and are then transported to the back of the nose where they enter cells and start an infection.

- Drink plenty of fluids. The Cold & Flu Council recommends drinking 2 litres a day. A raised temperature caused by a cold or flu can cause sweating and dehydration. Hot drinks are especially beneficial as they soothe sore throats and ease coughs by promoting mucus production.
- Listen to your body. Rest when you feel tired and unwell—this will help your body regain energy to fight back. Keep warm, but not hot. Get some fresh air.

Medication

Despite their frequent prescription, antibiotics do nothing for the cold or flu, as these infections are caused by a virus, not bacteria. (Antibiotics may be of benefit when used to fight a secondary bacterial infection.) However, there are some forms of medication that may help, but be sure to discuss your options with a doctor if you are taking other drugs already.

- Pain killers can ease headaches and muscle aches. (Children should not take aspirin because of the risk of developing Reye's syndrome, a serious disease that affects the brain and liver in particular.)
- Antihistamines can dry up mucus production but may make you drowsy—not recommended when operating machinery or driving.
- Decongestants are used to relieve nasal congestion and are available in numerous over-the-counter cold remedies. They work by narrowing blood vessels in the nose lining, reducing swelling, inflammation and mucus production.
- The use of cough medicines is not supported by scientific evidence; however, sucking lozenges, hot drinks and soups may help. Spicy foods may also help by promoting calmative airway secretions that soothe an inflamed throat.

Maud Farris-Luse (1887–2002) and Kamato Hongo (1887–2003)

When Maud Farris-Luse died in Michigan, United States, in 2002 aged 115, she had been recognized by *The Guinness Book of Records* as the oldest living person in the world. She remembered her first move to Indiana by horse-drawn carriage in the 1890s. She led an ordinary life, working as a factory clerk, a hotel maid and cook, and had seven children. Said to be mentally alert until she was 110, she never smoked or drank but loved fishing. When Maud died, Japanese Kamato Hongo took over her 'title' and entertained her family by singing a folk song from her bed on her 116th birthday in 2003. Her unusual habit of sleeping for two days in a row, then staying awake for two days, meant that she had missed her 115th birthday the year before. The love and warmth of her family was said to be the secret of her longevity.

Alternative action

Evidence of the effectiveness of alternative treatments for the common cold, including herbal remedies, is not conclusive but many are popular nonetheless. They include the following:

- Steam inhalation. Breathing in steam from a bowl or jug of hot water can be soothing to sore nasal passages.
- Echinacea. Some studies show this plant, originally used by Native Americans, can help a cold once it's set in, but whether it can prevent one forming is not yet substantiated. It may work through a combination of antioxidant and antiviral activity and by stimulating the white blood cells of your immune system.
- Garlic. Garlic was used in ancient times by both the Greeks and Egyptians. The Russians used it in World War I as an antibiotic. Some researchers believe it stimulates and activates white blood cells in humans and many of its components have been shown to have effect against the influenza virus.
- Elderberry. This plant has been used as an expectorant, a sore throat treatment, and for coughs, colds and nasal catarrh. Studies have shown it inhibits a number of flu virus strains and speeds up recovery from the flu.
- Zinc. Zinc lozenges may help by blocking the entry of the virus into body cells, but doubt surrounds the safety of the high dose that seems necessary.
- Vitamin C. Investigations into the preventative effects of vitamin C are not conclusive. It's thought at best that increased vitamin C may help to reduce the severity or duration of symptoms, but even this is not clear.

Out in the cold

A cold virus such as a rhinovirus can survive for up to three hours outside the nasal passages on objects and the skin.

A LIFETIME OF HEALTH

While colds plague us throughout life, other problems come and go with age. For instance, a paper published in the Medical Journal of Australia (MJA) in 2003 highlights asthma (almost 1 in 4 Australian children suffers from it) and behavioural problems as among the most prevalent chronic disabilities of childhood. By contrast, alcohol misuse, depression and anxiety disorders are the most prevalent chronic disabilities for Australians aged between 25 and 44. And the first two—alcohol misuse and depression—are also major risk factors in the two principal causes of death in this age group: road traffic accidents and suicide. The middle years, when, to quote the MJA, 'The accumulated interactions of genetic predisposition, environment and lifestyle commonly start to impact on health', are characterized on a population basis by conditions such as heart disease and chronic lung disease. Chronic illness in old age includes arthritis, hypertension (high blood pressure), ischaemic heart disease and diabetes.

WHAT CAN YOU DO TODAY TO IMPROVE YOUR HEALTH?

There is a wealth of information about health, from diets for the liver and exercises for the eyes to alternative medicines for cancer and the best way to get fit in your fifties. Although some aspects of your health seem in the hands of fate and others are most definitely locked in your genes, there are many ways you can optimize your health and hedge your bets. Many effective health measures need not be complicated and usually have multiple benefits. Eating more vegetables, for instance, can improve digestive health, help you control or even lose weight, and—depending on the type of vegetables—may reduce cholesterol and improve circulatory health as well as reduce the risk of cancer. Some of the simple steps to better health that you can take yourself are listed below.

Stop smoking

Tobacco smoke contains 43 chemicals known to cause cancer. Some of these directly cause damage to a gene known as 'p53', the main role of which is to prevent cancer cells forming. One-fifth of cancer deaths in Australia can be attributed to smoking. As well as lung cancer, smoking increases the rates of cancer of the lips, oral and nasal cavities, oesophagus, pharynx, larynx, pancreas, bladder, cervix, vulva and penis. Smoking also damages the circulatory system: it narrows arteries, making them sticky and causing a build-up of fatty deposits. It raises blood pressure and can lead to abnormal heart rhythms and chest pain. Smoking causes over 40 per cent of heart disease in people under 65 years of age. Smokers have four times the risk of suffering sudden cardiac death than do non-smokers.

Cut back alcohol

Experts seem to agree that a little drinking is healthy, but heavy drinking is definitely not. It's associated with heart and brain damage; cirrhosis of the liver; cancer of the liver, breast, mouth, throat, larynx and oesophagus; stomach ulcers; intestinal bleeding; depression; aggressive behaviour; and a higher chance of being involved in accidents on the road, at work and at home.

Most health authorities set a limit on healthy drinking at two drinks a day for women and four for men. Women, being generally smaller and with proportionately less body water than men, have a lower safe limit. They also run the risk of an increased tendency to breast cancer with increased alcohol intake. While drinking little and often is less damaging than binge drinking, consuming alcohol with a meal slows down the alcohol absorption and is an even better way to go.

Eat more fruit and vegetables

Fruit and vegetables are bursting with beneficial ingredients: vitamins, minerals, antioxidants and other phytochemicals ('phyto' is from the Greek for plant). It's likely that this accounts for the fact that diets rich in vegetables and fruit are protective against heart disease and cancer. Some phytochemicals prevent the formation of carcinogens; others prevent the oxidation of cholesterol, reducing cholesterol production. For example, saponins in beans (and also

Stop-smoking products

While a genuine desire to stop smoking is a quitter's best friend, help is available to boost your resolve—booklets, books, videos and advice that help you understand the underlying reasons for your smoking as well as plan a strategy to quit. In addition there are the following:

- Courses. These provide extra support, and teach skills to cope with temptation and withdrawal symptoms. They are particularly useful for someone who's tried quitting several times without success.
- Nicotine replacement therapy. This reduces nicotine withdrawal symptoms so you can concentrate on breaking the smoking habit. Options include nicotine chewing gum, patches, inhalers, roll-on products and the prescription drug Zyban.
- Other products. Some products offered by mail order companies are not only ineffective, according to Quit in Australia, they may also be poisonous. These include silver compounds (toxic with long-term use); Lobeline, a substance similar to nicotine; and herbal preparations including herbal cigarettes that may be a significant health hazard in themselves, containing substances similar to tobacco, including tar.
- Acupuncture. Treatment is designed to provide relief from withdrawal symptoms and is more effective when combined with counselling.
- Hypnosis. Cessation rates improve when hypnotherapy is used in conjunction with counselling and follow-up support and where there is a high motivation and expectation to succeed.
- Filters. There is insufficient evidence to promote these as a quitting aid, and some studies show that smokers compensate for the reduction in nicotine and tar by inhaling more deeply.

wholegrains) neutralize cancer-causing enzymes in the digestive tract; sulphur compounds in allium vegetables such as garlic, onions and leeks may reduce stomach cancer; and flavonoids in celery and onions fight oxidation and reduce blood clots.

Vegetables are naturally low in fat and come in a dazzling array of choice: leaves such as spinach and lettuce, bulbs like onions, roots such as radishes and sweet potato, stems including asparagus shoots, flowers such as cauliflower and artichoke, and 'fruits' such as eggplant (aubergine) and tomato. Fruit has a similarly healthy profile. See the section on healthy eating on pages 299–308 of this chapter.

Keep moving

Adequate exercise helps maintain a healthy weight, reducing the risk of many diseases linked to obesity. In addition, it reduces the risk of heart disease because it improves the blood cholesterol profile and lowers blood pressure. Weight-bearing exercise also reduces the risk of developing osteoporosis (brittle bones) by strengthening bones; improves the way the body deals with insulin (the hormone that controls blood sugar); improves fitness, tones muscles and increases strength; helps keep bowels regular; and generally makes you feel better about yourself and better able to deal with stress. See the detailed section on exercise on pages 299–308 of this chapter.

Sleep sufficiently

Sleep keeps your immune system and mental functions at their peak. Fatigue due to sleep deprivation is implicated in accidents on the road and at work. Without adequate sleep you lose concentration, experience more anxiety, are irritable and are less able to make good decisions. Sleep deprivation may even impair your memory. According to sleep researchers, daytime drowsiness is due to 'sleep debt'. This can accumulate over a period of weeks, requiring extra hours of sleep to 'pay it back'. See the detailed section on sleep on pages 321–329 of this chapter.

Relax

Stress exacerbates heart disease and high blood pressure and contributes to digestive problems such as irritable bowel syndrome, constipation, diarrhoea and ulcers. It also inhibits your immune system—some doctors feel recurrent cold sores and other infections and heightened allergic responses may often occur against a background of stress.

To counteract and keep on top of stress, take time out with relaxing activities or techniques. While the body's stress response is automatic, the relaxation response needs to be ushered in by specific processes. In the relaxation response the muscles relax, the pulse slows, the breathing rate and blood pressure fall. Some of the techniques that can induce relaxation include repetitive exercise, stretching, progressive muscle relaxation, yoga and meditation.

VOX POP: How significant is your health to keeping you happy?

'It's very important and I really appreciate it as I have a number of friends who don't enjoy the good health I do—like a mate who had a double lung transplant. He is so grateful for his new lease of life. He's an inspiration to be around. I let fitness activities drift from time to time, but I'm lucky in that my body stays in reasonable shape. Could be the vegetarian diet.' DL

'I enjoy good health and it's very important to me. I tend to react to flu or other illness with a certain indignation and irritation—how inconvenient that this nonsense should come along when I have deadlines and appointments…I cycle to work and back and walk a lot rather than catch a bus or taxi wherever possible. I used to be slim to the point of thinness but at about age 34, weight set in. I eat fruit and vegetables and fish. I don't like junk food anyway. I probably drink a bit more than I should.' PN

'I firmly believe that, "He who has health has hope, and he who has hope, has everything." I have a good fitness level, which helps keep fatigue at bay. Yoga and exercise are my passion. They help me mentally too.' CS

'Feeling healthy maximizes my enjoyment of life. When I feel fit, I feel good about my body and can cope better with stress. I like healthy food—especially vegetables, pulses and the staples— and try to keep alcohol to recommended limits. Keeping flexible reduces stiffness. Enough sleep makes everything more manageable. I walk everywhere, cycle regularly and practise yoga when I can. If I get the opportunity, I enjoy different pursuits like indoor rock climbing, caving or horse-riding. I'd like to lose a few kilos but am wary of the psychological effect of dieting.' MN

'I was diagnosed with rheumatoid arthritis twelve years ago, but accept it better now and try not to let it depress me. But it can be frustrating. I value my health more as I get older. I try to keep as healthy as possible by regular swimming, gentle walking and a healthy vegetarian organic diet. I also try to control my weight and keep a sense of humour. I definitely feel less stressed when I feel physically fit, and I feel fitter when I'm slimmer.' AS

EATING YOUR WAY TO HEALTH

The vocabulary of nutrition is complicated: omega-3 fatty acids, phytochemicals, probiotics, polyunsaturated fats, HDL cholesterol… But healthy eating need not be difficult. All it requires is for you to follow a few simple principles, isolate and work round problems like business lunches or the need to lose weight, and find practical ways to make it all easier. Solutions can be as simple as stocking the larder with the right foods, investing in a few low fat cookery books or finding out how to make food taste great with less fat and less salt. Here are some of the areas nutrition experts concentrate on.

FIXING FAT

We need some fat for the vitamins and other chemicals it contains. But too much saturated fat—the type found in highest concentrations in foods of animal origin, as well as in several plant oils including coconut oil and palm oil, and many snack foods like

Relaxation: the way to go

In his book *The Relaxation Response*, Dr Herbert Benson of the Harvard Medical School advises practising inducing the relaxation response—in which muscles are released of tension, and breathing and pulse rate slow—to guard against stress. The exercises can be used in reaction to a stressful situation (once you've got a moment and a bit of space to yourself!) but can also help you 'bring on' relaxation on a daily basis. Here are three ways to relax.

1 DEEP BREATHING

Using the diaphragm—not just the chest—to breathe helps focus the mind and is an effective way to relax. Deep inhalation can help divert attention from a stressful situation; holding the breath momentarily raises carbon dioxide levels, which in itself aids relaxation; while slow exhalation relaxes muscles. For best results, practise for five to ten minutes at a time, perhaps once or twice a day. To try diaphragmatic breathing:

(a) Get comfortable. Relax and close your eyes, keep your back straight with your chin tucked slightly in and your shoulders back but loose.

(b) Gently place your hands at the sides of your lower ribs, with fingers pointing towards your stomach.

(c) Inhale slowly through your nose, feeling your ribs move out to the side as you do so.

(d) Exhale slowly through your mouth, feeling tension flow out along with the breath.

2 DEEP MUSCLE RELAXATION

This is also sometimes called progressive muscle relaxation and involves tensing specific muscle groups then relaxing them. It helps you to recognize the different feelings of tension and relaxation, as well as train you to elicit relaxation. You can practise sitting in a chair or lying on the floor. The idea is to gradually move from head to toe, tensing then relaxing each of the muscle groups twice before moving on. At the end of the exercise, stay still for a few moments before opening your eyes and reflecting on how the exercise felt. Move down your body in the following order:

- forehead: wrinkle, raise eyebrows
- eyes and nose: close tight
- lips, cheeks and jaw: grimace
- hands: stretch arms out in front, clench fists
- forearms: push against an imaginary wall
- upper arms: tense the biceps by bending the elbows
- shoulders: lift
- back: arch
- stomach: tighten
- hips and buttocks: tighten
- thighs: press together
- feet: bend towards the body
- toes: curl tightly.

3 THE MINI

For everyday hassles, try one of these mini relaxations. First of all, get comfortable. Remember to let relaxation happen at its own pace, take note of sounds and let them pass, focus on easy, natural breathing.

(a) Count down. With head level and eyes open, choose a spot to focus on. Then count backwards in time with your breath, starting at five. With each breath gradually close your eyes until at 'one' they are shut.

(b) Shrugging it off. Raise your shoulders up to your ears. Hold for a count of four then drop back to normal. Repeat a few times, varying with shoulder rotations—first one shoulder, then the other, then both together.

(c) As light as a cloud. Focus on breathing and feel your mind open up. As your breathing becomes calm and regular, imagine the breath is a cloud entering you, filling you up then leaving your body.

biscuits and cakes—is unhealthy. It raises blood cholesterol, increasing the chances of a build-up of cholesterol and hardening of the artery walls (a condition called atherosclerosis), which can result in a heart attack or stroke. Confusingly, cholesterol—a fatty, waxy substance found in all the body tissues—comes in several forms, some of which are 'good' and some 'bad'. In simple terms, the bad (LDL, or low density lipoprotein, and VLDL, very low density lipoprotein) block arteries, while the good (HDL, high density lipoprotein) helps clear away bad cholesterol from the blood.

While saturated fat and another known as trans fat, found in some margarines, increase bad cholesterol, other fats appear to reduce it. These are known as mono-unsaturated (found in olive oil, avocados, peanuts and canola oil) and polyunsaturated fats (found in vegetable oils, margarines, fish, nuts and seeds). They feature highly in the Mediterranean diet which, studies have found, seems to protect against heart disease. To reduce your consumption of saturated fat:

● Choose low fat dairy products.
● Use less saturated fat in cooking.
● Prepare and cook foods using less saturated fat—grilling, rather than frying, for instance.
● Get to know the fat content of some of your favourite foods by consulting a fat and/or calorie and fibre counter.

Oily fish such as mackerel and tuna are high in omega-3 fatty acids, a fat component found in some polyunsaturated fats. Omega-3 is converted to substances such as prostaglandins, which act like hormones, and then to other substances involved in blood clotting, immune responses and inflammatory reactions. These are believed to be beneficial in a number of situations, ranging from coronary heart disease and organ transplant to some kinds of arthritis and asthma.

The other issue concerning fat is that whatever type it is, it is very energy dense. Too much fat in your diet can lead to weight gain. It may also be linked with some cancers including bowel cancer.

The lowdown on lowering cholesterol

There are many different factors that influence the level of bad cholesterol in the blood:

- Legumes and oats lower cholesterol, possibly because of the insoluble fibre they contain.
- Excessive alcohol consumption increases blood fat levels, increasing blood cholesterol.
- Some substances, such as saponins in chickpeas and other legumes, lower blood cholesterol.
- Exercise seems to boost good cholesterol.

BONING UP ON CALCIUM

Calcium is needed for healthy bones and to prevent osteoporosis, also known as brittle bones, a condition that affects 1 in 3 women. While calcium is found in highest concentrations in dairy foods such as milk, cheese and yoghurt, it is also found in tahini (a sesame seed paste used to make hummus), canned salmon, figs and almonds. The following foods inhibit calcium intake, something which may not be a problem if your intake is high, but could be important if your intake is marginal:

- salt
- caffeine (more than four cups a day)
- nicotine
- alcohol (more than two standard drinks a day)
- oxalates, chemicals found in spinach, rhubarb and peanuts
- phytates, chemicals found in legumes
- large amounts of fibre
- protein (a doubling of protein intake from 50 g to 100 g or from 1¾ oz to 3⅕ oz almost halves your calcium absorption)
- some medications, including antacids.

Weight-bearing exercise, such as walking, climbing stairs or carrying groceries, helps to prevent osteoporosis by increasing calcium deposits in the bones.

INVIGORATING IRON

Lack of iron is the most common nutrient deficiency in the world. In Australia, for instance, in the Australian National Nutrition Survey released in 1997, 66 per cent of women under the age of 45 and around half of all teenage girls consumed less than the recommended amount of iron. Iron is a crucial component of a number of molecules in the body, which transport oxygen in the blood and provide oxygen to the muscles. That's why lack of it can make you feel tired, weak and generally washed out. When iron levels are low enough, anaemia develops—along with

Lance Armstrong (1971–)

'The golden boy of American cycling', as Lance Armstrong became known, was a natural athlete from the start. He won the Iron Kids Triathlon when thirteen, and by sixteen was a professional triathlete. But in 1996, when he was 25, he turned his determination to another challenge: cancer. For five months Lance had ignored symptoms of pain and swelling in his groin, attributing it to his daily training of six to eight hours cycling. But when he began to cough blood and suffer severe headaches he was forced to seek medical advice. The diagnosis was barely believable: he had advanced testicular cancer that had already spread and produced a dozen golf-ball-sized tumours in his lungs as well as lesions on his brain.

The news paralyzed him with fear, but not for long. He took charge of his treatment, opting for an aggressive course of chemotherapy combined with surgery. He returned to cycling in 1998 and in 1999 won the month-long Tour de France. In 2003 he won it for the fifth time. With the help of friends, Lance established the Lance Armstrong Foundation in 1996 to help support cancer survivors and promote cancer research and awareness. 'I'm proof that everyone is at risk for cancer,' he says on the foundation's website. 'I was a 25 year old competitive bicyclist in prime condition.' But while cancer was his toughest opponent, the race against it was also his most rewarding.

shortness of breath, coldness, palpitations, and pins and needles.

Iron comes in two types: haem found in meat, and non-haem found in vegetables. While haem iron is absorbed better, there are many ways to improve the absorption of non-haem iron:

- Non-haem iron is better absorbed in the presence of haem iron, so even a little meat goes a long way to combating iron deficiency.
- Vitamin C enhances iron absorption. Eating vegetables or fruit with iron-rich foods is a good idea, whether that means a glass of orange juice with your iron-fortified breakfast cereal or a tomato salad with your steak.
- Substances that inhibit iron absorption include tannins in tea, phytic acid in bran and oxalic acid in spinach.

Vegetarians can obtain enough iron from plant foods but need to be aware of substances that interfere with absorption; for instance, it's a good idea to avoid drinking tea with a meal.

They should also ensure that they eat plenty of wholegrain cereals, legumes, nuts and seeds.

FABULOUS FRUIT

Despite efforts to get people to eat more fruit, many do not. In a National Nutrition Survey in 1996 in Australia, for instance, half the males aged between twelve and 44 and a third of children between four and eleven had not eaten any fruit the previous day.

Fruit is bursting with vitamins, minerals and numerous beneficial phytochemicals (plant chemicals). It also provides fibre, is low in fat and relatively low in energy. So, how can you go about increasing your fruit intake?

- Snacks. Perfectly packaged and easily portable for office or school lunches, fruit is also a low fat option for mid afternoon snacks at home.
- Breakfast. On top of cereal, in smoothies with yoghurt and milk, on its own with a glass of milk…fruit is an ideal way to start the day.
- Fruit salad, stewed or baked fruit. Fruit is the perfect healthy

dessert option, either on its own or with low fat yoghurt and dried fruit and nuts for variety.

- Garnishes and accompaniments. Chopped mango or banana gives a note of freshness to curries. Finely chopped apple and onion makes a garnish for thick vegetable soup. Salsas, such as peach with chopped mint and lemon juice, are the ideal accompaniment to barbecued food and Mexican dishes.
- In savoury dishes. Fruit is a feature of several cuisines including Moroccan, where apricots, apple, currants and quince may be added to meat stews. Fruits such as apple can be incorporated into salads. Orange juice adds warm notes to soups with ingredients such as carrots or lentils.

VEGETABLES FOR VITALITY

Five is the magic number of total fruit and vegetable serves we should be aiming for every day, according to numerous health authorities. If that sounds boring, consider the following ways of incorporating more vegetables in your diet:

- Steam with flavour. The nutrient value of steamed vegetables is next best to raw ones. If plain steamed vegetables do not inspire, try putting a bunch of basil or garlic slivers in the steamer.
- Bake. Drizzle with olive oil and add spices such as cumin or coriander seeds. Potatoes, sweet potatoes and other root vegetables such as turnip and parsnip are good candidates, so are eggplant (aubergine), fennel and pumpkin.
- Barbecue. Lightly brush eggplant (aubergine), capsicum (pepper) and mushroom with oil before cooking them on the barbecue grid. Corn on the cob can be soaked first in water, then barbecued with the protective leaves (but without the silky fibres).
- In stews. Don't forget the vegies when cooking meat stews. Zucchini (courgettes), capsicum, eggplant and tomato add a Mediterranean flavour. Turnips, swede, parsnips and carrots make the meat go further in a wintry casserole. Potatoes help thicken the sauce and onions add background flavour.
- Hearty salads. Try yoghurt coleslaw made with cabbage, carrot and apple; or tomato and basil with olive oil. Grated carrot, green

pawpaw, finely sliced onion and cucumber take on an Asian flavour with lemon or lime juice, a dash of fish sauce and fresh herbs. Salad ingredients can be dressed in a variety of ways.

- In soups. Cubed; blended; in medleys or just one or two flavours; on their own or with meat, fish, pulses or pasta—vegetables make for wonderful soups. Carefully choose your combinations and soup it up, from a delicate homemade stock to thick, almost porridge-consistency concoctions.

SUPER STAPLES

Bread, pasta and rice—sometimes called 'complex carbohydrates' or starchy foods—are a valuable part of a healthy diet. They are a low fat source of protein and most supply a range of minerals. Some grains, such as oats and barley, provide soluble fibre. Although low carbohydrate diets have become fashionable, authorities such as the World Health Organization recommend relatively high carbohydrate diets to maintain a healthy weight. Wholegrains are valuable for their fibre and nutrient content. They also tend to have a lower glycaemic index (GI)—a measure of the effect a food has on blood glucose. A low GI means a slow, steady release of glucose, valuable for managing diabetes, weight control and for endurance sports.

GI is another tool you can use to assist you in choosing healthy food alongside other criteria such as energy content, saturated fat level, fibre, vitamins and antioxidants. Cooked carrots, for instance, are sometimes condemned for their surprisingly high GI—but they remain a valuable food because of other nutrients. We are advised to include some low GI foods in our diets every day. GI values range from 0 to 100, with glucose at 100.

- Low GI (below 40) foods include milk, yoghurt, pasta, apple, mixed grain bread and lentils.
- Moderate GI (between 40 and 70) foods include ice cream, porridge, brown rice, potato, banana, grapes and wholemeal bread.
- High GI (over 70) includes breakfast cereals such as cornflakes and wheat biscuits, white rice, parsnips and honey.

What about...?

- Sugar. Often accused of being unhealthy for you, sugar is not all bad—it's the packaging that counts. Fruits are sugary but also contain fibre and a host of vitamins, minerals and antioxidants. But biscuits and cakes, which also contain sugar, tend to be high in fat, low in fibre and lower in nutrients altogether.

- Folic acid. Women who wish to become pregnant are advised to take a course of folic acid supplements for a month before conception and during the first three months of pregnancy. This is because of studies that show a link between folic acid deficiency and babies born with defects of the neural tube—a central nerve in the spine—the best known of which is spina bifida. Food sources of folic acid include lentils, chicken liver, chickpeas, spinach and oranges.

- Salt. High salt intake is linked to high blood pressure, osteoporosis and renal failure. As three-quarters of the salt eaten is from manufactured foods, it makes sense to switch over to fresh produce as much as possible if you want to cut back on salt consumption. You could also reduce the amount of salt you use in cooking and at the table.

- Fibre. Fibre has a host of benefits—from easing constipation to lowering cholesterol. It may also help to prevent bowel cancer. There are two main types: insoluble fibre (such as that found in bran) and soluble fibre (found in oats, apples and pulses).

WAYS WITH WEIGHT

Weight problems are at epidemic proportions in numerous countries worldwide. The International Obesity Task Force says that in Japan obesity in men has doubled over the past twenty years. In Samoa, 77 per cent of male urban dwellers are obese; while in Australia two-thirds of men are overweight or obese and more than 50 per cent of Australian women are overweight or obese. In the United States, 64 per cent of adults are overweight or obese. Our children are getting fatter too: in Australia, 1 in 5 children is obese or overweight.

The usual measure of obesity is the body mass index, or BMI. To calculate your BMI, divide your weight in kilograms by your squared height in metres. For example, a 1.6-metre person weighing 60 kilograms would have a BMI of $60/(1.6 \times 1.6) = 23$. The BMI is divided into the following categories:

- under 20: underweight
- 20 to 25: normal
- 25 to 30: overweight
- over 30: obese.

So, in the example above, the person's BMI of 23 would fall right in the middle of the healthy weight range.

Being overweight, especially obese, increases the chance of developing a range of illnesses including heart disease, diabetes, metabolic disorders, joint problems and high blood pressure.

There are no short cuts to losing weight, although theories abound and range from low carbohydrate, high fat diets to high fat, low carbohydrate diets! There are diets where you eat nothing but pineapple and others where you eat only eggs. The bald truth is that unless 'energy in' (food) is less than 'energy out' (exercise) you will not lose weight. So, to lose weight you need to move more and/or eat less. The best approach is to do both.

If you are thinking of trying to lose weight, consider your current diet first of all. Do you eat the sorts of foods recommended or can you identify problem areas—like pizza and pies most nights? It's not a bad idea to record everything that passes your lips for a week or so to gain a picture of where you could cut back without too much trouble. Take an honest look at how active you are. Can you identify ways to move more and shift fat too? Some of the approaches to weight loss include the following.

Prescribed diets

Look for ones with a balanced approach, where you eat from all the food groups (bread, pasta and rice; fruit and vegetables; meat and fish or vegetarian alternatives; dairy or alternatives). Avoid fad diets, including those that promise a dramatic weight loss or more than

1–1.5 kilograms (2.2–3.3 pounds) a week, or ones specifying less than 5000 kilojoules (approximately 1200 calories) of daily energy intake without supervision.

Clubs

If you like to follow 'rules' and enjoy the support of other slimmers, a group approach may be for you. However, some people find the public weigh-ins confronting, while others find the 'rules' too finicky to follow.

Focus on fats and alcohol

One way to reduce energy intake is to concentrate on cutting back on fats, which are energy dense, and alcohol, which provides empty calories. To cut back on fat, avoid fast food, cakes, pies and cream. Watch your portion size of cheese and trim the visible fat from meat. A fat counter booklet will help you get to know where fat hides. If you enjoy alcohol, it's probably better to cut back rather than cut it out altogether to increase the chances of sticking to a slimming regimen.

Petrol consumption, watching television and weight gain

In some countries, petrol consumption and the number of hours that are spent watching television have risen at similar rates to obesity levels. One paper from the long-running *Nurses Health Study* by researchers at the Harvard School of Public Health, published in the United States in 2003, analyzed the habits of and followed the weight of more than 50,000 women. Watching television was associated with increased obesity and type 2 diabetes (also known as adult onset diabetes). The trouble is that watching television means more than simply sitting around playing coach potato—it also has a hypnotic effect and thus lowers your metabolic rate in a way that other sedentary activities such as sewing, playing board games, reading and writing do not.

Light meals

Another way of reducing food intake overall is to make one meal—perhaps your evening meal—a very light one: a big bowl of salad, a plate of steaming vegetables with fresh herbs and a light sauce, a bowl of low fat soup, and so on. Have a bread roll or a baked potato with it so you don't feel entirely deprived.

Simply smaller

If the balanced approach suits you and your diet is quite healthy, just try to cut back on the amount you eat overall. Have one slice of meat instead of two, two spoons of rice instead of three, and so on.

Extra careful

After noting your food intake for a week, you may realize that it's not one biscuit at morning tea that's the problem, but three in the morning, four in the afternoon, and cheese and crackers before going to bed. If this is the case, you might be able to cut a lot of energy from your diet simply by cutting down on extras like confectionery, cakes, crisps and alcohol.

The benefits of breakfast

Breakfast is often hailed as an important meal for the slimmer as it kick-starts the metabolism after a night's rest. It is easy to make it a healthy meal, as there is a great selection of good choices available: cereals, bread, fruit, and so on. Additionally, people usually find that their resolve is higher in the morning, so it's a particularly good time for them to try to eat well.

WHEN YOU NEED TO PUT ON WEIGHT

As anyone who's tried to put weight on can tell you, it's surprisingly hard—and you may not get much sympathy from friends who have the opposite problem. However, some strategies may help.

- If you've recently experienced sudden weight loss, be sure to visit a doctor, especially if accompanied by other symptoms such as loss of appetite, pain or recurrent digestive problems.
- Don't skip meals. Even if you are not hungry, eat at regular times to try to regain a healthy appetite.
- Include energy foods like bread, rice and pasta—you won't put on weight if all you eat is salads and thin soups.
- Extras are OK. If you have a basically healthy diet, a few treats like a glass of wine or a chocolate bar will not do you any harm.
- Easy does it. Gradually increasing the amount you eat by increasing portion sizes can help.

The secrets to a successful diet

The National Weight Control Registry, a collaborative venture between the US universities of Colorado and Pittsburgh, has identified 2000 Americans who have lost weight and kept it off. The average registrant has lost 60 pounds (around 27 kilograms) and maintained the loss for five years. Half of the registrants lost weight on their own without any formal program or other help. Four common approaches to weight loss were:

- a low fat, high carbohydrate diet
- regularly monitoring your weight
- eating breakfast
- being physically active for at least an hour a day.

EXERCISE: A BODY DESIGNED TO MOVE

A bear, however hard he tries
Grows tubby without exercise.

'TEDDY BEAR', A A MILNE, *WHEN WE WERE VERY YOUNG* (1924)

The benefits of exercise are well documented. Those who are physically active are more likely to live longer, less likely to have a heart attack or stroke, have a reduced risk of developing diabetes, feel more energetic, manage their weight better, have a healthier blood cholesterol level, lower blood pressure, and stronger bones and muscles. They are more confident and happy, and sleep better. And that's just for starters. The list grows every year. In fact, recent research shows these additional benefits:

● Breast cancer survivors benefit from exercise. A Canadian study published in the *Journal of Clinical Oncology* in 2003 showed those who began an exercise program soon after treatment improved their mental outlook as well as fitness levels. The exercise group in the University of Alberta study trained on stationary bikes, working out three times a week. Researchers believe that the exercise helped reverse the side effects of cancer treatment, which included weight gain and inactivity, and also helped the patients feel more optimistic.

● Walking halves a diabetic's chance of dying. A US study of almost 3000 people with diabetes, reported in the *Archives of Internal Medicine*, found that those who walked for at least three hours a week had a 54 per cent lower risk of death from any cause, and a 53 per cent lower risk of heart-related death. Exercise helps prevent diabetes developing in the first place and, in those who have developed the condition, it helps improve blood sugar levels.

● A study published in the *Journal of the American Medical Association* found regular exercise lowered the risk of older people fracturing a hip. Researchers at Boston's Brigham and Women's Hospital followed more than 61,000 postmenopausal

How much exercise?

- Getting started. Thirty minutes a day of a moderate activity such as walking, swimming, gardening or playing golf is sufficient for you to start reaping the benefits. Even better news for those who don't like organized sport, or anything that feels like 'exercise', is that three slots of ten minutes have the same benefit as one 30-minute session.
- Losing weight. If you want to lose weight, the more exercise you can fit in, the greater the benefit. Some US experts recommend exercising for at least an hour a day if you want to lose weight.
- Greater fitness. If you are already active but want to improve fitness, consider the different components of fitness. A fitness program from the Harvard University Health Services recommends vigorous activity of twenty to 30 minutes' duration, five times a week.

nurses from eleven different states in the United States over a twelve-year period. They found that walking for an hour a day or jogging for three hours a week reduced the risk of fracture to a degree equal to that of taking hormone replacement therapy.

MORE THAN ACTIVE

While just 30 minutes of activity a day is enough to gain the benefits of exercise, a more sophisticated approach takes into account three categories of fitness: heart–lung endurance (pumping blood and breathing); strength (muscle strength and endurance); and flexibility of muscles and joints.

Heart–lung endurance

Also referred to as cardiac fitness, this is about the heart's ability to keep up with the demands of fast-moving muscles and the lungs' capacity to keep the body supplied with sufficient oxygen. Exercises that condition the heart and lungs get your pulse moving and your breath going faster. The benefits are improved heart and lung function, weight management, stress management, improved cholesterol, lower blood pressure, reduced risk of heart attack and stroke, prevention or control of diabetes, improved sense of wellbeing, and maintained bone density. Cardiac fitness exercises include:

- brisk walking
- running or jogging
- swimming
- cycling
- hiking
- skipping
- using equipment such as treadmills, stationary bicycles, stair climbers, ski and rowing machines
- aerobic classes or videos
- sports with lots of vigorous movement like basketball, football, singles tennis, skating or squash.

Burning up energy is the key to weight control—whether you are trying to burn your body's fat stores and lose weight or wanting to maintain your current weight. The following list samples a few popular forms of exercise and gives the approximate kilojoules or calories burned during a 30-minute session. The exact amount you burn will depend on your weight and how much you throw yourself into the activity.

ACTIVITY	KILOJOULES (CALORIES)
Aerobics	1400 (335)
Cycling	1500 (360)
Golf	700 (170)
Running	1500 (360)
Swimming	1000 (240)
Tennis, doubles	360 (90)
Tennis, singles	1000 (240)
Walking, with hills	700 (170)

Weighing it up

If you are starting out using weights, it's important that you consider the following questions:

1 HOW HEAVY?

Weights should feel heavy but you should be able to lift them eight times before having to rest.

2 HOW OFTEN?

Muscles need to rest between weight training sessions, so don't train two days in a row.

Muscle strength

Increased muscle strength allows muscles to exert a force for a brief time or for repeated times. Training gradually strengthens the muscle by increasing the strain put on it. The benefits are toned muscles, weight management, stress management, reduced risk of injury, reduced fatigue, slower loss of bone mass, improved posture, and finding everyday tasks easier. Everybody can benefit from strong muscles, old and young. The important thing is to start 'light' and gradually build strength. Exercises for muscle strength include:

- body weight exercises such as sit-ups, push-ups and leg lifts
- using free weights such as wrist and ankle weights and dumbbells
- using resistance equipment such as latex bands and stretchy tubes
- using adjustable weight machines.

Flexibility

Stretches aid flexibility whether morning stretches, limbering up exercises, cool down activities, stretching programs, yoga, ballet, tai chi or gymnastics. Apart from rewarding you with a greater range of movement, exercises for flexibility improve circulation, reduce the risk of injury from tight muscles, and are good for stress management and overall fitness.

BETTER EXERCISE

Whatever your chosen activity, a few basics will help reduce injury, and make exercising more pleasant and more effective.

A plan

If you want to change your current exercise regimen, draw up a rough plan to help you focus on the activities you think you'll benefit from. Think about what's realistic, considering the following:

- Your current activity level. Start small and work up.
- Your health. If you have a heart problem, are on medication or have a chronic illness, check with your doctor what sort of exercise program is right for you and what, if anything, you should be wary of or avoid.

Weaving exercise into daily life

Sometimes you need to get creative about slotting in exercise and making small changes that will make you more active. Try:

- walking part or all of the way to work
- exercising in your lunch hour, perhaps using any facilities at work
- scheduling in an exercise session at the weekend
- joining an adult education class in an activity you've always wanted to learn: ballroom dancing or abseiling, aqua aerobics or kick boxing
- morning yoga
- stretching at your desk
- using stairs instead of the lift
- using a bike for errands instead of the car
- locking some habits into your life—like a ten-minute stretch at the beginning of each day or a Friday night swim
- adding vigour to your housework, yard work and gardening
- a variety of activities: if you get bored with one activity, try others—maybe try some that offer companionship at the same time, such as nature walks or team sports.

- Your expectations. Do you want to shape up, reach your peak cardiac fitness or strengthen muscles?

Government health authorities are often a good place to start for fitness information, including recommended reading material and videos. The following guidelines from the President's Council on Physical Fitness and Sports, an American body, may also help you plan a weekly exercise schedule:

- Remember to warm up at every session. This can either be five to ten minutes of slow jogging, walking, knee lifts, arm circles, and so on or, alternatively, a slow version of the activity you're about to embark on.
- To improve your muscular strength you'll need a minimum of two twenty-minute sessions a week that include exercises for all major muscle groups.
- To increase your muscular endurance you'll need at least three 30-minute sessions a week including push-ups, sit-ups and weights.
- To improve your cardio-respiratory endurance (or heart–lung endurance), you require three twenty-minute bouts of aerobic activity (activity requiring oxygen) a week.
- Don't forget to work on your flexibility. Ten to twelve minutes of daily stretching is recommended.
- Remember to cool down properly after every session. Five to ten minutes of slow walking, or other low-level exercise, combined with stretching is ideal.

Warm up, cool down

Once you move beyond walking as your means of exercise, you'll need to warm up properly. This warms muscles, making them less prone to injuries such as being pulled or torn. It also eases you into activity by gradually increasing your heart rate.

Cooling down allows the heart rate and breathing to return to normal slowly. It also gives your body temperature time to regulate itself, prevents blood pooling in one place and reduces the risk of sore muscles.

Women only: a different kind of exercise

All women are advised to practise a specific type of 'workout' known as Kegel exercises. A simple tensing movement that strengthens the pelvic floor muscles, Kegel exercises are designed to keep incontinence at bay in later life. Particularly vital for women who have had children, they are an invisible, internal strengthening exercise and can be practised anytime, anywhere: in the shower, on the phone, in the car.

1   Contract the muscles of the pelvic floor for one second then release.
2   Repeat ten times to make a set.
3   Work up to repeating one set ten to twenty times a day.

Superior stretching

Dr Maria Fiatarone from Harvard University Health Services recommends holding a stretch for at least twenty seconds to increase flexibility. In addition:

- do not bounce
- relax the muscle being stretched
- try stretching further, but not so much that it hurts
- stretch smoothly and in a controlled fashion.

The training zone

Improving your fitness means training your heart muscles to pump

The talk test

If pulse rates are too high tech for you, try the talk test.

- If you can talk while carrying out aerobic exercise, you are exercising within safe limits.
- If you are so out of breath you can't hold a conversation, slow down.

The RICE rule

For self-treatment of minor sports injuries, apply the rule of RICE:

- Rest. Rest the injured limb.
- Ice. Apply ice to the injured area for at least twenty minutes.
- Compression. An elastic bandage on a sore joint or a firm bandage on a sore or cut helps to slow down bleeding and swelling.
- Elevation. Elevate the injury higher than the heart.

more strongly. After training, the hill that used to make you run out of breath when you walked up it briskly doesn't anymore. To improve your heart you need to work it out, but within safe limits.

Aim to work out at between 50 and 75 per cent of your maximum heart rate. To calculate your maximum heart rate, take your age away from 220. If you are twenty years old, your maximum heart rate is 200; but if you are 45 it is 175. In the above examples, the training zone of the twenty year old would be between 100 and 150 beats per minute; the 45 year old should aim for somewhere between 88 and 131 beats per minute.

If you are just beginning a fitness program, aim for 50 per cent of your maximum heart rate. As your fitness improves, gradually increase this to 60 per cent, then 75 per cent. To take your pulse, place two fingers on the inside of your wrist near the base of the thumb. Count the pulse for fifteen seconds then multiply by four.

Avoiding injury

- Easy does it. A gradual approach to getting fit reduces the risk of injury and pain. The more sedentary you've been, the more careful you need to be when starting to get fit again.
- Prepare. If you've planned a skiing or a cycling holiday, get ready for it by increasing the amount of time you spend on the bike each week or strengthening those thigh muscles ready for the slopes.

- Get the right gear. Make sure you have helmets for cycling and skateboarding, and well-fitting, supportive shoes for running and other sports that put pressure on your feet.
- Let old injuries heal. Wait for pain and swelling to subside completely before resuming training, and follow medical advice.

Times to avoid exercising

There are times when it is best to rest, for a variety of reasons:
- when you have the flu, or feel particularly tired or under par
- immediately following a meal or alcohol
- if you feel dizzy.

A GOOD NIGHT'S SLEEP

sleep that knits up the ravelled sleave of care...balm of hurt minds, great nature's second course, chief nourisher of life's feast.

MACBETH IN WILLIAM SHAKESPEARE, *MACBETH* (ACT II, SCENE II) (1606)

We love to sleep. It is a precious, delicious gift we only appreciate when deprived of it. We hate to be woken or kept awake by busy minds or crying babies. We curse barking dogs that wake us and seek cures to insomnia when it keeps our eyes open in the night. Sleep provides our life with a rhythm: letting us sink into the sheets at the end of the day, giving us the chance of a fresh start in the morning.

Our need for sleep is subtly but securely woven into our lives. After a few nights of sleeplessness, our concentration, ability to make good decisions, alertness and all sorts of mental abilities are seriously impaired—lack of sleep is a contributing factor in many tragic car accidents. How good a night's sleep you've had before exposure to the cold virus may be the deciding factor in whether or not you'll come down with it.

Hundreds of biological processes go on during sleep, making it almost impossible to separate sleep from the process of living.

Medical scientists can point to an intricate dance of biochemistry and hormonal activity that takes place while we sleep: the levels of hormones involved in our immune system, called interleukins, rises at night, so too the level of the cancer killer, tumor necrosis factor (or TNF). Other players in the front line of our immune system, natural killer cells, seem to decrease in number after a sleepless night. One study in San Diego found that people who stayed up till 3 am had 30 per cent less natural killer cells the following day.

The American Cancer Society took these observations a step further and studied the link between average sleep per night and longevity. It found that those who slept around eight hours a night had lower mortality rates than both long sleepers (nine to ten hours) and short sleepers (four hours or less). Clearly good sleep is one of our bread-and-butter needs, not a luxury.

But the fabric of our sleep can be pulled out of shape surprisingly easily. While we have the defence of being able to override our sleep urges in an emergency—an ability that may have helped us survive in wilder days—it is a double-edged sword. Nocturnal sabre-toothed tigers don't threaten a good night's sleep anymore, but television, electric lights and bringing work home on the laptop do.

BIOLOGICAL CLOCK

Our biological clocks are tuned each day to the light from the rising sun and the falling light of dusk. At certain times of the day your biological clock will keep you awake, at other times it is switched off. The hormone melatonin is an important cog in this biological timekeeper. Secreted by the pineal gland, it directs the body to prepare for sleep by letting it know it is dark outside.

Bright light, such as that from the sun, can reset our clock. But dim lights, like that from desk lamps, also have the ability to affect human cycles. What this means for modern humans checking their emails late at night or reading by the bedside lamp is that they can delay the biological onset of sleepiness. This can push many people past their biological bedtime, which would be fine if humans didn't need sleep so much. According to William C Dement, professor of psychiatry at Stanford University Medical

Combating jet lag
A few minutes of moderate exercise on getting out of bed will increase the temperature of your body and help it move into the current time zone. A few sit-ups, push-ups or a little jogging on the spot will all help.

School and director of the university's sleep laboratory, such regular skimping of sleep leaves you vulnerable to building a serious 'sleep debt'. This is a measure of how much sleep you've missed out on and an indication of how much your body craves sleep.

CAN'T SLEEP, WON'T SLEEP
According to Dement, half the human race has trouble sleeping at some point in their lives. Insomnia, meaning quite simply, a sleeping difficulty of one sort or another, has many causes, which can be complex and various. It's a widely used term that covers a range of different situations, but people usually use it to mean they have trouble falling asleep or staying asleep as long as they'd like to. This often has a flow-on effect to daily life, leading to daytime fatigue, irritability, anxiety, impaired concentration, and waves of drowsiness.

Noise can interfere with your sleep, although you usually become used to the noises around your home, particularly repeated noises such as trains or traffic. Body clocks can run too late—your body feels like it's 9 pm although it's midnight—making it difficult to fall asleep; or too early—you wake in the early hours and although still tired, just can't get back to sleep. Depression and other emotional problems are often accompanied by difficulty sleeping.

Getting a better night's sleep
There are no miracle cures for poor sleep patterns, but a variety of approaches—sometimes referred to by sleep researchers as 'sleep hygiene'—may improve your night's rest.

Measuring your sleep debt
1 MULTIPLE SLEEP LATENCY TEST

Sleep labs use a measure abbreviated to MSLT (Multiple Sleep Latency Test) as an indicator of a person's sleep debt. In layperson's terms it refers to how long it takes you to fall asleep in a quiet, dark room. If you are well rested it takes fifteen to twenty minutes; falling asleep within five minutes is an indication of serious sleep debt or a sleep disorder. In the lab this test is done by measuring a person's brain waves and noting when they change. This observable change occurs at the border of wakefulness and light sleep.

There is a way of trying to measure your MSLT yourself. Lie in comfortable clothing, shoes off, in a quiet, dim room. Drape one arm over the side of the bed while holding a metal spoon suspended over a plate. When you succumb to sleep you'll drop the spoon and, unless you are seriously sleep deprived, the clatter will wake you. Sleep labs get people to do these tests in the middle of the day, optimally at 10 am, noon, 2 pm, 4 pm and 6 pm. They then average the scores. The reason, they say, is that falling asleep in the evening has more to do with age than anything else: it's easier for an older person to fall asleep in the early evening than a young person.

- Wind down. Slowing down or relaxing a couple of hours before going to bed helps calm your mind. If there's lots of chatter inside your head, you probably need something to divert your mind—whether it's a light read, a session at your piano or perhaps a good drama on the television if you find that relaxing.
- Avoid caffeine before bedtime. Caffeine has a half-life in the body of between three and seven hours depending on an individual's body chemistry. That means if you drink a cup of coffee containing 100 milligrams of caffeine at 6 pm, by 11 pm you could still have 50 milligrams working around your body.

2 DAYTIME SLEEPINESS TEST

Another way of measuring your sleep debt is to measure your daytime sleepiness. You can get a rough idea by answering the following quiz. Determine your score in each situation as follows:

- Would never doze: 0 points
- Slight chance: 1 point
- Moderate chance: 2 points
- High chance: 3 points.

How likely are you to doze off in the following situations?

- sitting and reading
- watching television
- sitting, inactive, in a public place such as a theatre or in a meeting
- as a passenger in a car for an hour without break
- sitting and talking to someone
- sitting quietly after lunch without alcohol
- in a car, while stopped for a few minutes in traffic

Add up your total score:

- 0–5: slight or no sleep debt
- 6–10: moderate sleep debt
- 11–20: heavy sleep debt
- 21–25: extreme sleep debt.

- Keep a regular schedule. Following a pattern and going to bed at about the same time every night trains your sleep cycle.
- Relax. Relaxation techniques can help fight arousal and remove anxiety, improving the chances of good sleep. One of the most widely recommended techniques is progressive relaxation training (see page 300 for details).
- Stimulus control. Steer clear of stimulating thought and activities before bedtime. Late news, homework, paying bills, checking emails all get your brain working when it needs to be slowing down.

- Worry time. If you find it hard to switch off later in the evening, try allotting a 'worry time' before dinner. Write down everything that is causing anxiety and take a few minutes to think about how you might begin to address the problems. After your worry session, lead your mind astray by doing something calming and relaxing.

- Cognitive techniques. These are 'mind games'—counting sheep, for example—that provide enough distraction from interfering thoughts to induce sleep. Another exercise worth trying is to set yourself the goal of staying awake. This counteracts the fear of insomnia and relaxes you to such an extent that the sleep debt can take effect.

Want of breath

Sleep apnea—the potentially life-threatening breathing disorder that affects millions around the world, eighteen million in America alone—takes its name from the Greek word apnea, meaning 'want of breath'. The National Center on Sleep Disorders Research (NCSD) in Bethesda, Maryland, estimates 4 per cent of middle-age men and 2 per cent of middle-age women suffer disturbed sleep and daytime sleepiness because of the condition. It can also lead to depression, irritability and memory difficulties.

In central sleep apnea the brain fails to send appropriate signals to the muscles required for breathing. In the much more common obstructive sleep apnea, air cannot flow into or out of the nose or mouth, despite efforts to continue to breathe—for instance, where

Thomas Edison (1847–1931)

Thomas Edison, as inventor of the electric light bulb in 1879, can take some blame for the meddling of the biological clock and consequent sleep deprivation. He boasted that he needed only four hours' sleep a night, but he is said to have made up for this by napping regularly throughout the day.

Help! My biological clock's gone haywire!

A Stanford University student became the subject of a study in setting the biological clock straight when he arrived at the Stanford Sleep Disorders Clinic in 1975. As he complained to researchers William Dement and Charles Czeisler, he lay awake all night, finally falling asleep when dawn broke and his fellow students were beginning their day. The researchers asked him to sleep a few hours longer each day, so that his 'bedtime' moved from 6 am to 9 am, then to noon, and gradually through the afternoon until he was going to bed at 10 pm and waking at 6 am. Bingo! It took the team seven days to set him straight.

throat and tongue muscles relax in sleep. In both types, breathing stops momentarily, then starts again suddenly. It can happen up to 30 times an hour.

It's often spouses of sufferers who suspect something's amiss as sleep apnea is usually, although not always, accompanied by loud snoring and what seems like a struggle for breath. Diagnosis is usually by tests at a sleep centre, although it is not straightforward as there are many reasons for disturbed sleep. Treatment usually takes the form of one of the following:

- Behavioural therapy. For some people, avoiding alcohol, tobacco, and sleeping pills is enough to stop the airways collapsing and producing sleep apnea. People who are overweight can benefit from shedding some of the excess—even a 10 per cent reduction in body weight can reduce the number of disturbances a night. Pillows and aids to promote sleep in a side position can also help people who only experience breathing pauses when they sleep on their backs.
- Physical therapy. Nasal continuous positive airway pressure (CPAP) involves wearing a mask over the nose while asleep, which forces air through the nasal passages constantly and continuously. Some people with mild apnea benefit from dental appliances that reposition the lower jaw and tongue.

- Surgery. Options include the removal of the adenoids and tonsils, nasal polyps or other growths. There are also procedures that remove excess tissue at the back of the throat. Several procedures may be needed to bring benefits. 'None of them is completely successful or without risks,' says the NDSD.

The toll of night shifts

Although you can adapt your internal clock to some degree when faced with night shifts, you don't ever completely adapt. One problem is reverting to a daytime schedule over the weekend, to fit in with friends and family. Another is that people tend to sleep two hours less when working night shifts (i.e. in a daytime sleep) than when working normal shifts and sleeping at night. When shifts are rotated, as they often are, workers find they cannot fully adjust to any schedule.

How much sleep do you need?

Sleep researchers recommend various methods of honing in on your ideal time. One is to guess how long you think you need, then pick a bedtime at which you know you'll fall asleep easily. Allow fifteen minutes for falling asleep then set an alarm accordingly. For example, if you believe you need eight hours' sleep and know you'll fall asleep around 11 pm, set your alarm for 7.15 am. Then note your daytime drowsiness. If you are getting more tired, you need more sleep. If you find you are drowsy, add 30 minutes to your sleep and monitor your drowsiness again. This is a rather scientific way of going about it; you might find your own more suitable short cut—like going to bed earlier for several nights and keeping a note of your waking time. These 'one shot' measurements do not take into account that sometimes we need more sleep when we're exhausted.

Take a nap!

Researchers say naps make you smarter, faster and safer. A planned nap is a powerful tool to cope with fatigue and especially those times in your life when sleeplessness veers towards crisis level (family emergencies and when coping with wakeful babies, for instance). Many high profile high-achievers swear by the power of the nap including Winston Churchill, who napped in the afternoon to give him the energy to work into the night. However, there are a couple of secrets to successful napping:

- Timing. Don't try napping in the evening. In fact, napping anytime after the afternoon dip will interfere with going to sleep properly later on. Midday or early afternoon—like the traditional siesta of Mediterranean countries—usually works best.
- For how long? The longer the nap, the greater the benefit. Research at Stanford University found that a 45-minute nap improved alertness for six hours. Other investigations found similar results: a one-hour nap producing improved alertness for ten hours. And although in test situations, subjects don't always feel better after a nap, they invariably perform better.

THE PAIN OF PAIN

Until 1842, alcohol was the only pain killer used in Western medicine. Morphine was used in the American Civil War, but its addictive qualities curbed widespread use. Over-the-counter pain killers are now used in their millions every day for headaches, muscular aches and digestive pain. A number of alternative treatments for pain are also gaining popularity, particularly where people feel orthodox medicine has been unable to help. Acupuncture, Ayurveda (the traditional medicine of India), reflexology (Chinese foot massage), and the posture therapy called the Alexander Technique are all examples.

Taking good care of yourself—outside and in, mind and body— can have a surprising effect on pain. Reducing anxiety and stress can ease tension that causes pain, while keeping fit and supple can also help enormously. Relaxation techniques may help you distract your mind from the burden of pain. Continuing to lead a full life, despite the pain, can help stop the slide into depression. At times, people have to review their expectations of day-to-day life and learn to pace themselves: rests might have to be worked into the day, improvements may be the slow but steady kind.

TYPES OF PAIN

Pain is usually meaningful—the pain you feel if you fall warns you to take care and maybe take a rest too. But in some conditions, such as arthritis, the pain messages appear to have little use. Health professionals may refer to three types of pain.

Acute pain

Acute pain is often severe but usually lasts a maximum of a few days. It signals that the body needs to rest in order for tissue repair to take place. Conventional pain killers are usually all that's needed to relieve this kind of pain.

Chronic pain

This may last for months or even years. Pain messages are generated long after the initial cause for pain is gone or as part of the response to a disease such as cancer. Conditioning may occur because of constant tensing of muscles near the affected area,

---

Keeping track

A pain diary may help identify pain triggers if you suffer chronic pain but can't work out why. It may also help you and your doctor diagnose and better manage your pain. You need to record:

- the amount of pain
- a description of the pain (eg. dull, throbbing, sharp, etc)
- your action (eg. taking a pain killer or going for a walk)
- how your pain changed
- stressful events
- the location of the pain
- factors that appeared to ease the pain (eg. eating yoghurt after a stomach ache, taking a cooling shower).

which conditions the nervous system to perceive pain whenever the muscles are tensed.

Referred pain

When pain is felt at a point of injury, it is said to be localized. Sometimes pain from one part of the body—such as an internal organ—is felt elsewhere. Heart pain can be referred to the arm.

Pain can strike almost any part of the body, but the most common types of pain occur in the back and the head. Headaches and backache afflict everyone at some time and may have long-term effects.

HEADING OFF HEADACHES

Headaches are more than a pain in the neck—they can be debilitating and even traumatic, especially when experienced regularly. The Migraine Trust in the United Kingdom estimates 70 per cent of UK school children experience a headache at least once a year. In up to a quarter of children the headaches are recurrent. Some children lose half their schooling because of migraine. Some headaches are symptoms of a serious disorder so it's always worth seeing your doctor if you suddenly start having severe, regular or persistent headaches, especially if you suffer stiffness and have a fever, are confused and have lost some speech ability, or when headaches follow physical exertion. When you don't suspect they're a sign of something more serious but want to head them off anyway, how do you ease the pain without resorting to drugs?

- Eliminate triggers. If you suffer from headaches often, try keeping a headache diary, like the one described above for general pain. Can you identify any triggers? Particular types of food, particles in the air, pulsating lights and stressful events in the day are common possible causes.
- Relax away. Tension headaches may be relieved by relaxation techniques that ease anxiety and stress as well as relax muscles.
- State of mind. Unrealistic expectations, depression and anxieties can give you a headache. Try stepping back and taking a look at the way you are running your life.

What type of headache?

- Migraine. These are described as a process, from the time you 'feel a migraine coming on', when people report being oversensitive to light or notice changes in their mood; to the headache itself, a subsiding of pain and a feeling of being drained afterwards. The pain is severe enough to interrupt work.
- Tension headaches. This common headache is often associated with stress and fatigue, and may be accompanied by muscle tension.
- Mixed headache. These share features of both migraines and tension headaches and are frequently associated with pain-killerr overuse and sleep disturbances.
- Cluster headaches. Named because they cluster in several episodes for weeks, these are very painful—they can wake you from sleep—may be seasonal, and may originate behind or around one eye.
- Sinus headache. This is associated with inflammation of the sinuses because of allergy or infection. It's usually a deep dull ache around the nose and sometimes the temple and ears. Lying down with a hot compress may help.
- Rebound headaches. These frequent, even daily, headaches fade with medication but return as the medication wears off. Eventually, it is proposed, the drugs themselves perpetuate the headache. Cutting out the medication, even if it causes withdrawal symptoms, is necessary to break the cycle.
- Menstrual migraine. Some women migraine sufferers report migraines around the time of their period. This is due to fluctuations of hormones, particularly estrogen.

- Irregular sleeping habits. Some people suffer the weekend headache, caused by a change in sleeping routine, particularly a lie in. For others, a rest and a nap may be enough to stop a migraine or headache in its tracks.

BACKING AWAY FROM BACK PAIN

Eight out of ten people suffer back pain during their lives, according to Dr Anthony Campbell, former consultant physician at the Royal London Homeopathic Hospital and author of *Back: Your 100 Questions Answered*.

Back pain takes many forms—from a stiff neck to a twist caused when loading the car with shopping—and it can be remarkably hard to discover its cause. The back is incredibly complex and consists of dozens of muscles, bones, nerves and blood vessels; we still don't understand it completely.

Although many back episodes appear to come out of the blue, a general strategy to keep fit and strong helps, firstly by reducing the likelihood of injuring yourself and secondly by speeding up your recovery. Other strategies are discussed below.

Good back habits

Certain habits will minimize your chances of back problems—particularly when lifting and carrying:

- Always have a firm foothold.
- Do not stoop.
- Bend your knees.
- Keep your hips below your head—don't try to lift something you're reaching for with your head lowered. This usually means squatting.
- Get a good grip on the object to be lifted and move it slowly.
- Swivel your feet rather than twist your back if you need to turn.
- Carry objects close to your body.
- Squat or kneel to place an object down.
- Divide loads—such as shopping bags—equally, so you are balanced left and right.

Sleeping sound

Like Goldilocks, your back needs a bed that is 'just right'—neither too hard nor too soft, but supporting your back as you sleep. Pillows help support your neck.

Great gardening

When weeding or clearing the garden, don't bend over, instead kneel. Use a special kneeling pad if you have one. Don't overload the wheelbarrow as this puts strain on the lower back, and remember to give yourself breaks every now and then.

Superior sitting

Slouching is bad news for your back. An upright position that feels natural is the one to aim for. For desk work, the height of the desk and chair should allow your elbows to be at 90° to the desk. Specially designed back chairs move you into a radically different posture in order to encourage a good back position.

Exercise extra

Regular exercise strengthens bones, counteracts tension and tones muscles—strong abdominal muscles are beneficial to the spine.

Laurent de Brunhoff (1925–)

Babar's Yoga for Elephants, published in 2002, is the latest Babar creation from Laurent de Brunhoff. The book covers many basic poses suitable for humans as well as elephants, including the Salute to the Sun, which will, as Babar explains, 'help us all relax and draw strength from our inner elephant'. While it was Laurent's French artist father, Jean de Brunhoff, who invented Babar and wrote the first six books, it was Laurent who continued the tradition after his father's death in 1937. Laurent has since written 30 Babar books, which have been translated in seventeen languages. *Yoga for Elephants* was written to teach his wife, Phyllis Rose, the basic yoga positions.

With regards to your back, forms of exercise that use large muscle groups are great— walking, swimming and cycling, for example. (If you favour breaststroke, remember to keep your head down to avoid straining your back.) It is debatable, according to Campbell, whether specific back exercises are beneficial but, anecdotally, many people report feeling better for them.

When you feel as fit as you can, you feel better about yourself and cope better with the demands of a busy schedule. Taking steps to improve your health can broaden your experience of life too, especially if you get involved in new interests, whether Japanese cuisine, a community walking group or caving.

TAKING STOCK

Use this questionnaire to run through the many aspects of your
daily life that impact on your health—and to identify the trouble
spots that, with a little focus and a varied degree of determination,
you can start to fix.

1 General
(a) How would you descibe your health (eg. healthy and fit, no
problems, manage diabetes, on heart medication, etc)?
(b) How does your health impinge on other aspects of your life? Do
health considerations affect your choice of home, work and
financial situation?
(c) How important is health to you? Has your perception of its
importance changed with time?
(d) Have you ever had to fight bad health or illness? What was
the outcome?
(e) How do you keep as healthy as you can?

2 Mind and body
Does your physical health affect your mental health? Do you find that
you are less anxious or stressed when you feel physically healthy?

3 Relaxation
(a) Is it important to you that you incorporate relaxing elements
into your life?
(b) If yes, what do you do (eg. yoga, walks)?
(c) How does it help?

4 Exercise
(a) What does a normal day or week hold for you in terms
of exercise?
(b) Is it something you make sure you do?
(c) Do you feel you do enough?

5 Diet

(a) Do you think what you eat makes a difference to your health?

(b) If so, what do you think matters (eg. eat organic, low fat, vegetarian, etc)?

(c) Are there areas you feel you could change for the better?

6 Sleep/fatigue (if applicable)

(a) Have you ever had sleep problems?

(b) If so, did you work out what caused them?

(c) Did you find a way to sleep better/longer?

(d) Do you suffer from fatigue or low energy levels?

(e) If so, do you know what causes it?

(f) Have you found ways of boosting your energy levels or relieving tiredness?

7 Pain (if applicable)

(a) Do you suffer severe pain (eg. migraine, back pain, pain from illness or injury)?

(b) If so, what treatment have you tried for it?

(c) Is there more you could do to prevent pain in the first place?

There are more things in heaven and earth, Horatio,
Than are dreamt of in your philosophy

HAMLET IN WILLIAM SHAKESPEARE,
HAMLET (ACT I, SCENE V) (1601)

9. SOUL SEARCHING

SPIRITUALITY—THE QUEST FOR PURPOSE AND MEANING IN LIFE—IS AN ANCIENT PREOCCUPATION THAT HAS FOUND EXPRESSION IN DIFFERENT WAYS IN DIFFERENT CULTURES, FROM ANCIENT EGYPT TO ABORIGINAL AUSTRALIA. ITS FABRIC WEAVES MANY THREADS TOGETHER, EACH VERSION INCORPORATING IDEAS FOUND AT THE HEART OF RELIGION, PHILOSOPHY, PEACE MOVEMENTS, THE ARTS, AND EVEN ECOLOGY.

THE CHANGING FACE OF SPIRITUALITY

Science, logic, rationality and the material world take us only so far. We need more: a sense of wonder perhaps, mystery, beauty, and maybe just once in a while stepping outside the confines of our own experiences—an awareness that we won't find all the answers in one place. Church congregations may be shrinking in some parts of the Western world, but much research indicates an unprecedented desire for religious and spiritual growth among people at all levels of society and in all parts of the world. 'There is an intense search for spiritual moorings and a deep hunger for God,' George Gallup Jr, co-chairman of the Gallup polling organization, told a conference in 2002. There are several aspects to this search.

ANCHORING

American futurist Faith Popcorn identifies the 'anchoring' trend as a reaching back to spiritual roots, taking what was secure from the past so as to be ready for the future. People are looking beyond Western traditions to 'alternative' spirituality and healing, she says. In addition, 90 per cent of Americans say religion is important, and 72 per cent pray every day. The rise in Internet sites and software devoted to family genealogy is also a symptom of the need for personal anchoring, says Popcorn.

MEASURING UP

According to research, including some undertaken in Australia and the United States and reported in a paper published in 2003 entitled 'Religion, Spirituality and Health: How Should Australian Medical Professionals Respond?', religious beliefs prolong your life, lower cholesterol levels and reduce the incidence of some cancers. Religious people are also less likely to abuse drugs, including alcohol and cigarettes; are less likely to suffer depression or commit suicide; and are more likely to enjoy a happy marriage.

While researchers attempt to measure the biological effects of spirituality, some medical researchers are calling for an approach to healing that takes into account a patient's spiritual beliefs.

SCIENCE AND RELIGION

Are the explorations of science and religion at loggerheads? Can scientists find answers to everything or do they have to hand over to the spiritual realm on some issues? While the rise of science and theories such as the evolution of species were seen as a threat to the established church in the nineteenth century, scientists do not necessarily believe their work is at odds with religion. Tom McLeish, professor of polymer science at Leeds University, England, believes that the questions that are asked in science can be traced back to religion. He sees both as being part of the tradition of being human because, as he says in a Guardian newspaper article on 4 September 2003, 'we find ourselves in this puzzling, extraordinary universe of pain and beauty…able to explore it, by adopting the very successful methods of science.'

THE RISE OF THE SOUL

According to a 2000 report commissioned by the BBC on the state of British spirituality, entitled *The Soul of Britain*, belief in the soul increased significantly over the previous twenty years. In fact, the number of people who believe in the soul now exceeds that of those who believe in God—around 60 per cent believe we have a soul, but only 1 in 4 believes in God.

ISLAND MENTALITY

Over 400 years ago John Donne wrote, 'No man is an island, entire of itself' (*Meditation XVII*). But some would argue that today's preoccupation with the rights and independence of the individual—referred to as individualism—has created lonely 'human islands', prone to depression and even suicide. In his book *Learned Optimism*, psychology professor Martin Seligman from the University of Pennsylvania calls it 'the waxing of the self and the waning of the commons': self is the priority, but at the expense of investing in the community and the feeling of 'connection' that brings.

To counteract the forces of individualism, Seligman proposes 'moral jogging'—investing in the 'commons' and reducing depression at the same time. He suggests that you give to charity; do voluntary work; talk to the homeless; teach your children to give; and exercise your moral judgment by contacting people who act either honourably or despicably and letting them know what you think. These are all good examples of some of the threads of spirituality—religion, creativity, community and values—that can be woven into our lives.

VOX POP: On life, the universe and everything...

'I'm an atheist and am not convinced there is a higher power, but occasionally I'll see an astoundingly beautiful bit of the world and I can't see how it came by accident. I'm politically confused but being unemployed in the '80s and working in the health service since has given me a deep mistrust of the right wing. I've no time for racism or sexism.' TS

'Creativity is important to me as a writer but I have difficulty staying focused on one project through to completion. I've been involved in group occult ritual practice in the past but in recent years I've become more and more active in shamanic work. I believe in a universal flow, and if I'm on the right track, things fall into place and tend to be easy. But if it's all a big battle, I'm probably on the wrong track and need to think about alternatives. I also meditate, and do yoga and qi gong. I see life as a daily adventure, a wonder, a miracle that can be snatched from us at any moment, so it's worth enjoying it to the full. Creating and helping the people I care about bring meaning to my life.' DL

'It's wonderful being alive! The fact that we exist at all—that there is something other than nothing—seems so incredible that no explanation is quite sufficient to do it justice. The coincidences and "lucky breaks" in my life seem somehow to indicate fortunate harmony that I don't feel I deserve, and yet which seem to charge things with significance, reminding me that the universe is deeper than a mechanistic assemblage. I'm not a member of a church. I distrust people who feel they know what it's all about, whether they are members of organized religions or atheists. Doubts are positive when you see what certainties do to some people! I think it's up to us to give our lives meaning but I also think that our existence matters, and not just to us. My family and friends bring meaning to my life—the interplay of the seasons; light and shade; laughter and quiet reflection; variety; art and wit; memories; being needed.' PN

'I am a Christian. I follow Jesus. I have peace with God and know I'm loved and forgiven by God. That helps me give and receive peace and love. I believe God created a purposeful world with a place for everyone. But it's up to people to make the most of it and fulfil their role. Relationships are what bring meaning to my life—with God and all the people around me.' FC

'The spiritual side of my life is my top priority, along with good health. My deepening connection to who I am and what I am doing on the Earth plane at this time is most important.' JS

'I'm quite spiritual but not religious. I abandoned Catholicism once in my teens and again finally about fourteen years ago. I have political beliefs but lack a party-political home. Abandoning my religion caused me great spiritual pain: I felt the faith was bogus but belonging to the Church still comforted me. It took a long time to get over this sense of loss, and even though I'm over this now, the good old hymns still grip me. And I sometimes feel empty at Christmas and Easter. I don't believe life has an intrinsic meaning, but I do believe it's up to each of us to find or make a meaning. I have mine, but I'm open to persuasion. My life is worth living because of what I can do for others, especially for my wife. The pleasures of life are not what makes it worthwhile (that would be too shallow) but they do make the trip more enjoyable.' HB

'The spiritual realm is still a mystery to me but it's probably the one area where happiness is truly long-lasting and relevant.' ML

'I believe the spiritual is a case of horses for courses—it's very personal and up to the individual. I hate being preached at and I don't believe in people placing importance in religion: believe in yourself and your family and don't rely on something else to make your life good and happy.' CT

'The spiritual and non-material are very important to me. Yoga is my main activity, plus the reading about it, which includes the spiritual side. My husband is a jazz musician—I love being part of the music scene, it's such a wonderful creative arena.' CS

'I do not consider myself a Christian in that I do not believe in a God, I cannot make that leap of faith and certainly do not believe in Heaven and Hell. But I am undoubtedly a Christian culturally. I love churches and religious music and some of the rituals. I believe in many of the Christian values and try to follow them in my daily life. I'm interested in Buddhism, particularly some of the guiding principles, which I find both refreshing and practical in perspective. I believe it's up to us to give our lives meaning. My close family give me most meaning. I also love the natural world, the creative world and believe in giving back to the community, even if it's just making sure you say hello to your neighbours, feeding a friend's cat when they're on holiday and supporting local fundraising. While I like my creature comforts, I wouldn't describe myself as materialistic and without a life of ideas—whether it's theatre, reading or art—I would go mad.' AH

RELIGION

'Give me that old-time religion, it's good enough for me,' says the traditional spiritual. Religion is very much alive around the world but Western countries are seeing a decline in formal religious practice—people don't want the old-time religion, it seems! In the United Kingdom, formal church attendance fell from 4.74 million in 1989 to 3.71 million in 1998. Some of the criticisms aimed at the Church are an obsession with control, living in the past and a failure to be involved with humanity as a whole.

In his report in 2000, 'Understanding the Spirituality of People Who Don't Go To Church', David Hay of the University of Nottingham, England, says, 'Britain resembles many other Western European countries: it demonstrates a severe lapse in formal adherence to the Christian faith.' But this is just the surface picture, he believes. Significant proportions of the population say they have an awareness of a patterning of events (55 per cent in 2000), an awareness of the presence of God (38 per cent), an awareness of prayer being answered (37 per cent), and an awareness of a sacred presence in nature (29 per cent). A quarter said they had been aware of the presence of the dead, while another quarter said they had been aware of an evil presence. (A word on statistics: they don't always add up. Results depend on the questions asked, the level of trust built up between interviewer and interviewee, and the methodology.) At least two-thirds of the population, he concludes, nurture a hidden spirituality. 'How can this hidden spirituality be reintegrated into the community to provide the energy for its renewal?' he asks.

According to the website Adherents.com—the brainchild of Preston Hunter, a computer programmer with an interest in comparative and world religion—there are 10,000 distinct religions around the world, of which 150 have a million or more followers. Christianity has 33,830 different denominations, from Catholicism to Shaker. According to Hunter, around 85 per cent of the world population believes in God or a similar higher power. (The United States is usually cited as a country with a high belief rate, at around 95 per cent.) Among the believers, around two billion of the world's population profess to be Christian; over one billion Muslim; 750,000 million Hindus; twenty million Sikhs; and around fifteen million Jews.

PICK 'N' MIX RELIGION

The Unitarian Church combines readings from Buddhism, Sikhism, Taoism, Native American Spirituality, Islam, Hinduism, the Old and New Testaments, as well as secular humanism. It's been described by one of its own as, 'a forum in which people can be religious without the trappings of religion'. It attracts disaffected Christians, Buddhists, pagans, agnostics and even atheists—all looking for spiritual fulfilment in a communal atmosphere. One of its movements is known as Build Your Own Theology. Among its past followers are Thomas Jefferson, Benjamin Franklin and John Adams.

Traditional Christian organizations do not recognize the Unitarian Church, but many individuals will recognize its approach in their own gut feelings.

Learning your ABCs: the Alpha course

One of the newer movements to come out of the Christian church is the Alpha course, an eleven-week reintroduction to Christianity. Since its inception at Trinity Church, Brompton, London in 1991, the course has spread to more than 132 countries, from Australia to Zambia, India to Poland. It is estimated that around 3.8 million people around the world have been on an Alpha course, about a quarter of those in the United States and Canada. Described as an evangelical course—with its main aim to tell the good news about Christ—it has been taken up by both Anglican and Catholic branches of Christianity. The Alpha course is usually advertised as 'an opportunity to explore the meaning of life', and its success has been in part attributed to the friendly, welcoming flavour of the meetings—usually centred on a meal.

Thomas Moore, a former priest and now a psychotherapist and author who writes on matters of the soul and spirituality, asks why you cannot be pagan in your affirmation of life, Christian in your affirmation of communal love, Jewish in the way you affirm the sacredness of the family, Buddhist in your affirmation of emptiness, and Taoist in your affirmation of paradox. To those of us not familiar with the history of religions such an idea seems to go against the very nature of religion. After all, each religion appears to have one point of view that lays down the rules, guidance and principles for living and even comes with a set of 'must have' beliefs. But as religions have spread from country to country they have adapted as they've come face to face with folk theology or other mainstream religions. In addition, culture and philosophy chip away at religion so they change from place to place, forced to adapt and continually evolve if they are to survive. In some countries, such as Japan, faith is not always considered necessary to be religious. In some cases, the behaviour itself is enough. In addition, boundaries between religions are not absolute, and in some countries dual or multiple affiliations are not uncommon.

Take Korea as an example, a country with a recorded history dating back to 2333 BC. Korea has hosted a range of religions over time, and quite often at the same time: Shamanism, Taoism, Buddhism, Confucianism and, more latterly, Christianity. Around 400 AD, the main three religions were Shamanism, Buddhism and Confucianism, each with its own realm of influence. Confucianism was concerned mainly with social obligations and duties; Buddhism asked the big questions about the meaning of life; while Shamanism added a touch of everyday magic.

If you would like to take a walk along the religious path, you'll find local churches, the Internet, the library and bookshops are good places to start the search for more information on religions that interest you. You may prefer the pick 'n' mix approach or you might like to formally follow or learn another religious 'language' to deepen your existing experience and knowledge.

STORIES, RITUALS AND SYMBOLS

One of the fascinations of religion is its repeated use of symbolism and the comfort it brings followers though the use of rituals and stories. Here are a few examples from around the world.

Christianity

The Christian faith centres on Jesus Christ, whom followers believe came to Earth as the son of God around 2000 years ago. The image of Christ's death on the cross is the strongest symbol in the faith, reminding followers of Christ's rising from the dead. Another important symbol is the fish, because the first letters of the words 'Jesus Christ' in Greek spell 'fish'. Three fish together represent the Trinity: the Father, the Son and the Holy Spirit. In Holy Communion, bread symbolizes the body of Christ, while wine represents his blood.

The best known Christian story is that of the nativity—the story of Jesus' birth in a stable and the travels of the three wise men who followed a star to bring him gifts of gold, frankincense and myrrh.

Judaism

Judaism traces its history to around the fourteenth century BC and from the beginning involved a dialogue between God—or Yahweh—and the chosen people, the Jews. While Jews today are scattered across the world, they share a strong culture centering on Jewish history, law and family life. The main symbol is the Star of David, with its triangles representing sun, fire and masculine energy inter-linked with the moon, water and female energy.

The Passover festival commemorates the Exodus, when an angel of death passed over the Israelites, sparing their lives and leaving them free to leave Egypt. The ritual meal consists of: an egg, a reminder of spring and rebirth; lettuce, a symbol of frugal meals eaten in slavery; nut and fruit paste, representing the bricks and mortar used to build cities in Egypt; a shankbone, to recall the lambs killed in the first Passover; bitter herbs, to represent the bitterness of slavery; and matzo, a flat, unleavened bread to remind of the haste with which the Israelites left Egypt. A dish of

A challenging path

Faith can be a hard road to travel as this story from an Anglican minister, FC, clearly demonstrates.

I was raised in a Roman Catholic house but gave away my belief in God when I was ten and a car that had not seen me forced me and my bicycle off the road. When I saw that it was my scripture teacher I said, 'No more of this God stuff for me!'

I was an atheist until I was nineteen and moved to the city. I became hounded by spirituality, heard oppressive voices and became introspective: these experiences pulled back the curtains of my spiritual realm. At 21 I had a revelation of the one pure Holy God. It was invasive and overwhelming. I wasn't an atheist anymore but I was in a spiritual wilderness. I tried to leave the aesthetic life—grew dreadlocks, ate bananas and peanuts and hitch-hiked around Australia. I was a failure at it all and had to cut my hair after some court trouble. I was in despair and even more miserable than ever. I decided to go to a hut in the Victorian Alps. I shook my fist at the

salt water at the table represents tears shed by Jews during long years of captivity.

Hinduism

Hinduism, the main religion of India, has evolved over thousands of years and embraces a complex range of religious beliefs, philosophy and mythology. Brahma is the one eternal principle, and all gods and goddesses are aspects of Brahma. The three aspects of Brahma, the Creator; Vishnu, the Preserver; and Shiva, the Destroyer, form a trinity.

Hindu temple architecture is symbolic: the central tower represents a mountaintop (where the gods live), and the image of the god is found in the inner sanctum, which is called the *garbhagrah*, or womb chamber, and which is a maternal symbol.

heavens and said, 'I'm not leaving this mountain till I've worked it out.' I had explored Hare Krishna and read the Koran but on this mountain I became a Christian.

I decided to train for the ministry and at college had another very confronting period of doubt lasting many years. I was trembling with the inclination to convert to another religion that is what I call 'legalistic' in that it has lots of rules and ready-made answers. My wife said she'd leave me if I converted. I would have lost my wife, my kids, my job...it would have shipwrecked my life. I got an infection that had to be treated in hospital for four days. That stay transformed my life. I realized there was good and beauty in all things, but on the other hand all personal stories dissipate and are changed but the one story that doesn't change is Jesus'. He is God's story, and went the way of the flesh too. But the fact he was resurrected was God's way of showing he was eternal, comprehensive and everlasting.

FC says that having experienced such times in his life he can connect with other people's stories without feeling threatened.

Candles feature strongly in Divali, the festival of lights, which is celebrated in honour of Lakshmi, consort of Vishnu and goddess of abundance and good fortune.

Buddhism

The teachings of Gautama Buddha, born Prince Siddhartha in India in the mid sixth century, form the basis of Buddhism. Having renounced his worldly life, he sought enlightenment through meditation, which he eventually achieved after sitting under the Bodhi tree. Buddha means 'the enlightened one', and enlightenment leads to Nirvana, meaning literally, 'absorption into the cosmos'. While Buddhists do not in theory worship Buddha, they do pay homage to his teachings of non-violence and compassion in front of his image, which

Arthur Stace (1884–1967)

Anybody watching the New Year's Eve Sydney fireworks at the turn of the millennium in 1999 might have noticed the word 'Eternity' emblazoned on the Sydney Harbour Bridge. For 33 years the word had mysteriously appeared on Sydney pavements. It was the work of Arthur Stace, a thin little man who rose at 5 am each morning to repeat his one-word sermon with his piece of chalk and confound the press at the same time. Discovered one morning in 1956, his story finally emerged, 24 years into the mystery.

Arthur Stace was born in the Sydney suburb of Balmain to an alcoholic father and a mother who ran a brothel. As a child, he stole to eat, received no education, and at fourteen went to work in a coal mine (thought to be the old Balmain mine). By fifteen, he was a heavy drinker and had served his first jail sentence. His twenties saw him acting as a 'cockatoo', or lookout, for gambling houses and brothels. He served in World War I, returning in 1919 with shell shock and gas poisoning. He became, in his own words, a 'petty criminal, a bum and a metho drinker'. But, in 1930, during the Great Depression, he found himself wandering into a meeting for needy men taking place in an Anglican Church. He noticed a few well-dressed men standing near the door and, on hearing they were Christians, he decided to have 'a go at what they've got'. Describing the pivotal moment he later said, 'I went in to get a cup of tea and a rock cake, but I met the Rock of Ages.'

Two years later, on hearing a sermon with the words 'Eternity! Eternity!...Where will you spend eternity?', Stace felt the word ringing through his head and a powerful call to write it. Taking a piece of chalk from his pocket, he knelt down on the pavement outside the church and formed the letters 'Eternity'. Even though he could barely write his name, the letters came out smoothly in a beautiful copperplate script. Stace said he never understood how.

He found work as a cleaner and preached whenever he could, having memorized passages from the Bible. When he went into a nursing home in 1965, he remarked, 'I don't think I'll leave here under my own steam.'

appears in many forms. The laughing Buddha, or Mi Lo Fo, meaning 'friendly one', is laughing at fate. A rotund man, his fat folds are said to contain the wisdom of the universe. Buddha Muchalinda depicts a man meditating, with hands lightly resting in the gesture of meditation and legs in the lotus position, while the great snake, Muchalinda, protects the Buddha from the rain with his many hoods.

Islam

Islam is based on the teachings of the Prophet Mohammed, who lived in Arabia around 570 to 632 AD. His teachings were later recorded in the Koran. Devout Muslims follow the Five Pillars: declare their faith publicly, pray five times a day, give alms, fast during Ramadan, and make a pilgrimage to Mecca. The Hand of God, or the Hand of Fatima after Mohammed's daughter, represents the Five Pillars.

The star and crescent is the symbol of Islam, adopted in the fourteenth century and said to have originally represented the waxing moon once associated with the goddess Diana. The star, a symbol of sovereignty and divinity, was added later.

CREATIVITY AND THE ARTS

There really is no such thing as Art. There are only artists.
E H GOMBRICH, *THE STORY OF ART* (FIRST PUBLISHED IN 1950)

Whether you are making it—and, by making it, finding an important means of self-expression—or partaking of it, the arts bring magic and passion to our lives. Many people want to write, paint, design a beautiful garden or sculpt. There's many an artist hiding inside a nurse, labourer, parent or accountant.

The obstacles can seem overwhelming, however: family responsibilities, financial obligations, a sense of it being hard to justify, or simple career ambition getting in the way. Once the sheltered days of school are left far behind, time seems more and more difficult to find, but finding some support mechanisms can help pave the way for a more creative life.

LEADING THE CREATIVE LIFE

When you feel that a creative life is the one you really want to lead, but are frustrated you can't make it happen, take another look at how the problems of time, money and space affect your life.

Money

Rare is the artist who can support himself through his or her art, let alone a family at the same time. Most people who consider themselves artists have found a compromise between pursuing their art and earning a living. Some like to work in a field related to their art, such as teaching or working in an art shop, as a studio technician or as a designer. Others prefer the steadiness of an office job or other work they can walk away from at the end of the day and that does not interfere with their art.

Time

Time can seem difficult to carve out. Sometimes people put their art last, but make sure it still happens. Some people put it, literally, first. They rise early, before the rest of the household, and enjoy a couple of creative hours before tackling the rest of the day's chores and responsibilities. Even if you can only snatch fragments of time, make sure that you keep the creative process happening. While working in isolated bursts can be frustrating, in some cases the gap between creative periods gives you the distance to evaluate your work as well as the motivation to ensure you work efficiently during the scraps of time you have.

When you can't seem to create the time for writing, making art or playing music as you wish, remember these points:

- Ideas count. There's a time for everything. Sometimes it's not the time and place for practising art, but the ideas are still flowing. Capture your ideas and inspirations by keeping a visual

Creators need...

In order to flourish, some creative people find they need:

- Community. Whether this is through a class, supportive friends or artist friends, it helps your creativity to share the doubts and ambitions of others and have contact with people who understand your frustrations and joys.

- Focus. Goals might be what you need to keep the focus on your creativity. It might be something as simple as making a commitment to continue to follow a creative pursuit throughout your life or to create enough works to have a small exhibition for friends and family. You could perhaps subscribe to a theatre season to ensure you see plays you enjoy, that stimulate you and refresh your spirit.

diary where you note ideas, sketch images and stick postcards, photographs and other items you come across. Many creative people, including writer Graham Greene, have kept dream diaries to capture the strange and creative world they experience while asleep.

- Work at it. Gather what you need to play music, have your piano tuned, sign up for singing classes...keep working towards your goal. While inspiration counts, many artists say they can't afford to sit around and wait for it; it's just as important to put the hours in. If a two-hour slot opens up for you, make the most of it.

Space

Virginia Woolf said every writing woman needs 'a room of her own', and she wrote a book with the same title. That luxury is not always possible, however, and we may have to apply a little creativity to finding other solutions. Some possibilities include:

- making art or writing in your living space
- living in a studio
- creating a work space at home.

The home studio requires discipline to make it work but can be particularly handy if your available hours are erratic. On the other hand, a studio away from home may aid concentration and allow you to leave work out ready for the next visit. Remember, your creative space doesn't need to be large, it just needs to exist.

EMOTIONS AND REJECTION

Pursuing any creative pursuit can be exhilarating, exhausting, inspiring or draining. You experience the highs of achievement and the lows of self-doubt and rejection. How can you deal with this seemingly endless roller-coaster of emotion?

Maintain the momentum

Start new work at the time of the day you generally experience a good energy level. If you sag at the end of the day, don't kid yourself that this is the time to embark on a new project. Learn to prioritize and not to spread yourself too thin. Take advantage of the galvanizing effect of deadlines—whether real or self-imposed—if they work for you. Try to keep working at a steady pace, even when motivation flags.

Retain resilience

Try to keep a flexible approach and avoid too much attachment to an ideal world—it does not exist. You can probably make do with less space than you think you need; if children or other responsibilities mean you can only find half an hour at a time, see if you can find work that fits the time available. Temporary obstacles can give you perspective. There will always be times when you may simply need to go through the motions or sit it out until the situation improves.

Concentrate on the task

When you sit down to spend half an hour, or four hours, at a project give it all your focus and rein in your attention when it wanders.

Discipline yourself

Seeing a project through, even though it takes more time than you could possibly have imagined, nurtures your spirit by giving you pride in your tenacity and confidence in your ability to take on another project. Doing the job, rather than talking about it, is one way of making sure your energy is channelled into getting the job done. Endlessly talking about a project is draining; observing yourself following a plan is energizing.

Stay flexible

Changing tack is sometimes required. The material you've been working with may no longer be available, you can't find the right equipment, or your writing seems to be going nowhere. When you can adapt to a new situation, you may find you enter a more creative phase.

Be open to discovery

New situations—like finding yourself at home sick or unemployed for a spell—can be turned around and made to work for you rather than against you. Mistakes are often the fuel for a creative solution, producing better results than the ones originally planned.

Reward yourself

The less importance you put on external rewards, rather than those you give yourself when you feel you deserve it, the less your self-esteem will fluctuate according to the praise of others. If you can separate your work from the expectations of reward, you have a better chance of continuing the art.

COMMUNITY AND VALUES

There are many other ways people seek to find meaning in life.
One way is by reaching out and creating community—and reversing
Seligman's 'waning of the commons'.

CHARITY BEGINS AT HOME

A strong family life is the foundation of community for many
people. The relationships there provide stability and security as well
as intimacy and trust. Outside the immediate family are other
opportunities to connect: kindergarten and school; Neighbourhood
Watch and street parties; for some, a church; for others, a
basketball game or reading group.

Charities create sometimes highly influential and valuable
connections across the world. For example, UNICEF, the children's
charity, was founded in 1946 after World War II left many European
children facing famine and disease. It was created by the United
Nations to provide food, clothing and health care. Almost 60 years
on, it consists of more than 7000 people working in 158 countries to
advocate for measures to give children the best start in life;
promoting education for girls, immunization, and curbing the
spread of HIV/AIDS, for example.

Rachel Carson (1907–64)

American naturalist and science writer Rachel Carson combined
scholarly achievement with writing talent and received many awards
for both. But it is her book *Silent Spring*, published in 1962, for which
she will be remembered. The story of the use of toxic chemicals in the
countryside and the widespread destruction of wildlife by pesticides,
fungicides and herbicides was highly controversial—she was attacked
by the chemicals industry and some in government as an alarmist. But
Silent Spring was also highly influential. The pesticide controls that
were later introduced in the United States owe much to her work, as
do the beginnings of the environmental movement.

VOLUNTARY WORK

Volunteers report experiencing a lift in mood when they help people. They also are less easily depressed and get sick less often.

In her book *Everyday Passions: A Conversation on Living*, Uniting Church minister Dorothy McRae-McMahon describes how after her bright two-year-old son was brain-damaged and never spoke again she felt she had a choice. Either she tried to get more rest to cope with the very demanding life a growing, brain-damaged child presented—and reduce her life—or she stretched her boundaries by adding to her life. She chose the latter and, because she was largely restricted to the house during the day, she became a Life Line volunteer at night. Later, she and a friend organized a monthly lunch for elderly women who had little chance of getting out. McRae-McMahon joined the Vietnam War peace movement and edited a bimonthly newsletter. 'These activities were a big effort,' she writes, 'but they saved my life.' Tiredness was a healthy reaction, not one of depression and boredom.

GETTING INVOLVED

The fundamental message behind every successful movement—regardless of whether its concerns are environmental, political or charitable—has great meaning for the organization's followers and gives a context to the beliefs and work of the individual members. The communities formed by the movement or organization's followers bring further meaning to the followers' lives. Below are just a few examples.

Greenpeace

'Greenpeace exists because this fragile earth deserves a voice,' the non-profit organization says on its website. It began in 1971 when a group of volunteers and journalists sailed in a small boat called the *Phyllis Cormack* into Amchitka, a tiny island near Alaska where the US government was conducting underground nuclear tests. Amchitka was the last refuge for 3000 endangered sea otters as well as being home to bald eagles, peregrine falcons and other wildlife. While the bomb was detonated, the *Phyllis Cormack* sparked a flurry of public interest and the island was later declared a bird sanctuary.

The Greenpeace flagship, the *Rainbow Warrior*, takes its name from a North American Cree Indian legend. It tells of a time when humanity's greed made the earth sick and a tribe of people known as the Warriors of the Rainbow rose up to defend her.

Greenpeace now has 2.8 million supporters in 41 countries. Among the issues they campaign for are: to stop climate change, to protect ancient forests, to save the oceans, to stop whaling, and to encourage sustainable trade.

Gaia

The central concerns of the environmental movement—such as conserving energy and water, and reducing the use of poisonous chemicals—are variously important depending on your perspective. Many aspects, including being frugal with resources, make sense economically. For some people, however, it's more about looking after Mother Earth. 'Believing in the earth is now one of the most widespread spiritual movements in the post Baby Boomer West,' says Rachael Kohn in her book *The New Believers: Re-imagining God*, published in 2003.

English scientist James P Lovelock coined the term 'Gaia' for our planet in an effort to engender a sense of reverence and caring for the earth, particularly among fellow scientists who, he felt, saw the earth as nothing but an object of study. His idea was taken up and expanded upon by a branch of the green movement, some of whom see the planet in a religious light.

Amnesty International (AI)

AI was founded by British lawyer Peter Benenson in 1961. It researches and takes action focused on preventing and ending, to take a phrase from its website, 'grave abuses of the rights to physical and mental integrity'. It also aims to secure 'freedom of conscience and expression, and freedom from discrimination'.

Among the abuses it opposes are hostage-taking and the torture of prisoners. It aids asylum seekers and campaigns for more accountability within the international military, security and police relations. AI has more than one million members in more than 140 countries. At its 'nerve centre' in London, it employs 410 staff members who are aided by 120 volunteers from more than 50 countries. Its many specialized networks include the International Lawyers' Network and the Health Professionals' Network.

MYTHS AND STORYTELLING

Fairy tales, Greek myths, creation stories from the Dreamtime… stories add a richness to human life and form a connection from one generation to the next. Early mythology attempts to make sense of nature—like why the sun moves in the sky or how the earth was created. Much of it is concerned with eternal cycles of life and death. In their language of the imagination, stories often resonate or ring true in a deep way, giving insight into and identity within our own lives.

American anthropologist Joseph Campbell, who died in 1987, believed the world's mythologies could be distilled into the unifying theme of the hero's journey. For him, stories were a metaphorical way of expressing how we meet the challenges of day-to-day life. First, there is the call—in everyday language, a disastrous or upsetting event that pulls you out of ordinary experience. This takes you to a foreign place, which is distressing, but you may find comfort in companions or allies. The dark night of the soul descends with all its trials and tribulations—this is the disintegration of your old way of looking at things. The supreme ordeal is about coming to terms with, for example, your own death or the limits of your control on other things. Then you begin the journey back to normality. A reward or elixir may carry healing power, especially as you now have something to share with others.

This model attracted great interest in Hollywood, and Campbell's classic hero journey is repeated on screen after screen in films such as *Star Wars*.

SIMPLE LIVING

American Duane Elgin's 1981 book *Voluntary Simplicity: Toward a Way of Life that is Outwardly Simple, Inwardly Rich* sums up many of the issues that concern what has been labelled 'the simple living movement'. It's about embracing some or all of the simple living tenets: frugal consumption, ecological awareness and personal growth. A central aspect is rethinking the relationship with money and reversing the trend to spend more than you earn and stay at a job you are uncomfortable in.

MORALS, ETHICS AND VALUES

Individual material gain makes life more comfortable, but many argue that the price has been a loss of spiritual, family and moral values—particularly for young people trying to find purpose and meaning in their lives. In an Australian Broadcasting Corporation interview in 2003 on the Radio National program 'Encounter', Richard Eckersley of the National Centre for Population Health says our value system has been turned on its head, with the consequences of increased depression and other psycho-social problems among young people. Traditionally, he says, virtues were concerned with building and maintaining strong harmonious personal relationships and social and spiritual attachments, and the strength to endure adversity. Vices, on the other hand, have been about the unrestrained satisfaction of individual wants and desires. But in modern Western cultures, Eckersley argues, vices have become virtues, and vice versa.

A VAST NETWORK FOR THE EXPLORING

On the surface, the pigeonholes created by advertising and brand awareness may seem significant, with their target audiences and population demographics. But, scratch the surface, and there's a lot more going on: the layers of human life—with their relationships, personal histories and family philosophies—are more complex than age, income and suburb. Take the website Awakening Earth, for example. It provides

Carl Jung (1875–1961)

In his memoirs, *Memories, Dreams, Reflections*, Swiss psychiatrist Carl Jung describes how—in many stages—he built a tower of stone for himself at Bollingen, near Zurich. It eventually became a sacred place for his 'soul work', where he could paint on the walls, write his dreams and enjoy his memories. It had no electricity. Instead, Jung tended the fireplace and stove himself, and lit the old lamps in the evening. He pumped water from the well, chopped wood and cooked food. 'These simple acts make man simple,' he wrote. 'How difficult it is to be simple.'

links to a vast number of organizations concerned with sustainability, politics, the media and more. A sample of sites includes the Center for a New American Dream, which promotes positive change in the way goods are produced and consumed; the United Nations Environment Program, whose activities cover atmosphere and terrestrial ecosystems; the Union of Concerned Scientists, an alliance of 50,000 scientists and citizens that augments rigorous scientific analysis with innovative thinking to build a cleaner world; Adbusters, a Canadian organization that produces advertising parodies and articles; Global Giving, which connects social investors with social entrepeneurs; and More than Money, which provides a service for people with wealth who are interested in using their money for social change.

The same applies more locally too. The opportunities to bring positive change and contribute are there for the finding. JB is going to campaign to plant a row of trees on a barren piece of council land near his new home. The neighbourhood centre needs good English speakers to help with conversation classes. The ladies of Cracoe, Yorkshire, whose story inspired the 2003 Disney-backed film *Calendar Girls*, have raised £600,000 for leukaemia research with their Alternative WI Calendar.

Most people, whether or not they believe in a soul, need to transcend daily life in one way or another. Connecting to a greater community and exploring the natural, spiritual and human worlds can change your outlook and bring meaning to your life—and do you a world of good at the same time.

TAKING STOCK

When materialistic concerns threaten to engulf you, try looking beyond to stretch your experience of life. Take a moment or two to think about some of the issues these questions raise.

1 Beliefs

(a) Do you have strong beliefs or values that are an important part of your life?

(b) Are these religious, political, ethical or other spiritual beliefs?

(c) How do these beliefs and values affect your life in practical ways?

2 Creativity

(a) Do you feel the need for a creative outlet?

(b) If so, what is it and what is the flow-on effect to the rest of your life?

(c) What difficulties do you face in meeting this need?

(d) How could you find new ways of feeling creative?

3 Meaning

(a) Do you think life has a meaning or is it up to us to give our lives meaning?

(b) What brings meaning to your life?

4 Community

(a) What forms your community? Family, friends, clubs, school acquaintances, youth centres?

(b) How do you maintain ties with your community?

(c) Are there ways you could explore that would strengthen these bonds?

_____

_____

_____

_____

_____

_____

_____

_____

_____

_____

_____

_____

_____

_____

_____

_____

_____

_____

This chapter will be devoted to those tricks which, because of an essential subtlety, are easy of execution and yet have a strong effect.

BRUCE ELLIOTT, CHAPTER 1, 'SWEET SIMPLICITY',
MAGIC AS A HOBBY (1950)

10. LIFE TOOLS

SOMETIMES AN ARTICLE YOU
READ OR A COMMENT BY
A FRIEND GIVES NEW
PERSPECTIVE TO YOUR
SITUATION AND HELPS YOU
TO SHAKE OFF THE OLD AND
BRING IN THE NEW. THIS
CHAPTER PRESENTS AN
ECLECTIC MIX OF IDEAS. ONE
OF THEM MIGHT JUST BE THE
KEY TO CHANGE THAT YOU'VE
BEEN LOOKING FOR.

NEW LIGHT ON OLD PROBLEMS

In Michael Gow's play *Sweet Phoebe*, a designer couple living in a designer flat have everything running smoothly: their careers are successful, there is talk time, dinner time and time allotted for intimacy. Into this overly ordered life comes a little dog, Phoebe. Gradually more than a few 'dog-ears' appear in the flat—balls are left on the floor and talk time is rescheduled to walk time. A little spontaneity shines into the couple's life. But disaster strikes when Phoebe goes missing…The play has a happy ending, but the couple is forced to face and ultimately survive chaos along the way. You can't help thinking at the end of it all that they are better people. Never mind the tears, just look at the personal growth!

At times we could all do with a sweet Phoebe to help shed new light on old problems, kick-start change and refresh the spirit.

BEATING PROCRASTINATION

If once a man indulges himself in murder, very soon he comes to think little of robbing; and from robbing he next comes to drinking and sabbath-breaking and from that to incivility and procrastination.

THOMAS DEQUINCEY,
MURDER CONSIDERED AS ONE OF THE FINE ARTS (1827)

Procrastination, the great thief of time, afflicts all of us at times and some of us all the time. Picture the writer who works from home and who will clean the bathroom rather than sit down and start the 6000-word article needed next week; the student who goes to a party when he should be revising for tomorrow's exam; or the employee who reads every page of the weekend paper instead of completing his tax return. A little procrastination might be normal—sometimes it's our own conscience sorting the wheat from the chaff of our endless 'to do' list—but a lot of procrastination gets in the way of living and can sabotage our efforts. Procrastination is such a problem on the student campus that it is the subject of a surprising

The serious side of laughter

If you can laugh at it, you can survive it. Seeing the funny side boosts your sense of wellbeing, helps motivate people at work, inspires hope, and helps you cope better with crisis and tragedy. It is also said to boost creative thinking and give a sense of perspective. There's no doubt either that humour releases tension. CM found humour made dealing with cancer more bearable:

Being diagnosed with cancer is a traumatic experience—the anxiety, the frustration of waiting for test results, the treatment. It takes its toll on everyone. I became very aware and sensitive to the feelings of those around me, especially my husband and family. The atmosphere was often very heavy and sad. I soon discovered humour was the best remedy to help break down the tension. Laughter does not trivialize a serious situation. There were also tears and anger. But making the occasional joke opened up the topic to people who might find cancer a hard subject to discuss.

We know instinctively that laughter is often the best medicine. But does science back us up? In an interview with the *Journal of Nursing*

volume of research. In his book *Do It Now: Break the Procrastination Habit*, American psychologist William Knaus describes a study in which 90 per cent of students were found to procrastinate over their studies. Of these, a quarter were defined as 'chronic procrastinators' and ones at risk of dropping out of college.

Some of the underlying reasons that people avoid tasks, or keep putting them off, even though they are important, are not difficult to fathom given a little investigation:

- Poor time management. You think you've got more time left than you actually have or you think the job will be done more quickly than is possible. Alternatively, you believe you can only start when the time is right, when you feel in the mood.
- Feeling overwhelmed by a task. A large, complex task or one

Jocularity in 1997, Dr Lee Berk, professor and medical research scientist at the School of Medicine and Public Health at Loma Linda University, California, outlined the research to date on the psychoneuroimmunology of mirthful laughter. One study involved two groups of medical students. One group watched a humorous film, the other sat in a neutral environment. Blood samples were taken before and after the session. People who'd watched the funny film showed signs of an increase in a range of cells involved in the immune system, including activated T-cells, natural killer cells and the antibody immunoglobulin A (IgA) which helps fight upper respiratory tract infections. Retired hospital administrator Don Marquis described in the same journal how humour in the hospital helps staff recover from shocking situations.

How can you tap into your funny side?

● Keep in touch with your inner clown.

● Make time for humour—read the odd joke, watch a comedy.

● Tell a joke.

that you are not sure you're equipped to handle is one that can be all too easy to avoid.

● Difficulty concentrating. Day-to-day distractions can make it hard to get on with jobs. It can be especially difficult for people with lots of responsibilities—family or work ones—to put aside unfettered time.

● Fear, anxiety and other negative beliefs. Fear that you'll fail or that the result won't be good enough can mean you spend time worrying rather than taking action to ensure you won't fail.

● Boredom. If the task bores you, you're more likely to find reasons not to complete it.

● Perfectionism. Unrealistic standards can jeopardize progress and make you feel that a setback is a catastrophe.

- Intrinsic problems with the task. It's harder to work on a project you feel has been imposed on you or which you feel is neither meaningful nor relevant. Equally, it can be difficult to get going on a task that you feel is poorly defined.

So how can you break through the procrastination barrier?

Understand your procrastination

If possible, pinpoint why you are reluctant to tackle a certain task or challenge. Facing your demons can diminish their power by letting you fight them with logic. You may fear failure in a course you've just started, but you are guaranteed it if you never hand in your course work. If the task quite simply bores you, but you have no option other than to eventually complete it, try spicing it up by attacking it little and often until the task is done. Make it more enjoyable by putting on music, as long as it doesn't interfere with your concentration, or getting a friend to join you.

Set priorities

When you are faced with numerous jobs that have to be done—as most of us are—work out which ones come first. This helps you move smoothly from one job to the next without wasting time dithering. If you find it hard to prioritize, at the beginning of the day write a list of jobs that need doing or that you'd like to do. Then number them in order of importance and indicate which ones could reasonably wait until tomorrow or maybe next week. Save yourself some heartache by straight away crossing out tasks that are not really necessary. Having set the day's priorities, work through them one by one. If you run out of time, move the remainder on to tomorrow's list and start again tomorrow. Flexibility and constant review is the key.

Another approach to a long-term task, such as a PhD, is to look at your 'wish list' of areas you want to cover and divide it into categories: those areas you can cover; those you'd like to cover but know realistically you'll only touch on; and those that you are unlikely to be able to do. Concentrate on the issues you know you can cover and accept you cannot do it all.

Throw your hat in

'A journey of a thousand miles starts with a single step,' said the Chinese philosopher Confucius. Throwing your hat in, incidentally, is an expression stemming from the custom of throwing your hat into the boxing ring as a sign of accepting a challenge to fight. In

Simon Wiesenthal (1908–)

While a concentration camp prisoner in World War II, Simon Wiesenthal, a Jew, had an unusual and troubling encounter. A young SS soldier who was dying in a hospital bed sought absolution from a Jew so he could die in peace. It was Wiesenthal who was brought to his bedside. The soldier had much to confess and, many hours later, Wiesenthal sensed he faced a choice—to give his forgiveness or not. He left the room without uttering a word but the decision haunted him. Should he have forgiven the dying man? Was it even in his power to forgive him?

Years after the war had ended, Wiesenthal told his story in a book he called *The Sunflower: On the Possibilities and Limits of Forgiveness*. The title is drawn from his thoughts as a prisoner being marched from one place to another, past the graves of German soldiers. From each grave grew a sunflower—a connection between life and death that for Wiesenthal was a symbol of their freedom in stark contrast to the mass grave, with no sunflowers, that he imagined he would finish in. In the second half of the book, Wiesenthal asks what others would have done in his shoes.

The twentieth anniversary publication (1996) presents 53 responses from theologians, political leaders, jurists, psychiatrists, human rights activists, Holocaust survivors and victims of attempted genocide in Bosnia, Cambodia, China and Tibet. Respondents range from the Dalai Lama and Primo Levi to Desmond Tutu and Harry Wu. Arthur Waskow turns his attention to the dying man. 'What would it mean for me to "forgive" you?' 'Ultimately...we have to live with ourselves,' comments Dith Pran. What would you have done?

the fight against procrastination, think of a small act—that first step—as a symbol of rising to the challenge. When a task seems daunting, think of it as a series of small steps rather than one amorphous whole. Break the job down into its elements and work through them. If you've always wanted to write a family history, get yourself an A4 notebook and start jotting down ideas: who you should talk to, where you can find out more. Perhaps sketch out the part of the family tree you already know and work out a plan of attack. Take breaks so that you work at maximum concentration then rest. A rule of thumb for intellectual tasks is 45 minutes on, fifteen minutes off.

Motivate yourself

It's easier to rally motivation if you create the best possible environment. If you have a desk job to do, make sure you have good lighting and a quiet space. Tidy your desk. Whatever job needs doing, gather together the correct tools before you start to minimize the time you waste going back and forth.

Plan your time

Once you've broken a job down into its smaller components, try to realistically estimate the time it will take. Some researchers recommend doubling this figure by 100 per cent. There are those who muddle through life without calendars and diaries but most busy people swear by them. If you need help planning your time, invest in a page-a-day diary and a wall calendar with enough space to write details of appointments and events. Get into the habit of using a diary to work backwards to help you plan when you need to start tasks. Remember to build in buffer zones for unexpected or unwanted delays such as illness.

'50 THINGS TO DO BEFORE I DIE'

Time is a sort of river of passing events, and strong is its current.

MARCUS AURELIUS ANTONIUS, ROMAN EMPEROR (121–180 AD)

Start where you are

'Don't be so predictable', 'Don't wait in ambush', 'First train in the preliminaries' and 'Don't wallow in self-pity': these are just a few examples of a special kind of teaching from the wide world of Buddhism. Called *lojong* teachings, these particular 'mind training' gems are from the *mahayana* school and are organized around seven points that contain 59 pithy maxims. Within these simple phrases lies the possibility of an entire change of attitude.

In her book *Start Where You Are: A Guide to Compassionate Living*, American Buddhist nun Pema Chödrön gives them a contemporary interpretation. Permeating her writing is the theme of starting with what you have, whether it's rage, jealousy or poverty. These are like clouds temporarily blocking the heat and brilliance of the sun, she says. The key to the *lojong* sayings is to ponder them and to wonder about them. Taken to their full, they provide subject matter for a special type of meditation called *tonglen*. They have value in everyday thinking too.

In a chapter entitled 'Lighten Up', Chödrön explores two slogans: 'Always maintain a joyful heart' and 'If you can practise even when distracted, you are well trained.' The first is about using every situation that arises as reason to 'wake up'—if you can do this, you can also remain cheerful. The second points out that it's training that allows you to remain cheerful or joyful, even when distracted. Curiosity, paying attention to the world, taking an interest, and nurturing a sense of humour all help support a joyful mind, says Chödrön. An easy way to lighten up is to do something different, something out of your usual pattern—whether it's taking a look at the sky out of the window, splashing cold water on your face, or singing in the shower. It could be the best gift you give yourself.

All too often we are swept along in the river of our life and hardly even seem to come up for breath, let alone to check we are following the course we really desire.

Put some time aside to come up for breath and toss some ideas around, just for the sake of it, noting down 50 things you'd like to do before you die. This is an enlightening and thought-provoking exercise. The first ten items might come easily—perhaps a couple of places you've always wanted to travel to, a book you've always been meaning to read, a letter to a relative that you've let pass for too long. However, as your list lengthens, you may find it sobering to realize that unless you make these things happen, they won't. The point is not to ruthlessly pursue these dreams, small and big, but to reflect. Some of them will be simple, like taking a course of lessons in sculpture. Some may be eccentric, perhaps learning to do a handstand in the second half of your life. Others may be indulgent and never really seriously pursued—the dream of the sports car that fades in importance. Alternatively, the mere action of writing down on paper that you'd like to do some voluntary work may be enough to make you pick up the phone to contact a local community centre.

By pushing the list to 50—without taking it too seriously— you will move past the obvious ideas into fields that involve other people in your life, small matters that will make a difference (like fixing the shower door) or acts that may lead to more adventurous changes (approaching an agency that specializes in overseas appointments).

If you compile this list from time to time, you may find it interesting to see which ideas drift away and which new ones make their appearance.

WHAT GOES AROUND COMES AROUND

Not in the sky nor in the ocean's middle,
Nor if you were to hide in the cracks in the mountains,
Can there be found on this wide earth a corner
Where karma does not catch up with the culprit.

FROM THE CHAPTER ON KARMA, THE SANSKRIT *DHARMAPADA*

'Karma'—a key concept in Buddhist and Hindu thought—is used with a variety of subtleties. Literally meaning 'action', it is usually described as the law of cause and effect, which states that every intentional action of the body, voice or mind has a corresponding result. At its simplest: a good action brings good results, and a bad one, suffering. The lines quoted above underline the fundamental message that your deeds stay with you and you cannot escape them: evil deeds eventually issue bitter fruits.

The knowledge that your actions affect you, the doer, as well as the recipients of those actions brings a heightened importance to your everyday choices. What tone of voice do you use when you complain about a faulty product? Do you do a neighbour a favour by taking their empty garbage bin off the footpath?

Buddhism takes the idea further. With its belief in reincarnation, it proposes that the seeds of your actions can bear fruit in future lives, so suffering in this life can sometimes be because of bad actions in a past one.

Aspects of this concept, call it cosmic justice or divine retribution, find expression in sayings from around the world: 'As you sow, so shall you reap,' says the Bible (Galatians 6:7); 'Ashes fly back in the face of him who throws them,' says a Nigerian proverb. Literature, legend and myth are littered with examples of people getting their comeuppance or just desserts. French writer Emile Zola's murderous couple are ruined by guilt in his novel *Thérèse Raquin*, similarly, Shakespeare's *Macbeth*. On the other hand, the goodness of fairytale characters Cinderella and Snow White shines through and they eventually marry their prince and live happily ever after, despite rough patches with lots of housework!

Another meaning of karma, used in theosophy, is the unbroken sequence of cause and effect. Each effect is, in turn, the cause of a subsequent effect, creating a chain of events. This complex ripple effect is also known as the doctrine of inevitable consequence.

While karma has sometimes been defined as fate or destiny in the West, Buddhist teachings stress the opposite. Every step of the way you are faced with the choice of planting 'good' seeds and 'bad' seeds. At a simple everyday level, the fruits of these actions—the 'what goes around comes around'—are often visible. When you're feeling cross and bothered, people will respond to you in a similar vein and the day seems filled with obstacles. When you approach problems with an open mind, or even a smile, they often unravel in a quicker and smoother fashion.

COACHES FOR LIFE

Forensic accountants, audiologists, Hispanic marketing specialists… and life coaches. These are the jobs on the rise mentioned on a Yahoo US recruitment website, Hotjobs, in 2003. 'Life coach' is also one of the fastest growing job descriptions in Australia, despite the current relatively small estimate of 12,000 life coaches worldwide.

What exactly is a life coach? It's someone you pay to help you fix up your life by setting goals and finding ways to achieve them. This could range from injecting life into tired relationships, getting out of a career rut, attaining the peak health that eludes you or launching out on the adventure you've always wanted to have but you've not yet dared to tackle.

The role of life coach emerged from corporate America in the 1980s. Executive coaches started to help overloaded managers motivate staff, manage time and surpass sales expectations. The trend has spread to such an extent that now anyone with the fee can have their own life coach.

Who can be a coach? To quote Fortune magazine on 21 February 2001: 'That's the scary part: pretty much anybody.' Some come from therapy, while some in the business field have dropped out of management consultancy. An increasing number of courses—mostly the on-line variety—promise diplomas or similar qualifications in life coaching in as little as three to six months. These courses do not appear to have entry requirements. As a career, 'colleges' suggest it is suited to good listeners; people who are interested in others; counsellors and therapists; and people who want to supplement their income by working from home, as much personal life coaching is undertaken via phone or email.

The many websites offering courses do not reveal much in the way of trade secrets but, once qualified, marketing yourself is all-important. You can choose from advertising, calling on your network of friends and colleagues, using an existing client base, conducting seminars, working with the media, undertaking public speaking, and, of course, Internet-based marketing.

But does life coaching work? Gordon Spence, a PhD researcher at the University of Sydney, thinks it might. He recruited 64 people for a ten-week study conducted at Sydney University's Coaching Psychology Unit and divided them into three groups. Group one received one-on-one coaching; the second had group coaching; while the third did not experience coaching. Those with individual coaching reported getting nearest to their goals in the time period and all who had received coaching—one-on-one or group—reported greater levels of goal attainment than those who had not. Says Spence, 'People felt more in control of their lives and became more open to new experiences.'

If you are thinking of approaching a life coach, you should consider these points:

- Serious problems require specialist help. If you are depressed rather than 'down', for instance, remember that life coaches are not trained psychologists. They may be a good sounding board or even motivator, but they have no medical training, and possibly very little training of any sort.
- Word of mouth is probably the best reference system. Someone who helped a friend of a friend may be a better bet than someone from the Internet.
- Take advantage of free initial consultations if you are unsure that it's right for you. Resist pressure to take it further if you are not entirely comfortable.

- Make sure you are clear about the cost and what you are committing yourself to in terms of ongoing payments and time frame. Some life coaches offer discounts if you sign up for blocks of three months or more.
- Be sure about how the sessions will run and, before you commit, make sure you have discussed what reasonable expectations you might have.
- There are a few accreditation schemes such as the International Coach Federation. However, 'using a life coach with this or similar accreditation does not guarantee professionalism and quality,' says Spence. 'There is no uniformly recognized body. You have to remember life coaching is an industry, not a profession.'

THE ART OF FORGIVENESS

The act of forgiveness can variously be defined as: to cease to blame or hold resentment against someone or something; to grant pardon for a mistake or wrongdoing; to free or pardon someone from penalty; or, in the sense of Old English, to free from the obligation of a debt.

Forgiveness does not diminish harm done to you, but it releases you from the bitter bonds of blame. It's also easier said than done: 'To err is human, to forgive, divine,' said Alexander Pope in his *Essay on Criticism*, written in 1711.

The winding paths to forgiveness can often include understanding. You may feel more ready to forgive an act or a person when you understand why someone acted the way they did. Forgiveness may also encompass empathy and compassion, but in no case does it include the condoning of an act. The ability to forgive—being a deep feeling rather than a judgment—is far from automatic, even if you wish you could forgive someone. Sometimes it requires you simply to be open and wait. Some acts take a few days to forgive; others, a lifetime. When it happens, you may often sense a new beginning, a freedom to move on, or as Stephanie Dowrick quotes Michael Leunig in *Forgiveness and Other Acts of Love*: 'There is a crucifixion and a resurrection every day...'

Are there stepping stones along the path to forgiveness? Giving up the fantasy that your own suffering causes suffering to the other person and will teach them a lesson can sometimes help. Some people have found the final step in forgiveness is when they accept their own imperfections and their own need to be forgiven, even if they have only 'wronged' in lots of small ways rather than one highly visible act of evil.

At the heart of forgiveness is the fading to nothing of the wish that another person be harmed because of what they have done to you. People who have forgiven talk of having stopped hating, and feeling a sense of freedom as a result. It's about finding peace and accepting the reality of the act or situation. Sometimes the process of forgiving requires you to look at the offence or act in a cold, objective light, to really see it for what it was—no more and no less.

Letting go of the past and bringing your life fully back to the present is also a way to shift your thinking and begin the process of forgiveness. Businesswoman CS took many years to forgive a former business partner over cheating and slandering. She says her first step was hearing the lyrics of a song which talked of keeping 'hurts' in a cupboard in our hearts and bringing them out time and time again to examine and replay them. She realized then that the key to getting on with her life was to forgive. A second step came when she realized it was the cheating rather than the slandering by which she was most hurt. It bothered her that she'd let money have such a hold on her life and her feelings.

Sometimes what's needed is to let go of the view that everything in life should be roses—and to accept that even the loveliest of roses bear thorns. The yin and yang in each individual was referred to by Martin Luther King when he said in one of his classic sermons, published in 1963 in his book *Strength to Love*:

We must develop and maintain the capacity for forgiveness. He who is devoid of the power to forgive is devoid of the power to love. There is some good in the worst of us and some evil in the best of us.

When you cannot forgive others they have a hold on you, whether you like it or not. And even small, everyday grudges may become seeds that germinate over time. Weeding out insignificant grudges as soon as they take root, well before they grow, may prevent them running wild. Hatred tightens and twists experience whereas forgiveness and peace, if you can find it, opens and lets life flow on again. By forgiving, you let the load go and are lightened.

MEDITATION MATTERS

Meditation is deeply rooted in Eastern life. It has many forms and there are numerous ways of describing its essence: 'bringing the mind home' is how Sogyal Rinpoche, author of *The Tibetan Book of Living and Dying*, chooses to describe it. The Buddha, he says, taught 84,000 different ways to tame the mind and its negative emotions. But Rinpoche confines himself to outlining three main methods: meditating on an object, saying a mantra and watching the breath.

The Beatles and their friendship with the so-called 'giggling guru', the Maharishi Mahesh Yogi, helped spread the popularity of meditation in the West. Today, it is increasingly accepted as having health-giving properties. Regular meditation is said to reduce stress, enhance concentration, and help control negative emotions. In addition it promotes relaxation, releasing muscular tension, which in turn relieves pain and increases mobility. Meditation also lowers high blood pressure. It stimulates the immune system, including increasing the production of white blood cells. As healing works best when the body is relaxed or sleeping, so meditation speeds recovery after illness and surgery. By opening constricted air passages, meditation aids asthmatics and hayfever sufferers and finally, by producing a feeling of calm, it increases the circulation to the digestive tract, the skin and the brain by reversing the fight or flight reflex. In addition to the medical benefits, people who practise meditation also report enjoying more moments of tranquillity, an improvement in sports and performance levels, and being better connected to their creative side.

Meditation can be approached at many levels. Anyone can have a go—it doesn't have to be part of a philosophical exercise or for hours at a time in strange twisted poses. In his book *Teach Yourself to Meditate*, Eric Harrison, a teacher of meditation from Perth, Australia, recommends aiming for fifteen minutes a day, four times a week to start making gains from meditating. You don't need any special equipment or even, necessarily, quiet. Some teachers suggest sitting cross-legged on the floor, or on a chair with a straight back. Hands should rest lightly on the knees. Many teachers recommend keeping the eyes open (you are less likely to fall asleep), and gazing downwards at an angle of around 45°. Some of these exercises are 'on the move'/'in the midst of the day' meditations, which don't require a special posture.

You may be surprised, particularly if this is the first time you try meditation, at just how often your mind wanders. Teachers advise that, like a puppy on a lead for the first time, you should bring your mind back each time it wanders—however many times it takes.

Watching the breath

This is meditation at its simplest. The idea is simply to 'rest' your attention, very lightly, on the breath. Sogyal Rinpoche points out the significance of the breath in Judaism, where *ruah* ('breath') means the spirit of God. In Buddhism, he says, prana, or 'breath', is said to be the vehicle of the mind. Keep your focus, without trying to fix concentration too hard, on the out-breath, avoiding mental commentary where possible.

Counting breaths

The idea of following your breath sounds ridiculously simple—until you try it. Then you'll see how the mind wanders. Counting the breath is a way of reining in the mind for longer periods. The aim of this exercise is to focus on each breath, feeling it fill your body and being aware of every sensation as you breathe in and out.

- Set aside fifteen minutes in a quiet place, in a comfortable position such as on a straight-backed chair.

- Spend a minute or two slowly scanning your body to release tension. In particular, inwardly examine your eyes, mouth, shoulders, hands and belly.
- Take a deep breath and sigh. Let your belly loosen. Explore the movement of the breath and enjoy its spontaneity.
- To help concentrate, count your breaths up to five or ten then start again. If you lose count, return to your breath and begin counting again—without annoyance. To counteract sleepiness, open your eyes a little or straighten your posture.
- Let your body relax. Be lightly aware of sensations such as heaviness and lightness, tingling and gentle breathing.
- Emerge slowly from the meditation, sitting quietly with your eyes open for a minute, taking care to notice if you feel different from when you started.

Spot meditation: waiting

You are late and in a hurry. The traffic lights turn red, you are in a long queue at the supermarket or the train is delayed. Instead of getting angry, follow this exercise:

- Smile and consider yourself lucky for being given a minute or two to do nothing.
- Let your body slow down and relax.
- Take a deep sigh, lingering on the out-breath.
- Let your face and belly soften.
- Breathe softly.
- Find the tension in your body and gently shake it free.

When the wait is over, move on.

Spot meditation: slowing down

For a few minutes, make a conscious effort to do everything a little more slowly than normal. Choose a simple activity to practise this on, such as getting dressed, having a shower, watering the plants or walking through the park.

Give yourself a start and a finish, with a few seconds at the end before taking up normal speed again. Notice your movements and be aware of your breathing. Keep the mind in the here and now by focusing on each sensation as it passes.

Sound meditation

Find a place to sit where you won't be disturbed. Close your eyes and listen. Focus on faraway sounds, maybe traffic sounds on distant streets, then come gradually closer until you are listening to something near you (such as a clock ticking in the room), then your own breathing.

Food meditation

A practice for mindfulness—that well-tuned awareness of the here and now—that is akin to meditation is eating a meal in slow motion, savouring the texture, colour, taste and sensation of each mouthful. The snack version might focus on a raisin (a meditation teacher in the United States has introduced students to this one— they take around ten minutes to eat a single raisin!); or an orange eaten slice by slice.

VOX POP: On tricks that help you gain new perspective

'I keep a daoist saying on a scroll near my desk. It says congming hutu. I bought it in Central China. It means "intelligence or understanding through chaos". It's like a proverb and is about 1000 years old. It helps me with acceptance—that I should not try to change things at home and work. It's about the opposite of organization and control: stop and enjoy the world instead of trying to control it (which is why everyone is so frustrated).' KF

'My ability to diffuse a situation through humour—I was diagnosed with cancer when still a young adult—has made me feel stronger to face the hard times and easier to relate to those I care about. I couldn't imagine going through such a painful experience without a little light relief.' CM

'Getting up early has revolutionized my life. I figured most evening hours were not well used, so I reset my body clock, went to bed earlier and stretched my day by getting up at 5 and working at least two hours before the children were up. It's helped me meet a deadline that needed a few months of extra time. Now that I'm nearing the end of that I think I'll keep up the habit as a way of writing a novel. I know that won't happen unless I carve out dedicated time. I also get to hear the birds sing, which I love.' MN

'I like that idea of Maslow's hierarchy of needs—you've got to get the basics right before you can move on to the higher stuff: cooking and sleeping areas at home need to be right before you can get a space together to study. If you are worried about where your next meal is coming from, it's hard to be really creative, and so on.' FL

'Sometimes when I seem to be saying one mean thing after another to my husband (maybe with good reason!) I give myself the half-hour challenge. I say to myself, "If I can't withhold from saying anything negative for even 30 minutes then I'm really pathetic." Sometimes it's enough to break an unhelpful cycle of thought.' HA

LOOKING FOR THE STARS

Two men looked out from prison bars
One saw the mud, the other saw the stars

AUTHOR UNKNOWN

Do you see stars or mud? Is your glass half full or half empty? When you are late for an appointment and see a taxi that you fail to hail, is it a sign that taxis are available or is it the last taxi in town? When you meet setbacks, do you bounce back, seeing them as a temporary challenge or do they represent a permanent defeat? In short, are you a pessimist or an optimist?

Anne Deveson (1930–)

An Australian filmmaker and writer who has also worked in social justice organizations, Anne Deveson has a special interest in resilience. Her youngest child was born 11.5 weeks premature and given a 5 to 10 per cent chance of surviving. Her eldest son Jonathan was diagnosed with schizophrenia at seventeen and died at 24. While researching her book *Resilience*, published in 2003, she was 'tested' again when a new loving relationship was cut short by her friend's death from cancer.

Resilience comes from the Latin re-silere, 'to spring back', and encompasses a mosaic of meanings: the ability to confront adversity and still find hope and meaning in life; facing reality with staunchness; making meaning out of hardship rather than crying out in despair; an innate self-righting mechanism. The idea of resilience is much discussed in child welfare circles. Why do some children rise above problems of poverty and lack of opportunity, while others are depressed and enter into a lifetime of unemployment?

The reasons are many, believes Deveson, but central to resilience is the stabilizing influence of a child's community. As the old adage says, 'It takes a village to raise a child.' Giving opportunities to children where they can shine also helps. Interestingly, resilient children know how to recruit people to help them. Resilience is a cloak of many colours, believes Deveson: some people's cloak is bold and bright, others wear a more muted version. Her own is brightly coloured if a little torn, 'but it will keep going for several more years.'

Psychologist Martin Seligman from the University of Pennsylvania has studied optimists and pessimists for more than 25 years, from the way they think to how it affects their lives and even health. He presents many of his findings in a book, *Learned Optimism*, including his theory that pessimists are more prone to depression because they are more likely to feel helpless, which can slide into a feeling of hopelessness. Optimists, he proposes, do better at school and university, are better salespeople, have a better health record and may even live longer.

But what is optimism? Is it simply looking at the sunny side of life? Key optimistic characteristics include:

- an ability to see events in their least threatening light
- seeing problems as temporary and a surmountable challenge
- regaining energy quickly after a setback
- believing that defeat is not their fault.

Pessimists, on the other hand:

- imagine the worst after a setback
- give up easily
- believe bad results are entirely their own fault
- see problems as long term.

The underlying difference between pessimists and optimists, says Seligman, is the difference in what he calls their 'explanatory style'—the way people explain to themselves the world and occurrences in it. It encompasses ideas such as 'permanence'. The optimist will see bad events as temporary: 'I'm exhausted' rather than 'this is the end of the line'; and good situations in a permanent light: 'I'm talented' rather than 'I tried hard that time'. Explanatory style also includes the element of 'pervasiveness': universal versus specific. Universal viewpoints such as 'nobody likes me' are pessimistic, while specific viewpoints such as 'Mrs Bloggs doesn't like me' are typically optimistic responses. The hope-filled perspective sees light at the end of the tunnel whereas the hopeless view cannot accept that a situation might change. The final element is that of 'personalization'. The pessimist takes things personally—'I'm stupid'—whereas the optimist is skilled at externalizing blame—'It's your fault.'

A study described by Christopher Peterson, professor of psychology at the University of Michigan, and colleagues, in their book *Learned Helplessness: A Theory for the Age of Personal Control*, is one of many that back up the health benefits of being an optimist. It evaluated 122 men who had just suffered their first heart attack for levels of pessimism and optimism. Eight years on 21 of the 25 most pessimistic had died, compared to only six of the 25 most optimistic. Other research shows optimists make a faster recovery after surgery and suffer fewer complications during and after surgery.

The good news is that, although your explanatory style may be learnt as a child, it's not set in concrete. If Seligman is to be believed, you can learn to become more optimistic in your outlook—and reap the benefits in health, happiness and at work. His premise shares much with the techniques of cognitive behaviour therapy in which you train yourself to dispute negative thought patterns. Instead you learn to come up with alternative views and explanations, examine the implications of a situation, and analyze the usefulness of a belief.

But don't desert pessimism altogether. As pessimists are often realists, it pays to maintain your sense of objectivity, especially when contemplating taking a risk or in a situation where you are listening to others' problems. Flexible optimism—with the skills and ability to switch it on and off—will help you see the stars without slipping on the mud.

Change is inevitable—but with a flexible outlook you can make the most of it. At times it's up to you to make the change, whether it's fixing a leak in the roof of your home, seeking a new job after a redundancy, deciding to renew family links, or resolving to get fit enough to run a marathon. Each morning is a new beginning. There is no need to be a prisoner of the past. Start where you are.

For all sad words of tongue or pen,
The saddest are these: 'it might have been!'
JOHN GREENLEAF WHITTIER, *MAUD MULLER* (1854)

SAMPLE QUESTIONNAIRE

1 Relationships

- Husband—good, although he's fed up with youngest not getting to bed early enough and therefore there isn't much adult time. Keep an eye on the situation; maybe think about better bedtime schedule once over major workload. Consider meeting for lunch while children at school/day care.
- John—good but problems over getting homework and piano practice done. Normal for his age, basically doing brilliantly at school and fine at piano, keep up the support, not really a problem.
- Oliver—sweet and cuddly but difficult to get him to bed at night. Let him stay up later but get him to go to bed in his own bed then wind back the bedtime; wake him up at 7 am.
- Friends—difficult to keep up with them because of busy schedule. Phone Fiona and suggest we meet for coffee.
- Family—they live overseas but we keep in quite good contact.

Bottom line: Great.

2 Health

- Weight—I'd like to lose 4 kilos. Cutting back on alcohol would help, also doing some extra exercise every other day.
- Flexibility—would like to get back to doing stretching exercises in the morning. Space and time are the main problems. Try keeping dining room floor tidy, get the boys to pick up their toys. Consider it essential for back maintenance.
- Fitness—doing quite a bit of walking and some cycling, could do with something more intense. See above. Either run or cycle

or swim on work days or in morning before husband has gone to work.

- Alcohol—drinks have slipped up a bit, should cut back to maximum two a day. Reintroducing yoga should help me relax better, be more in touch. Make sure I have interesting alternatives in the house (eg. flavoured teas, soy drinks, mineral water and fresh lime).

Bottom line: Feeling a bit tubby, need to make a big effort to reintroduce some good habits.

3 Work

- Challenged and slightly concerned about deadlines, particularly whether the final result is good enough. I am perfectly capable of the task. It's a challenge but possible if I keep the pace up and don't let myself get down. Looks like the deadline can be partly extended and that will allow me to meet it.
- Frustrated at times that I can't give it more time. It's what I've chosen, fits in with family life. In an ideal world, husband could step in more but his own deadlines make it difficult.
- Interesting.
- Flexible.
- Could lead to other things.

Bottom line: Pressured but should ease off in the next couple of months.

4 Finances

- Generally OK. Cash flow bit dicey at times but big picture good. A few bills to pay in the next few days.
- Late on tax returns. Under control, but need to email accountant about latest reminder from Tax Office and decide what to do.

Bottom line: Tax a bit of a worry but generally OK. Expecting small inheritance, which is a very welcome boost.

5 Home

- Constant battle with mess. Hate it when people pop around and it's chaos. Carry on trying to keep on top of it. Get the boys to pick up toys. Kitchen and bathroom OK; keep the dining room fairly neat as that's the 'public' room. Don't worry about bedrooms.
- Too small. We will move once lump sum through and we know what we've got to play with. Keep looking at options for moving. Stash some items in cupboards or boxes if no room.
- Nice place, feels like home, like the decor.

Bottom line: Great location, plan to move but have to sit tight for a few months.

6 Soul

- Art — not doing much, have lots of ideas, frustrated that I can't do much in the time. Particularly busy work time. Could get into the habit of carrying around a sketchbook and pencil, and do some drawing here and there, eg. when kids playing. Buy a plastic zip bag to put them in. Continue to record ideas with the hope I'll get time for them later.
- Guitar — out the window. It's a great relaxation and good to switch off the mind 'chat' of other problems. Make yourself do ten minutes after John's done his piano — could also make you more sympathetic to his difficulties with practising.
- Work has a creative side.
- Family life is challenging but immensely enriching.

Bottom line: Some creativity in my life but could do with more outlets for it. Should later; planning a sabbatical year, which will be amazing.

Overview

A busy time but most things hanging in there. A wait and see period for a number of areas of my life, but things should ease up in a couple of months.

THE MONEY CHECK-UP

How financially fit are you? Do you have financial flab that you could trim and make savings? It's time to take the money check-up and find out.

1 Where are you now?

(a) Assets

What are your assets? A home is a main one if you own one. You could also include home contents, a car, and any other assets of significant value such as heirloom jewellery or a valuable collection.

(b) Liabilities

What are your liabilities? These may include: home loan, personal loans (including car finance), credit card debts, store card debts, and so on.

(c) Wealth

Subtracting your liabilities from your assets gives you the balance: your wealth. Is this a sobering or a comforting figure?

(d) The half-hour budget

A budget is nothing more than a list of your predictable expenses in a year, from mortgage repayments or rent to school lunches and supermarket bills. Use the table on pages 394–397 to calculate your household budget. Depending on how honest you are—or how well you know your spending habits—it will show you what you need to be earning after tax to stand still or, if you seem to be heading backwards, by how much you are overspending and where your trouble spots are. Use the final column, 'Action', to note any ideas you have to reduce the amount you spend in a particular area. Adapt the table to suit your own needs: perhaps you regularly spend money on drinks after work, or specific items you have a soft spot for such as books or plants. If you are not sure where your money goes, try keeping a record for a week or two—you may be surprised. Undertaking this exercise once in a while can put you back in control of your spending. If you are happy spending $500 a year on magazines or golf balls, fine. If not, you have identified a drain on your wallet and can attempt to stem the flow.

2 Better banking

(a) Bank fees

Scrutinize banking fees, including savings plans, and take note of charges such as operating and exit fees. According to a 2001 article in *Choice* magazine, bank customers paid Australian banks $430 million in transaction fees in 2000. To assess the accounts you are currently using, scan through a series of statements and roughly tot up what you are paying in fees every month. If the calculation makes you uncomfortable look closer at what the fees are for and, with your bank if necessary, work out how you can minimize fees. If you have more than one account, review your needs and consider closing some and/or consolidating the accounts to save fees. You may be charged for:

- account-keeping fees (often when an account falls below a minimum balance)
- use of ATMs (you may be charged for every transaction or have a certain number of 'free' transactions a month; fees may be payable for using ATMs other than a bank's own)
- EFTPOS
- cash withdrawals over the counter
- one-off fees (eg. extra copies of a statement, fast cheque clearance)

- cheque accounts may incur fees for each transaction (if you don't need cheques regularly, it may be cheaper to pay occasional bank fees for bank cheques).

(b) Accounts

Is your money in the right type of account? Apart from working out the best way to avoid fees, there are other considerations:

- Generally, it's not a good idea to have thousands of dollars sitting in an everyday bank account that pays low interest.
- All-in-one accounts—which cover a home loan, overdraft facility, and so on—into which your salary is deposited may mean cash is working for you in terms of reducing the interest on your home loan. If this type of account appeals ask about charges, how interest is calculated, and so on.

3 Credit cards

The best way for a consumer to use a credit card is to pay off the balance each month as you avoid interest and late payment fees. Many people do not use them like this, however, and according to the US consumer magazine *Consumer Reports*, many US families are floundering in credit card debt of over $8000. Many people would be better off without a credit card, but the convenience of them, especially for Internet and phone purchases, makes them hard to give up.

(a) Which credit card?

When choosing a credit card consider the following:

- What interest rate is charged?
- When does interest accrue? Some have a period of grace, others start clocking up interest as soon as the cash till closes and your purchase has been approved.
- Is there an annual fee?

(b) If you don't pay off your balance each month:
- Choose a card with a low interest rate, stick with one only and avoid increasing your credit limit.
- Avoid cash advances as they usually incur interest immediately.
- Pay off as much as you can each month—at the very least the interest and any fees—otherwise your debt will never reduce.

(c) If you do pay off your balance each month:
- Consider a charge card.
- Look for the most interest-free days.

4 Insurance

(a) Do you have adequate insurance?

(b) Are the policies you have in line with your needs? Are they competitively charged? Do they cover what you think they do? Regularly reviewing the amounts you are insured for— for instance, in contents insurance—can avoid any serious disappointment in the case of a claim.

ANNUAL BUDGET

EXPENDITURE	AMOUNT	FREQUENCY (annual/quarterly/monthly/weekly)
1 HOME		
Mortgage or rent		
Insurance:		
building		
contents		
Local rates		
Gas		
Electricity		
Water		
Telephone		
Furniture		
Appliances		
Maintenance		
Other		
2 CAR		
Registration		
Insurance		
Maintenance		
Petrol		
Lease/loan payments		
3 FAMILY FINANCE		
Personal loans		
Credit cards		
Store cards		
Lay-by payments		
Other debts		
Insurance:		
health		
life		
income protection		
other		
SUBTOTAL		

TOTAL ANNUAL COST	ACTION

ANNUAL BUDGET

EXPENDITURE	AMOUNT	FREQUENCY (annual/quarterly/monthly/weekl
4 FOOD AND GROCERIES		
Supermarket		
Butcher		
Alcohol		
Tobacco		
Eating Out		
5 OTHER EXPENSES		
School fees		
School excursions, etc		
Extracurricular activities		
Adult education		
Hobbies		
Childcare		
Pets		
Treats and sweets		
Sport		
Public transport		
Memberships		
Newspapers, magazines		
Clothes		
Gifts:		
birthdays		
Christmas		
other		
Hairdressing		
Holidays		
Cinema/theatre		
Other entertainment		
Medical		
Dentist		
GRAND TOTAL		

TOTAL ANNUAL COST	ACTION

BIBLIOGRAPHY

Alexander, Christopher, Sara Ishikawa & Murray Silverstein with Max Jacobson, Ingrid Fiksdahl-King & Shlomo Angel, *A Pattern Language: Towns, Buildings, Construction*, Oxford University Press, New York, 1977.

Allen, Robert, *Zen Reflections*, MQ Publications, London, 2002.

Biddulph, Steve & Shaaron Biddulph, *The Making of Love*, Doubleday, Australia and New Zealand, 1999.

Bolles, Richard Nelson, *What Color Is Your Parachute? A Practical Manual for Job-Hunters & Career-Changers*, Ten Speed Press, California, 2003.

Brand, Stewart, *How Buildings Learn: What Happens After They're Built*, Penguin, New York, 1994.

Bruce-Mitford, Miranda, *The Illustrated Book of Signs & Symbols*, RD Press, Australia, 1996.

Cady, Roger & Kathleen Farmer, *Headache Free*, Bantam, United States and Canada, 1996.

Cairnes, Margot, *Staying Sane in a Changing World: A Handbook for Work, Leadership and Life in the 21st Century*, Simon & Schuster, Sydney, 2003.

Cameron, Julia, *The Artist's Way: A Course in Discovering and Recovering Your Creative Self*, Pan, London, 1995.

Campbell, Dr Anthony, *Back: Your 100 Questions Answered*, Newleaf, Dublin, 2001.

Carnegie, Dale, *How to Stop Worrying and Start Living*, Vermilion, London, 1998.

Carson, Rachel, *Silent Spring*, Penguin, London, 1962.

Chödrön, Pema, *Start Where You Are: A Guide to Compassionate Living*, Element, London, 2003.

Clitheroe, Paul, *The Road to Wealth*, Viking, Australia, 2001.

Clitheroe, Paul in association with Chris Walker, *Making Money: The Ten Steps to Financial Success*, Viking, Australia, 2003.

Conze, Edward (ed. & trans.), *Buddhist Scriptures*, Penguin, London, 1959.

Crystal, David (ed.), *The Cambridge Biographical Encyclopedia*, 2nd edn, Cambridge University Press, Cambridge, UK, 1998.

Csikszentmihalyi, Mihaly, *Flow: The Classic Work on How to Achieve Happiness*, Rider, London, 2002.

Dement, William C & Christopher Vaughan, *The Promise of Sleep: The Scientific Connection Between Health, Happiness, and a Good Night's Sleep*, Macmillan, London, 1999.

Deveson, Anne, *Resilience*, Allen & Unwin, Sydney, 2003.

Dibble, David, *The New Agreements in the Workplace*, The Emeritus Group, New York, 2002.

Dowrick, Stephanie, *Forgiveness and Other Acts of Love*, Penguin, Melbourne, 2000.

Eastman, Moira, *We're OK! Secrets of Happy Families*, Collins Dove, Australia, 1994.

Ecob, J R, *The Story of Mr Eternity*, The Herald of Hope, Sydney, 2000.

Edelman, Sarah, *Change Your Thinking*, ABC Books, Sydney, 2002.

Exley, Jo Ella Powell (ed.), *Texas Tears and Texas Sunshine: Voices of Frontier Women*, Texas A&M University Press, Texas, 1985.

Forster, Margaret, *Significant Sisters: The Grassroots of Active Feminism 1839–1939*, Penguin, London, 1986.

Gach, Gary, *The Complete Idiot's Guide to Understanding Buddhism*, Alpha, US, 2002.

Galinsky, Ellen, *Ask The Children: The Breakthrough Study That Reveals How to Succeed at Work and Parenting*, Quill, New York, 2000.

Gibran, Kahil, *The Prophet*, Heinemann, London, 1926.

Gillet, Dr Richard & The British Holistic Medical Association, *Overcoming Depression*, Dorling Kindersley, Great Britain, 1987.

Gleick, James, *Faster: The Acceleration of Just About Everything*, Little, Brown and Company, US, 1999.

Goleman, Daniel, *Emotional Intelligence: Why It Can Matter More Than IQ*, Bloomsbury, London, 1996.

Gombrich, E H, *The Story of Art*, 16th edn, Phaidon, London, 1995.

Hamilton, Clive, *Growth Fetish*, Allen & Unwin, Sydney, 2003.

Hamilton, Clive, 'Overconsumption in Australia: The rise of the middle-class battler', Discussion Paper No. 49, The Australia Institute, Canberra, November 2002.

Hamilton, Clive & Elizabeth Mail, 'Downshifting in Australia: A sea-change in the pursuit of happiness', Discussion Paper No. 50, The Australia Institute, Canberra, January 2003.

Handy, Charles, The Age of Unreason: Thinking the Unlikely and Doing the Unreasonable, Arrow Business, London, 1995.

Handy, Charles, The Hungry Spirit, Beyond Capitalism—A Quest for Purpose in the Modern World, Arrow, London, 1998.

Harrison, Eric, Teach Yourself to Meditate, Simon & Schuster, Sydney, 1993.

Harvard University Health Services, Good Health Management, President and Fellows of Harvard College for Accor Asia Pacific, Sydney, 1996.

Haynes, Alison, Food Glorious Food, Choice Books, Sydney, 2003.

Hinnells, John R (ed.), The New Penguin Handbook of Living Religions, Penguin, London, 1998.

I Ching (Book of Changes), Richard Wilhelm (trans.), Routledge & Kegan Paul, London & Henley, 1985.

Jung, C G, Memories, Dreams, Reflections, Flamingo, London, 1983.

Kindersley, Barnabas & Annabel Kindersley, Children Just Like Me, Dorling Kindersley, London, 1995.

King, Dr Rosie, Good Sex, Great Loving: Finding Balance When Your Sex Drives Differ, Arrow, Australia, 1998.

Kitchener, Betty & Anthony Jorm, Mental Health First Aid Manual, Centre for Medical Health Research at the Australian National University, Canberra, 2002.

Kohn, Rachael, The New Believers: Re-imagining God, HarperCollins, Sydney, 2003.

Leunig, Michael, Common Prayer Collection, Collins Dove, Australia, 1993.

Lowe, Jonquil, Be Your Own Financial Adviser, Which? Books, London, 2002.

Mackenzie, Vicki, A Cave in the Snow, Bloomsbury, London, 1999.

McKissock, Mal & Dianne McKissock, *Coping with Grief*, ABC Books, Sydney, 1995.

McRae-McMahon, Dorothy, *Everyday Passions: A Conversation on Living*, ABC Books, Sydney, 1998.

Matthew, Colin (ed.), *Brief Lives: Twentieth-Century Pen Portraits from The Dictionary of National Biography*, Oxford University Press, Oxford, 1997.

Mendelson, Cheryl, *Home Comforts: The Art and Science of Keeping House*, Scribner, New York, 1999.

Merson, John, *Stress: The Causes, the Costs and the Cures*, ABC Books, Sydney, 2001.

Mobbs, Michael, *Sustainable House: Living for our Future*, Choice Books, Australia, 1998.

Moore, Thomas, *Care of the Soul: A Guide for Cultivating Depth and Sacredness in Everyday Life*, HarperPerennial, New York, 1994.

Moore, Thomas, *Soul Mates: Honoring the Mysteries of Love and Relationship*, Harper Perennial, New York, 1994.

Oliver, Paul, *Dwellings: The Vernacular House World Wide*, Phaidon, London, 2003.

Pakula, Hannah, *An Uncommon Woman*, Phoenix Giant, London, 1997.

Parker, Robyn, 'Why marriages last: A discussion of the literature', Research Paper No. 28, Australian Institute of Family Studies, Melbourne, July 2002.

Pearson, David, *The New Natural House Book*, HarperCollins, Australia, 1998.

Rinpoche, Sogyal, *The Tibetan Book of Living and Dying*, rev edn, Rider, London, 2002.

Rybczynski, Witold, *Home: A Short History of an Idea*, Pocket Books, Great Britain, 2001.

SPRC, 'Caring differently: A time use analysis of the type and social context of child care performed by fathers and by mothers', Discussion Paper No. 117, September 2002.

SPRC, 'The time cost of parenthood: An analysis of daily workload', Discussion Paper No. 116, September 2002.

Seligman, Martin E P, *Learned Optimism*, Random House, Sydney, 1992.

Servan-Schreiber, Jean-Louis, *The Art of Time*, Bloomsbury, London, 1988.

Skynner, Robin & John Cleese, *Families and How to Survive Them*, Mandarin, London, 1989.

Solomon, Andrew, *The Noonday Demon: An Anatomy of Depression*, Vintage, London, 2002.

Terkel, Studs, *Working People Talk About What They Do All Day and How They Feel About What They Do*, The New Press, New York, 1974.

Tillyard, Stella, *Aristocrats: Caroline, Emily, Louisa and Sarah Lennox, 1740–1832*, Vintage, London, 1995.

Tyson, Eric, *Personal Finance for Dummies*, Hungry Minds, New York, 2000.

Warner, Sally, *Making Room for Making Art: A Thoughtful and Practical Guide to Bringing the Pleasure of Artistic Expression Back into Your Life*, Chicago Review Press, Chicago, 1994.

Weekes, David & Jamie James, *Eccentrics*, Phoenix, London, 1995.

The World Health Organization, *WHO ICD-10 Classification of Mental and Behavioural Disorders: Diagnostic Criteria for Research*, 10th revn, WHO, Geneva, 1992–4.

Wiesenthal, Simon, *The Sunflower: On The Possibilities and Limits of Forgiveness*, Schocken, New York, 1997.

Wood, Beatrice, *I Shocked Myself: The Autobiography of Beatrice Wood*, Chronicle Books, San Francisco, 1988.

INDEX

G

H

Published by Murdoch Books Pty Limited

Murdoch Books Pty Limited Australia
Pier 8/9, 23 Hickson Road, Millers Point NSW 2000
Phone + 61 (0) 2 8220 2000 Fax + 61 (0) 2 8220 2558
Website: www.murdochbooks.com.au

Murdoch Books UK Limited
Erico House, 6th Floor North, 93–99 Upper Richmond Road,
Putney, London SW15 2TG
Phone + 44 (0) 20 8785 5995 Fax + 44 (0) 20 8785 5985

Chief Executive: Juliet Rogers
Publisher: Kay Scarlett

Design Manager: Vivien Valk
Project Managers: Sarah Baker, Siobhán Cantrill
Editor: Anouska Jones
Designers: Jacqueline Duncan, Sarah Odgers
Cover photographer: Joe Filshie
Cover stylist: Georgie Dolling
Production: Maiya Levitch

National Library of Australia Cataloguing-in-Publication Data:
Haynes, Alison. Change: how to kick-start the future and refresh the spirit.
Bibliography. Includes index. ISBN 1 74045 787 0. 1. Life skills. 2. Self-actualization
(Psychology). I. Title. 158.1

Printed by Star Standard Industries (Pte) Ltd
Printed 2006.
Text © Alison Haynes 2006.
Design © Murdoch Books Pty Limited 2006.

All rights reserved. No part of this publication may be reproduced,
stored in a retrieval system or transmitted in any form or by any means,
electronic, mechanical, photocopying, recording or otherwise, without the
prior written permission of the publisher.

ACKNOWLEDGMENTS
Thanks are due to CollinsDove, a division of HarperCollinsPublishers, for permission to
reprint from Michael Leunig's Common Prayer Collection (1993); to Caroline Hunt,
Senior Lecturer at the School of Psychology, the University of Sydney, for reading the
section on depression treatments; to all at Murdoch Books for being so pleasant and
easy to work with despite deadline pressures, in particular to project manager, Sarah
Baker; and to editor, Anouska Jones, for her 'can do' attitude. Extra special thanks to
those who shared their stories, opinions and thoughts with me, and whose comments
form the Vox Pops; and to my friends, family and husband Peter, who helped me
'debrief' regularly throughout the researching and writing.